AF876236

Secured Credit and the Harmonisation of Law

CORPORATIONS, GLOBALISATION AND THE LAW

Series Editor: Janet Dine, *Director, Centre for Commercial Law Studies, Queen Mary College, University of London, UK*

This uniquely positioned monograph series aims to draw together high quality research work from established and younger scholars on what is an intriguing and under-researched area of the law. The books will offer insights into a variety of legal issues that concern corporations operating on the global stage, including interaction with WTO, international financial institutions and nation states, in both developing and developed countries. Whilst the underlying foundation of the series will be that of company law, broadly-defined, authors are encouraged to take an approach that draws on the work of other social sciences, such as politics, economics and development studies and to offer an international or comparative perspective where appropriate. Specific topics to be considered will include corporate governance, corporate responsibility, taxation and criminal liability, amongst others. The series will undoubtedly offer an important contribution to legal thinking and to the wider globalisation debate.

Titles in the series include:

Corporate Governance and China's H-Share Market
Alice de Jonge

Corporate Rescue Law – An Anglo-American Perspective
Gerard McCormack

Multinational Enterprises and Tort Liabilities
An Interdisciplinary and Comparative Examination
Muzaffer Eroglu

Perspectives on Corporate Social Responsibility
Edited by Nina Boeger, Rachel Murray and Charlotte Villiers

Corporate Governance in the 21st Century
Japan's Gradual Transformation
Edited by Luke Nottage, Leon Wolff and Kent Anderson

National Corporate Law in a Globalised Market
The UK Experience in Perspective
David Milman

Transnational Corporations and International Law
Accountability in the Global Business Environment
Alice de Jonge

The Corporate Objective
Andrew Keay

Secured Credit and the Harmonisation of Law
The UNCITRAL Experience
Gerard McCormack

Secured Credit and the Harmonisation of Law

The UNCITRAL Experience

Gerard McCormack

Professor of International Business Law, University of Leeds, UK

CORPORATIONS, GLOBALISATION AND THE LAW

Edward Elgar

Cheltenham, UK • Northampton, MA, USA

© Gerard McCormack 2011

All rights reserved. No part of this publication may be reproduced, stored in a retrieval system or transmitted in any form or by any means, electronic, mechanical or photocopying, recording, or otherwise without the prior permission of the publisher.

Published by
Edward Elgar Publishing Limited
The Lypiatts
15 Lansdown Road
Cheltenham
Glos GL50 2JA
UK

Edward Elgar Publishing, Inc.
William Pratt House
9 Dewey Court
Northampton
Massachusetts 01060
USA

A catalogue record for this book
is available from the British Library

Library of Congress Control Number: 2011924303

FSC
www.fsc.org
MIX
Paper from
responsible sources
FSC® C018575

ISBN 978 1 84980 397 7

Typeset by Servis Filmsetting Ltd, Stockport, Cheshire
Printed and bound by MPG Books Group, UK

Contents

Preface

This book addresses international harmonisation efforts in secured credit law and asks whether the most comprehensive international standard – the United Nations Commission on International Trade Law (UNCITRAL) Legislative Guide on Secured Transactions (2008) – is suitable for adoption at the national level. It explores the hypothesis that American law and lawyers have shaped the content of the Guide to the extent that it is not suitable for translation into other laws.

The clear objective of the Guide is to facilitate secured financing. The possibility of taking security rights over the assets of the debtor is thought to expand the availability as well as to reduce the cost of credit, thereby producing benefits for both creditor and debtor as well as for the overall economy. The Guide is very facilitating and enabling, and permits the creation of security in all sorts of situations. Security is seen as a good thing, through enhancing the availability of lower-cost credit. This perspective colours the approach adopted in the Guide on particular issues though, at the same time, it is recognised that beneficial economic results cannot be achieved by legislation alone – the legal and administrative infrastructure in a particular jurisdiction, including mechanisms for the enforcement of security, play a crucial role. In broad terms, the Guide follows the approach outlined in Article 9 of the American Uniform Commercial Code, and in the Personal Property Security Acts in Canada and New Zealand that have been modelled on Article 9. While the Guide is not an exact mirror image of Article 9, it is far closer in tone and spirit to Article 9 than the UNCITRAL Legislative Guide on Insolvency is to the comparable provisions of the US Bankruptcy Code. It is submitted that this closeness in approach is likely to militate against the prospects of the Secured Transactions Guide gaining widespread international acceptance.

The first chapter is introductory and looks at the nature and role of UNCITRAL as well as at recent controversy over UNCITRAL working methods. It considers the concepts of unification, harmonisation and modernisation and the legal instruments that are used to achieve these goals. It also addresses why the UNCITRAL agenda appears to have shifted from unification and harmonisation to modernisation, and considers the implications of this shift. The second chapter considers the case for and against harmonisation and modernisation of international trade law and asks where these are realistically achievable goals. The chapter also explains the concept of path-dependency and how this may influence the harmonisation and modernisation agenda. Chapter 3 turns the spotlight more particularly on secured transactions, or secured credit law as it is variously called, and asks why harmonise and modernise in this area? UNCITRAL suggests that doing so will lower the cost and expand the availability of credit. Harmonisation and 'modernisation' are assumed to equal 'liberal' security regimes and the facilitation of secured credit. In this chapter, the modernisation equals liberalisation agenda is subjected to greater scrutiny.

Chapter 4 looks at the main features of Article 9, which is often seen as a beacon for law reformers worldwide. It also considers the influence of Article 9 on other common law jurisdictions and the English common law and, in general terms, the civil law approach towards security rights. Chapter 5 assesses previous harmonisation efforts in the sphere of secured transactions and sets them against the background of the UNCITRAL Guide. The focus is on two particular instruments – the European Bank for Reconstruction and Development (EBRD) Model Law on Secured Transactions and the Organisation of American States (OAS) Model Law. Chapter 6 provides a critical evaluation of the main provisions of the Guide looking at the Guide in the context of other international and national secured transactions instruments including the EBRD Model Law and Article 9. The discussion addresses the overall philosophy of the Guide and how this is exemplified in particular provisions, including the scope of assets that may be collateralised, all-assets security, creation and third party effectiveness of security rights, quasi-securities and priorities.

Chapter 7 compares the UNCITRAL Secured Transactions Guide with its Guide on Insolvency. The main features of the Insolvency Guide are examined and analogies drawn with the key features of the US Bankruptcy Code. A central message is that the Insolvency Guide is not as closely aligned with US law as the Secured Transactions Guide. While the Insolvency Guide is arguably too legalistic on corporate restructurings, there appears to be greater recognition of diversity and the accommodation of different approaches than in the Secured Transactions Guide. The concluding chapter tries to explain why this may be the case and also the likely influence of the Secured Transactions Guide.

I have racked up many debts in the writing of this book, not least to Presy and to Amelia and Anthony. To them I owe profound thanks. I have also incurred many professional debts. Orkun Akseli, Spiros Bazinas, Hugh Beale, Andy Campbell, Jenny Clift, Neil Cohen, Frederique Dahan, Andrew Keay and Claire Kelly have helped in numerous ways. So too have many others and I hope that they will not be offended by the absence of any express reference. The usual disclaimer of responsibility applies with added force since some of those that I have thanked may not be entirely comfortable with the final product. I would also like to thank the Leverhulme Trust and the British Academy for facilitating the research on which the book is based and the University of Leeds for providing a hospitable working environment.

Gerard McCormack

1. Introduction

The United Nations Commission on International Trade Law (UNCITRAL) has recently produced a Legislative Guide on Secured Transactions.[1] The clear objective of the Guide is to facilitate secured financing. The possibility of taking security rights over the assets of the debtor is thought to expand the availability as well as to reduce the cost of credit, thereby producing benefits for both creditor and debtor as well as for the overall economy. The Legislative Guide is very facilitating and enabling, and permits the creation of security in all sorts of situations. Security is seen as a good thing, through enhancement of lower-cost credit availability. This perspective colours the approach adopted in the Legislative Guide on particular issues though, at the same time, it is recognised that beneficial economic results cannot be achieved by legislation alone – the legal and administrative infrastructure in a particular jurisdiction, including mechanisms for the enforcement of security, play a crucial role. In broad terms, the Legislative Guide follows the approach outlined in Article 9 of the American Uniform Commercial Code, and in the Personal Property Security Acts in Canada and New Zealand that have been modelled on Article 9. While the Legislative Guide is not an exact mirror image of Article 9, it is much closer in tone and spirit to Article 9 than the UNCITRAL Legislative Guide on Insolvency is to the comparable provisions of the US Bankruptcy Code. It is submitted that this closeness in approach is likely to militate against the prospects of the Secured Transactions Guide gaining widespread international acceptance.

This introductory chapter consists of five parts. The first part looks at the nature and role of UNCITRAL. The second at recent controversy over UNCITRAL's working methods. The third part considers

[1] The Guide went through the UN General Assembly approval process in December 2008 – UN General Assembly Resolution 63/121 – though the editorial revisions were only completed in 2009 and an intellectual property annex was 'pre-released' in 2010. For the content of the Legislative Guide see the UNCITRAL website – www.uncitral.org – and for background see B Foéx, L Thévenoz and S Bazinas eds *Reforming Secured Transactions: The UNCITRAL Legislative Guide as an Inspiration* (Geneva, Schulthess, 2007); U Drobnig 'Study on Security Interests' (1997) 8 UNCITRAL Yearbook 171 and S Bazinas 'UNCITRAL's Work in the Field of Secured Transactions' in J Norton and M Andenas eds *Emerging Financial Markets and Secured Transactions* (London, Kluwer, 1998).

the substantive work of UNCITRAL and how it came to promulgate a Legislative Guide on Secured Transactions. The fourth part looks at the concepts of unification, harmonisation and modernisation. The fifth part considers the legal instruments used to achieve harmonisation and/or modernisation of the law across international frontiers. This is followed by a brief conclusion.

UNCITRAL – ITS ESTABLISHMENT AND MISSION

UNCITRAL was established by means of a resolution of the United Nations General Assembly in 1966 and has as its object 'the promotion of the progressive harmonization and unification of the law of international trade'.[2] It was established as a Commission of the United Nations General Assembly. In setting up UNCITRAL, the General Assembly reaffirmed its 'conviction that divergences arising from the laws of different States in matters relating to international trade constitute one of the obstacles to the development of world trade'.[3] The resolution was grounded on a belief that 'the extensive development of international trade' could best be furthered by removing 'divergences arising from the laws of different States'. Harmonisation and unification of trade law were seen as instruments to facilitate international trade rather than goals in themselves. International trade was said to advance 'the interests of all peoples' and 'particularly those of developing countries' because 'international trade co-operation among States is an important factor in the promotion of friendly relations and, consequently, in the maintenance of peace and security'. Harmonisation and unification of international trade law was to be achieved through promoting the adoption of international Conventions and uniform laws as well as standard contract provisions, general conditions of sale, standard trade terms and other measures.[4]

---

[2] Official Records of the General Assembly, Twenty-first Session, Resolution 2205 (XXI), A/RES/2205(XXI), 17 Dec. 1966 which is available on the UNCITRAL website, www.uncitral.org.

[3] *Ibid.*

[4] Resolution 2205(XXI) included the following paragraphs:

> 'Noting at the same time that progress in this area has not been commensurate with the importance and urgency of the problem, owing to a number of factors, in particular insufficient co-ordination and cooperation between the organizations concerned, their limited membership or authority and the small degree of participation in this field on the part of many developing countries,
>
> Considering it desirable that the process of harmonization and unification of the law of international trade should be substantially co-ordinated, systematized and accelerated and that a broader participation should be secured in furthering progress in this area.'

As well as the harmonising function, UNCITRAL was also designed to play a coordinating role – acting as a sort of clearing house for other international organisations active in the field.[5] The need for such a clearing house is illustrated by the fact that 'the treaty collections are littered with Conventions that have never come into force, for want of the number of required ratifications, or have been eschewed by the major trading States'.[6] In the immediate aftermath of the Second World War, Harold Gutteridge, a noted comparatist, commented about the

> waste of effort and confusion that has, at times, been caused by the existence of competing agencies, engaged in the work of unification. The remedy for this state of affairs would seem to lie in the establishment of a rallying ground for unificatory activities . . . which would coordinate and supervise activities of this nature and also facilitate the collection of any information that might be required, either from governmental or other sources.[7]

Before the creation of UNCITRAL, the UN General Assembly requested the Secretary-General to produce a comprehensive report on the need for such a body.[8] The relevant resolution spoke of legal divergences and conflicts constituting an obstacle to the development of world trade. The resultant report by Clive Schmitthoff addressed the need for 'the progressive harmonization and unification of the law of international trade'.[9] Reference was made to harmonisation as a technique for 'reducing conflicts and divergences in international trade law' with unification described as '[t]he most effective method of conflict avoidance'. The report talked about harmonisation and unification as the 'preventive method' of private international law because it had the purpose of avoiding legal conflicts thus eliminating the need to rely on allegedly obscure choice of law rules.

---

5 See JA Estrella Faria 'The Relationship Between Formulating Agencies in International Legal Harmonization: Competition, Cooperation, or Peaceful Coexistence?' (2005) 51 Loyola Law Review 253 at 255–256.

6 See R Goode 'International Restatements of Contract and English Contract Law' (1997) Uniform Law Review 231 at 232. Goode identifies several reasons for this: 'failure to establish from potential interest groups at the outset that there is a serious problem, which the proposed Convention will help to resolve; hostility from powerful pressure groups; lack of sufficient interest of, or pressure on, Governments to induce them to burden still further an already over-crowded legislative timetable; mutual hold-backs, each State waiting to see what others will do, so that in the end none of them does anything'.

7 H Gutteridge *Comparative Law* (Cambridge, CUP, 2nd edn, 1949) at 146. According to Roy Goode 'Harmonised Modernisation of the Law Governing Secured Transactions: General-Sectoral, Global-Regional' (2003) 8 Uniform Law Review 341 at 345: 'These words remain as true today as when they were penned some 54 years ago.'

8 UN Resolution 2102 (XX), available online at www.uncitral.org.

9 The 'Schmitthoff Report' (UN Doc A/6396) reprinted in (1966) 1 UNCITRAL Yearbook 2 and available online at www.uncitral.org and associated links.

Schmitthoff saw both harmonisation and unification as achievable goals in that the similarity of international trade law transcended the division of the world between free enterprise and centrally planned economies – the West/East divide – and between civil law and common law origin countries. The primary obstacles to harmonisation and unification were identified as being the existence of a plethora of international law reforming institutions whose work overlapped and whose membership represented developed and not developing nations – the North/South divide. Schmitthoff suggested a UN-related law reform body on the basis that it would provide more inclusive representation of the world's legal and economic systems and accordingly better coordination among other international actors. A United Nations Commission on International Trade Law, established as a UN offshoot, would gain legitimacy and clout from the international representativeness of the UN and therefore function effectively as a coordinating entity.

Legitimacy could be described as 'a generalized perception or assumption that the actions of an entity are desirable, proper, or appropriate within some socially constructed system of norms, values, beliefs, and definitions'[10] and it has been argued that the legitimacy of international organisations such as UNCITRAL rests on the three foundations of representativeness, procedural fairness and effectiveness.[11] The notion of representativeness is bound up with the idea that those responsible for the framing of the new global norms are in some way representative of the kinds of jurisdictions to which these norms are addressed. The notion of procedural fairness implies catholic participation and 'voice' – peripheral and core actors, the weak and the strong, are all allowed to take part in the norm-making process in ways that are seen to be fair. Effectiveness implies proposals translated into action or, to put it another way, that the accomplishments of an international organisation in the past are likely to be turned into probable future successes.[12]

---

[10] See M Suchman 'Managing Legitimacy: Strategic and Institutional Approaches' (1995) 20 Academy of Management Review 571 at 574.

[11] See T Halliday 'Legitimacy, Technology and Leverage: The Building Blocks of Insolvency Architecture in the Decades Past and Decades Ahead' (2007) 32 Brooklyn Journal of International Law 1081 at 1084, referring to I Hurd *After Anarchy: Legitimacy and Power in the United Nations Security Council* (Princeton NJ, Princeton University Press, 2007). See generally S Wheatley *The Democratic Legitimacy of International Law* (Oxford, Hart Publishing, 2010).

[12] Other scholars have argued that UNCITRAL acts 'incrementally' and count this incrementalism as among its strengths – see J Pottow 'Procedural Incrementalism: A Model for International Bankruptcy' (2005) 45 Virginia Journal of International Law 935, who refers to the UNCITRAL Model Law on Cross Border Insolvency as fundamentally procedural in focus and sets out the merits of a process of incremental proceduralism.

Essentially, UNCITRAL functions at four levels – the Secretariat, the Working Groups, the UNCITRAL Commission and finally at the top of the hierarchy, the UN General Assembly.[13] The latter ratifies Commission decisions, often without additional deliberation, and this ratification, by virtue of the all-inclusive representative status of the General Assembly, gives a powerful symbolic imprimatur to UNCITRAL texts.

The UNCITRAL Commission has a membership of 60 States elected by the General Assembly for a term of six years. It is intended to be representative of the various geographic regions of the world; the principal legal and economic systems and developing as well as developed countries. The Commission sets out the work programme of UNCITRAL. Items may find their way into the work programme following representations from governments, or after consultation with non-governmental organisations (NGOs) or trade associations. For instance, following discussions at a 2010 international colloquium attended by representatives from governments, international organisations and the private sector, the UNCITRAL Commission decided to continue work on secured transactions, giving priority to the preparation of a text on registration of security rights.[14]

The Commission also finalises and adopts texts that have been sent to it by the Working Groups where the bulk of substantive work is done in the shape of 'policy decisions' and the drafting of relevant instruments. The Working Groups consist of official national delegates from UNCITRAL's own membership, invited observers from other UN Member States, together with intergovernmental and NGOs that have an interest in the topics under discussion. No nation that wishes to participate in the Working Groups is excluded and it is the custom for observers to participate fully in the discussions. In practice both the Commission and Working Groups arrive at their decisions by consensus rather than by putting matters to a vote. This consensual mode of decision making has, however, recently come under challenge.

Finally, at the ground level is the UN Secretariat, which comes from the International Trade Law Division of the United Nations Office of Legal Affairs, based in Vienna. It consists of a small group of legally qualified

---

[13] See generally R Goode, H Kronke and E McKendrick *Transnational Commercial Law* (Oxford, OUP, 2007) at 206–208; J Honnold 'Process and Value of the Unification of Commercial Law: Lessons for the Future Drawn from the Past 25 Years' in *UNCITRAL, Uniform Commercial Law in the Twenty-first Century* (New York, United Nations, 1995).

[14] See UN Doc A/CN 9/702 (April 2010) and A/CN 9/WG VI/WP 44 – 'Registration of Security Rights in Movable Assets' (August 2010).

officials from a range of nationalities. The Secretariat plays a facilitative role in assisting the Working Groups and Commission in its work.

UNCITRAL WORKING METHODS

Recently there has been considerable controversy over UNCITRAL working methods though the controversy has not been on familiar fault lines as such, pitting the richer countries of the North and the West against those of the South and the East.[15] Rather the main protagonists have been France and the US. France has called for revision of UNCITRAL's de facto working methods[16] whereas the US is basically content with the status quo.[17] The controversy does not appear to have led to any pronounced substantive changes though there have been clarifications of practice that may have gone some way towards meeting French concerns.

Essentially, there were three bones of contention raised by France. The first concerned the consensual mode of decision making which the UNCITRAL secretariat suggested is conducive to achieving a larger cooperation among countries having different legal, economic and social systems and also ensuring that UNCITRAL instruments were generally acceptable.[18] It stressed, however, that consensus was not the same as complete agreement and a decision could fairly be said to have been arrived at by consensus even though not all States were fully in accord with all aspects of a proposal. According to a note prepared by the Secretariat '[t]he basis of consensus is that efforts are made to address all of the concerns raised by participants so that the final text is acceptable to all', but the doubts articulated by a single State were not sufficient to prevent a consensus being formed on the basis of what was otherwise

---

[15] C Kelly (2009) 'The Politics of International Economic Law: Legitimacy and the UNCITRAL Working Methods' ExpressO available at: http://works.bepress.com/claire_kelly/15.

[16] 'France's Observations on UNCITRAL's Working Methods' UN Doc A/CN 9/635 (2007). France believed that it was necessary to clarify UNICTRAL's rules of procedure either by specifically referring to the UN rules applicable to all subsidiary organs, or by adopting rules unique to UNCITRAL. Reference was made to UNCITRAL's drafting stages as its 'legislative process'. See also 'UNCITRAL Rules of Procedure and Methods of Work: Proposal by France' A/CN 9/697 (2009).

[17] 'UNCITRAL Rules of Procedure and Methods of Work: Observations by the United States' UN Doc A/CN 9/639 (2007).

[18] 'UNCITRAL Rules of Procedure and Methods of Work: Practice with the Implementation of the Applicable Rules of Procedure' UN Doc A/CN 9/638/Add.4 (2007) and see also 'UNCITRAL Rules of Procedure and Methods of Work: Note by the Secretariat' A/CN 9/676 (2009) and A/CN 9/697 (2010). Note too, UN General Assembly Official Records Sixty-fifth session, Supplement No 17 (A/65/17) Annex 111.

the prevailing view of the meeting. France did not object to the consensus mode of decision making but sought clarification on the meaning of consensus, suggesting that consensus was deemed to have been arrived at too easily.[19] It contended that 'there cannot be a consensus without the consent of all delegates'.[20] The UNCITRAL Secretariat has now propounded the following working definition of 'consensus':

> Consensus is generally understood to mean adoption of a decision without formal objection and vote. Consensus may not necessarily reflect unanimity of opinion, namely, complete agreement as to substance and a consequent absence of reservations, and should therefore be distinguished from unanimity, i.e., the decision-taking by a vote wherein no negative votes are cast, albeit with abstentions. . . . Consensus in the Commission is based on the substantially prevailing view, a flexible notion that does not embody a pre-defined mode of calculation and is characterized by the absence of a formal objection resulting in a request for a vote.[21]

There is some wriggle room in this definition but this is likely to be the case with all attempted definitions of 'consensus'. Clearly the concept lacks the clarity of meaning of a decision by a simple majority vote. Nevertheless, the French view of the term does not seem to have been taken on board, or fully taken on board, in the Secretariat formulation.

While fuzzy and manipulable to a degree, the notion of consensus-based decision making has certain advantages. A unanimity requirement could stymie sensible decision making. It would constitute a particularly perverse form of minority rule, giving each and every State a veto power, no matter how insignificant the issue, but a simple majority requirement would go too far in the other direction, undermining the legitimacy of UNCITRAL and the possibility of its texts gaining general international acceptance. The UNCITRAL Secretariat itself has noted that it 'would not be conducive to the harmonization of commercial laws if some provisions or instruments were approved by a small majority'.[22]

France was perhaps on sounder ground in its second point when it queried the role of non-UNCITRAL members, particularly special interest groups, in the UNCITRAL decision-making process. It was argued that because of the technical and specialised work undertaken by UNCITRAL, experts from NGOs through the expertise they possessed

---

[19] 'France's Observations on UNCITRAL's Working Methods' UN Doc A/CN 9/635 (2007) at para 5.11d.

[20] *Ibid.*

[21] 'UNCITRAL Rules of Procedure and Methods of Work: Note by the Secretariat' A/CN 9/676 (2009) at paras 11, 12.

[22] *Ibid* at para 9.

influenced the entire process[23] and participated on a 'de facto equal basis with Member States in the sessions of the working group to produce the draft instrument'.[24] The influence of experts and NGOs was also increased by the funding constraints faced by UNCITRAL, which was generally not able to fund participation in its activities by States. Financial factors therefore effectively shut certain poorer States out of the decision-making process whereas well-resourced private sector organisations with an interest in the subject-matter under discussion were free to attend and participate and had the financial wherewithal to do so.[25]

The French complaint was also with the expansion in the number of NGOs that were allowed to participate. In the past only a small number of NGOs with a stated interest in the field of international trade were active within UNCITRAL, but more recently the field had opened up to a larger number of NGOs, 'more obviously national in nature'[26] and these groups have had a potentially decisive say on the outcome of UNCITRAL deliberations.[27] To counter the influence of these interest groups, France put forward certain proposals including provision for 'in camera' meetings where requested by a Member State.[28] It also proposed that the sphere of influence of experts should be confined to informal events such as colloquia and seminars, and only Member States should be permitted to draft and circulate documents.[29]

Having identified the problem of interest group capture it is submitted that the detailed proposals advanced by France do not do much to address the problem, or at least raise issues of their own that may be as

---

23 'France's Observations on UNCITRAL's Working Methods' UN Doc A/CN 9/635 (2007) at para 3.1. France was particularly concerned about the fact that when UNCITRAL undertook to draft an instrument, experts, or the groups represented by them, often initiated the process and provided most of the technical information that was considered by the respective working groups. These experts were not representatives or delegates of any Member State. Moreover, the working groups generally operated without any guidelines and the draft instruments that they submitted to the plenary session were only altered if a strong current of opinion favoured such changes.

24 *Ibid* at para 3.1.

25 *Ibid.*

26 *Ibid* at para 6.1.

27 NGOs participating in the Working Group on Insolvency Law included the American Bar Association and the American Bar Foundation – see UNCITRAL Report of Working Group V (Insolvency Law) and Working Group VI (Security Interests) on the work of their second joint session at para 7, UN Doc A/CN 9/550 (2004). The preface to the Legislative Guide on Insolvency Law also acknowledges that '[NGOs] participated actively in the preparatory work'.

28 'France's Observations on UNCITRAL's Working Methods' A/CN 9/635 (2007) at para 6.2.

29 *Ibid* at para 3.2 stating that NGOs should only be permitted to circulate information documents unless otherwise requested or authorised by Members.

troubling. For instance, provision for in-camera deliberation seems to run counter to the UN professed ethos of openness and transparency and raises the spectre of deals being stitched up behind closed doors. The US was able to knock this proposal quite easily, stating: 'One of the hallmarks of the . . . successful work methods has been . . . [the] open and public process. Transparency and participation by knowledgeable and affected groups, including international and non-governmental organizations and private sector representatives, in working group meetings are key to UNCITRAL's success.'[30] On the circulation of documents, again France does not appear to have had much joy. In the guidelines issued by the UNCITRAL Secretariat, it is stated that[31] '[w]ritten proposals by the observer organizations may be circulated by the Secretariat to the commission and/or its relevant subsidiary organ unless decided otherwise by the Commission or the subsidiary organ concerned'. The theoretical position has not changed but there may be alterations in practice.

At the very least, however, the French challenge to the UNCITRAL working practices has served to highlight the influence exerted by NGOs on the deliberative process. But the very nature of UNCITRAL as a specialist organ of the UN puts a premium on gaining specialist technical inputs from affected parties. As one commentator remarks, while 'the participation of experts might give greater support to one State's position over another's, as long as the contributor is an expert and other experts are also permitted to participate, it would seem to serve . . . input legitimacy'.[32] On the other hand, the participation of 'experts' may mean a greater imbalance of power and influence within UNCITRAL, especially if the supposed expert organisations are perceived to be generally national rather than international in character.

The UNCITRAL Secretariat has said that the notion of 'international organizations' has been interpreted broadly as 'encompassing regional and subregional organizations, as well as other organizations with demonstrated international expertise'.[33] This introduces considerable flexibility, but the Secretariat has opened the door even further by stating

---

30 'UNCITRAL Rules of Procedure and Methods of Work: Observations by the United States' A/CN 9/639 (2007) at para 20.

31 'UNCITRAL Rules of Procedure and Methods of Work: Note by the Secretariat' A/CN 9/676 (2009) at para 32. The 2010 document A/CN 9/697 is terse on the point merely stating (at para 11) that the 'Secretariat shall decide on the appropriate form that the assistance of outside experts may take depending on the needs of the Secretariat'.

32 C Kelly (2009) 'The Politics of International Economic Law: Legitimacy and the UNCITRAL Working Methods' ExpressO available at: http://works.bepress.com/claire_kelly/15.

33 'UNCITRAL Rules of Procedure and Methods of Work: Note by the Secretariat' A/CN 9/676 (2009) at para 26.

that while it generally considers the international focus and membership of the organisation, the main criteria to be taken into account include its ability to contribute meaningfully to the deliberations in view of its recognised competence, experience or interest in the subject-matter under consideration and its role in representing a particular sector or industry.[34] Effectively, this means that interest groups whose orientation is primarily national may participate, and the US-focused Commercial Finance Association (CFA) has played a leading role in the Secured Transactions Guide, sponsoring receptions and symposia and providing experts for the UNCITRAL working group sessions.[35] Those participating in the working group on Insolvency Law included both the American Bar Association and the American Bar Foundation. Such bodies provide subject specialist knowledge and technical input but their very knowledge and expertise is liable to overwhelm most, if not all, national delegates. Such bodies may also have financial resources and commitment to the issues under discussion far exceeding that of national delegates. Evening up the playing field is not an easy prospect however, except by means of the increase of financial resources available to UNCITRAL for subsequent disbursement to poorly resourced States and groups seeking to participate in UNCITRAL activities. This matter links up with wider issues about UN funding that go far beyond the realm of legal harmonisation.

Similarly broad issues were implicated in the third issue raised by France, which related to the use of English language as the de facto working language within UNCITRAL. France considered that as Working Group documents were circulated solely in English, the status of French as an official UN language, and other UN languages, was being ignored. UNCITRAL offered some concessions in this regard providing for the possibility of translation of drafts and other relevant documents but only where resources permitted.[36] Given, however, the status of English as the international language of business, it is difficult to see its supremacy within UNCITRAL diminishing. This is not likely to change even if the global influence of the US recedes, for emergent powers such as India and China are more conversant with English than with French, whose position as the language of diplomacy and business belongs more to the past than the foreseeable future. The fact that UNCITRAL work

---

[34] *Ibid* at para 28.

[35] See generally the CFA website: www.cfa.com.

[36] 'UNCITRAL Rules of Procedure and Methods of Work: Note by the Secretariat' A/CN 9/697 (2010) at para 14: 'The UNCITRAL secretariat is committed to endeavour, resources permitting, to provide at such meetings translation and interpretation in as many official languages as appropriate.'

is expanding beyond international trade law, narrowly conceived into business law more generally, also seems likely to strengthen the dominant status of the English language within the organisation.

THE SUBSTANTIVE WORK OF UNCITRAL

The best-known instrument promulgated by UNCITRAL has probably been the Vienna Convention on Contracts for the International Sales of Goods,[37] which has gained a wide measure of international acceptance and adoption. The US, though not the UK, is among the list of adopting countries.[38] But apart from the Sale of Goods Convention, UNCITRAL has also produced international instruments on many areas of procedural and substantive law such as international arbitration,[39] e-commerce,[40] international payments,[41] procurement and infrastructure development,[42] international transport of goods,[43] and insolvency[44] as well as secured credit.[45]

On secured credit, UNCITRAL in the 1970s commissioned Ulrich Drobnig to produce a comprehensive report detailing the legal treatment of security interests in many jurisdictions.[46] In the light of previous international harmonisation efforts, Drobnig's report was not optimistic about the likelihood of framing international rules governing security interests, or even Model Laws, and gaining general acceptance for the

---

[37] United Nations Convention on Contracts for the International Sale of Goods (1980).

[38] For a list of the nations that have adopted the CISG in one form or another see the UNCITRAL website.

[39] UNCITRAL Model Law on International Commercial Arbitration (1985).

[40] UNCITRAL Model Law on Electronic Commerce with Guide to Enactment (1996) and UNCITRAL Model Law on Electronic Signatures with Guide to Enactment (2001).

[41] United Nations Convention on International Bills of Exchange and International Promissory Notes (1988); UNCITRAL Model Law on International Credit Transfers (1992); United Nations Convention on Independent Guarantees and Stand-by Letters of Credit (1995).

[42] UNCITRAL Legislative Guide on Privately Financed Infrastructure Projects (2000); Model Legislative Provisions on Privately Financed Infrastructure Projects (2003).

[43] United Nations Convention on the Carriage of Goods by Sea (1978) – the 'Hamburg Rules' and see now the 2008 United Nations Convention on Contracts for the International Carriage of Goods Wholly or Partly by Sea – the 'Rotterdam Rules'.

[44] UNCITRAL Model Law on Cross-Border Insolvency with Guide to Enactment (1997); UNCITRAL Legislative Guide on Insolvency Law (2004).

[45] See generally S Bazinas 'UNCITRAL's Work in the Field of Secured Transactions' above, note 1.

[46] 'Study on Security Interests' (1977) 8 UNCITRAL Yearbook 171; UN Doc A/CN 9/ SER A/1977.

same. The report suggested that it was likely to be only a small minority of cases where moral persuasion or intellectual insight into the virtues of harmonised rules would persuade States to adopt them though insistence by international financial institutions might induce acceptance in a greater number of cases. In the wake of the Drobnig report, UNCITRAL concluded that worldwide unification of the law of security interests in goods was in all likelihood unattainable.[47] This was because the laws of States differed fundamentally at the time on matters such as the degree of formality needed to create a security interest; the extent to which non-possessory security was recognised; the validation of all-assets or floating security; the availability of a single unitary security interest over all the assets of the debtor; the extent to which security interests needed to be publicised by registration; and the possibility of out-of-court enforcement of security interests upon the debtor's default.

The possibility of harmonising secured transactions law was revived in 1992 with a specific suggestion for harmonisation in the area of receivables financing.[48] This suggestion led to two reports and the commencement of work on harmonisation. In 1995, UNCITRAL decided to develop uniform rules and mandated a Working Group to embark on the exercise.[49] The result was the United Nations Convention on the Assignment of Receivables in International Trade, completed in 2001.[50] The Convention tries to create certainty on the cross-border assignment of receivables, partly through ensuring the validity of cross-border bulk assignments as well as the assignment of future receivables.

UNCITRAL in 2000 once again started work on security interests more generally, not least because of the perceived inadequacies of domestic laws to support modern financing practices.[51] It was noted that, in many States, there were limits on the use of non-possessory security rights in credit transactions. These limits included restrictions based on the identity of the debtor, the potential creditor, or the nature of the asset to be encumbered.[52] In addition, there was a lack of clarity on priority rules that ranked secured creditors compared with competing claimants and problems relating to the enforcement of security rights. In cross-border

---

47 See generally H Buxbaum 'Unification of the Law Governing Secured Transactions: Progress and Prospects for Reform' (2003) 8 Uniform Law Review 321 at 322.

48 'Uniform Commercial Law in the Twenty-first Century', UNCITRAL Proceedings, New York, 18–22 May (1992) at p 271.

49 (1995) 26 UNCITRAL Yearbook 228.

50 United Nations Convention on the Assignment of Receivables in International Trade (2001).

51 UNCITRAL Report on the work of its thirty-third session (A/55/17).

52 *Ibid* at para 41.

transactions it was noted that divergent domestic conflicts of law rules increased the risks associated with credit transactions and, by extension, the cost of credit. After a further study conducted in 2001, UNCITRAL instructed one of its Working Groups to commence work on the development of 'an efficient legal regime for security rights in goods involved in commercial activity, including inventory'[53] and this work has led to the Legislative Guide.

UNCITRAL is not the only international legal organisation working on the design of an 'efficient' legal regime for secured transactions. The European Bank for Reconstruction and Development (EBRD) in 1994,[54] the Francophone countries of West Africa (OHADA) in 1997,[55] and the Organisation of American States (OAS) in 2002[56] have all produced Model Laws or Uniform Acts and done follow-up work of greater or lesser intensity. The World Bank has formulated principles for Effective Insolvency and Creditors Rights Systems (revised in 2005).[57] The World Bank and a World Bank sister organisation, the International Finance Corporation, since 2002 have produced a series of reports designed to evaluate the ease of doing business across the globe. As part of the evaluation process, the *Doing Business* reports have made use of a ten-point template measuring the degree to which secured credit and bankruptcy laws in particular jurisdictions 'protect the rights of borrowers and lenders' and thus facilitate secured lending.[58] More recently the World Bank Group has collaborated in the production of a diagnostic toolkit on 'Secured Transactions Systems and Collateral Registries'.[59] The Hague Conference

---

53 UNCITRAL Report on the work of its thirty-fourth session (A/56/17) at para 358.

54 See its website www.ebrd.com and for some of the later work done by its 'secured transactions' team see 'Publicity of Security Rights: Guiding Principles for the Development of a Charges Registry' (2004) and 'Publicity of Security Rights: Setting Standards' (2005) and see generally J-H Röver *Secured Lending in Eastern Europe: Comparative Law of Secured Transactions and the EBRD Model Law* (Oxford, OUP, 2007).

55 OHADA stands for 'Organisation pour l'Harmonisation du Droit des Affaires en Afrique' and for the Model Law 'Acte uniforme adopte e 17 Avril 1997, portant organisation ses sûretés – 151 articles (JO Ohada no 3 du 1er Octobre 1997)' see its website: www.ohada.com.

56 See its website – wwww.oas.org – and for later work see 'Model Registry Regulations under the Model Inter-American Law on Secured Transactions' (2009). See also the work of the Asian Development Bank – www.adb.org – which has produced a 'Guide to Movables Registries' (2002).

57 See www.worldbank.org and the principles are also available as Annex 5 to *Secured Transactions Systems and Collateral Registries* (International Finance Corporation, Washington, 2010).

58 The template is available as Annex 3 to *Secured Transactions Systems and Collateral Registries* (International Finance Corporation, Washington, 2010).

59 International Finance Corporation, Washington, 2010.

on Private International Law in respect of intermediated securities,[60] and the International Institute for the Unification of Private Law (UNIDROIT)[61] more generally, have also been active in the secured transactions sphere. UNIDROIT's work has led to international Conventions on International Factoring, International Financial Leasing and more recently on international interests in mobile equipment (the Cape Town Convention).

So UNCITRAL is not alone in its efforts and, while there is the risk of duplication and overlap, UNCITRAL work gains added credibility and legitimacy from its perceived representatives and its institutional aura as a United Nations organ. Its work in the secured transactions sphere has not stopped with the Legislative Guide however, nor even with the elaboration of an intellectual property annex. At a 2010 colloquium several possible topics for further work were considered including preparation of texts on registration of security rights in movable assets; security rights in non-intermediated securities as well as a possible Model Law on secured transactions or a contractual guide on secured transactions.[62] Subsequently it was decided to give priority to the registration project on the basis that there was an urgent need for guidance to States in connection with the establishment and operation of security rights registries.[63] UNCITRAL cautioned that secured transactions law reform could not be implemented effectively in practice without an efficient publicly accessible security rights registry. It was also considered that the Legislative Guide was not sufficiently detailed on the various legal, administrative, infrastructural and operational questions that needed resolving before a registry could be implemented successfully.[64]

The focus of these international efforts has increasingly been on the 'modernisation' rather than the 'harmonisation' of secured credit law, or particular aspects thereof. For instance, the Preamble to the UNCITRAL Legislative Guide refers to a modernised law of secured credit worldwide whereas the original mission of UNCITRAL spoke of 'unification' and 'harmonisation' of international trade law. The question arises whether

---

60 'Convention on the Law Applicable to Certain Rights in Respect of Securities Held with an Intermediary' (2006) – available on the Hague Conference website: www.hcch.net. The Hague Conference styles itself as the World Organisation for Cross-border Co-operation in Civil and Commercial Matters.

61 See www.unidroit.org.

62 See UN Doc A/CN 9/702 (April 2010) and A/CN 9/WG VI/WP 44 – Registration of Security Rights in Movable Assets (August 2010).

63 See UN General Assembly Official Records Sixty-fifth session, Supplement No 17 (A/65/17) at para 264.

64 *Ibid* at para 265.

the goalposts have shifted or whether the concept of 'modernisation' is encompassed in the notions of 'unification' and 'harmonisation'? This issue will now be addressed.

HARMONISATION, UNIFICATION AND MODERNISATION

There is considerable ambiguity and divergence of opinion on the precise meaning of harmonisation.[65] Jacob Ziegel, e.g., has remarked that harmonisation in this field of law is a word with 'considerable elasticity [and i]n its most complete sense it means absolute uniformity of legislation among the adopting jurisdictions'.[66] According to Loukas Mistelis 'harmonisation is a process which may result in unification of law subject to a number of (often utopian) conditions being fulfilled, such as, . . . wide or universal geographical acceptance of harmonising instruments, and with wide scope of harmonising instruments which effectively substitute all pre-existing law'.[67] David Leebron defines harmonisation as 'making the regulatory requirements or governmental policies of different jurisdictions identical or at least more similar'.[68]

The official UN records on the establishment of UNCITRAL speak of the 'progressive unification and harmonization'[69] of international trade law to be accomplished by various instruments. According to the Schmitthoff report, harmonisation was a technique for 'reducing conflicts and divergences in international trade law' and unification was the 'most effective method of conflict avoidance'.[70] It is implicit in this analysis that harmonisation involves the convergence of legal rules toward a common standard and that, over the long run, harmonisation would move towards

---

[65] For different definitions of 'harmonisation' see P Glenn 'Harmony of Laws in the Americas' (2003) 34 University of Miami Inter-American Law Review 223 at 246; M Boodman 'The Myth of Harmonization of Laws' (1991) 39 AJCL 699 at 707. See also C Baasch-Andersen 'Defining Uniformity in Law' (2007) 12 Uniform Law Review 5–56.

[66] J Ziegel 'Harmonization of Private Laws in Federal Systems of Government: Canada, the USA and Australia' in R Cranston ed *Making Commercial Law: Essays in Honour of Roy Goode* (Oxford, Clarendon Press, 1997) 131 at 133.

[67] L Mistelis 'Is Harmonisation a Necessary Evil? The Future of Harmonisation and New Sources of International Trade Law' in I Fletcher et al. eds *Foundations and Perspectives of International Trade Law* (London, Sweet & Maxwell, 2001) 3 at 4.

[68] D Leebron 'Claims for Harmonization: A Theoretical Framework' (1996) 27 Canadian Bus LJ 63 at 66.

[69] Resolution 2102 (XX), but Resolution 2205 (XXI) which actually establishes UNCITRAL speaks of 'progressive harmonization and unification'.

[70] The 'Schmitthoff Report' (UN Doc A/6396) reprinted in (1966) 1 UNCITRAL Yearbook 2 and available online at www.uncitral.org.

a unification of legal rules. In other words, all jurisdictions would have the same legal rules applying to a particular transaction.

One could argue that the same vision of harmonisation permeates the UN General Assembly resolution creating UNCITRAL.[71] This resolution asserted that 'the extensive development of international trade' was best advanced by removing 'divergences arising from the laws of different States'. This definition conceives of harmonisation in terms of the convergence of non-uniform national laws around an agreed-upon international standard. At the same time however, it is a pragmatic and progressive definition in that harmonisation is not sought for its own sake but because international trade is seen as favouring the interests of all peoples and particularly those of developing countries. International trade cooperation among States is considered to be an 'important factor in the promotion of friendly relations and, consequently, in the maintenance of peace and security'.

The overriding goal is facilitation of international trade and friendly relations among States, with harmonisation and unification of laws serving as means towards this end. Such a characterisation leaves some room for flexibility as well as a degree of ambiguity about exactly what is comprised in the notions of harmonisation and unification. The UNCITRAL website[72] offers certain definitions and suggests that 'harmonisation' can be thought of as the process through which domestic laws are modified to enhance predictability in cross-border commercial transactions whereas 'unification' is seen as the adoption by States of a common legal standard governing particular aspects of international business transactions. Harmonisation is also distinguished from unification in terms of the international instruments most likely to be employed. Model Laws or Legislative Guides are seen as examples of texts that are drafted to harmonise domestic law, whereas a Convention is seen as an international instrument that is adopted by States for 'the unification of the law at an international level'. There is room for a more nuanced analysis however. A Convention may not be an effective instrument of unification in that few States actually implement it. A Model Law, on the other hand, despite its softer character, may actually bring about more unification in practice in that more States are prepared to enact its provisions, whether in whole or in part.

'Modernisation of laws' as an objective was not actually spelled out when UNCITRAL was created in 1966, but if the expression 'progressive'

---

71 Resolution 2205 (XXI).

72 Available at www.uncitral.org/uncitral/en/about/origin_faq.html.

in the relevant resolution is given substantive content one could argue that it implies 'modernisation'. The resolution emphasised that the progressive harmonisation and unification of trade law followed from the United Nations' broader agenda of economic development and the promotion of friendly relations among countries.[73] Call it 'mission creep' or the express iteration of implicit principles, UNCITRAL now defines its mission as the 'modernization and harmonization' of trade law.[74] 'Modernization' has been expressly incorporated within UNCITRAL's core function. Since 2000, in its annual reports to the UN General Assembly, UNCITRAL has set out the view that the progressive modernisation and harmonisation of international trade law reduces, or removes, legal obstacles to the flow of international trade as well as contributing significantly to 'universal economic cooperation among all States on a basis of equality, equity and common interest'.[75]

There may be considerable difference, however, between harmonisation and unification of existing bodies of national law and modernisation of such laws. Harmonisation might only intrude minimally on the legislative sphere of national States through the identification of common approaches among existing domestic laws. The consensus in the late 1960s understood 'progressive harmonization and unification' of trade law to mean the reconciliation of divergent practices and the expression of emerging international norms. The focus now on 'modernization and harmonization' sees UNCITRAL in a more pro-active light actively striving for the reform of global commercial law.[76]

Law reform efforts of this kind may involve so-called 'in with the new' modernisation. Existing legal instruments at the national level are seen as inadequate to keep pace with technologically-driven or market-led innovations and indeed, regulation or prescription at the national level may be insufficient to cope with the task at hand in view of its international dimensions. Given the fact that the challenges and problems are transnational in nature, the ideal solution may be at the transnational level bringing about an internationally compatible and harmonised result. Electronic commerce is a good example of this. UNCITRAL in the form of a Model Law

---

[73] See Resolution 2205 (XXI).

[74] See www.uncitral.org.

[75] See Resolution adopted by General Assembly on Report of the United Nations Commission on International Trade Law on the work of its 42nd session, A/RES/64/111 (December 2009).

[76] S Block-Lieb and T Halliday 'Harmonization and Modernization in UNCITRAL's Legislative Guide on Insolvency Law' (2007) 42 Texas International Law Journal 475 at 475–478.

has addressed national legislatures about the shape and content of new regulations that are required by changed exigencies.[77]

There are other notable examples of 'in with the new' modernisation in the case of work done by other international actors. Where assets by their very nature regularly move across national borders, there is a plausible argument that security interests over such assets should be governed by a single set of rules that apply irrespective of where the encumbered asset, the security giver and the security taker are located.[78] In this context, governments negotiated and adopted, under the auspices of UNIDROIT, the 2001 Cape Town Convention on International Interests in Mobile Equipment and various equipment-specific protocols. The Convention sidesteps the diversity of national laws on secured transactions by creating an international interest that gives financiers priority in the debtor's insolvency. This international interest is recognised in all contracting States upon registration in an accessible international register. But the Convention also highlights some of the dangers associated with the entire modernisation process. The background includes the privatisation of many national airlines with finance increasingly coming from private rather than state sources and a desire by these private actors for recognition and protection of their security interests in such high-value assets. In the process leading to the Convention, interest groups representing the aviation industry were particularly active and their involvement may have led to 'bright line' rules in the Aircraft Protocol protecting security interests. The danger is of interest group capture and a perception that the rules are designed to suit the preferences of richer nations that play host to powerful lending institutions.[79]

These dangers are perhaps even more acute in the case of 'out with the old and in with the new' modernisation. In this scenario, there is a framework of national law on a particular topic but this law is considered to be inadequate by UNCITRAL or other international actors. It is not

---

77 See UNCITRAL Model Law on Electronic Commerce (1996) which according to its Preamble is intended to assist 'all States significantly in enhancing their legislation governing the use of alternatives to paper-based methods of communication and storage of information and in formulating such legislation where none currently exists'.

78 See generally L Weber and S Espinola 'The Development of a New Convention Relating to International Interests in Mobile Equipment, in Particular Aircraft Equipment: a Joint ICAO-UNIDROIT project' (1999) 4 Uniform Law Review 463.

79 See generally R Cranston 'Theorizing Transnational Commercial Law' (2007) 42 Texas International Law Journal 597 at footnotes 49–55. For analogies with the American Article 9 drafting process see A Schwartz and R Scott 'The Political Economy of Private Legislatures' (1995) 143 University of Pennsylvania Law Review 595; E Janger 'Predicting When the Uniform Law Process Will Fail: Article 9, Capture, and the Race to the Bottom' (1998) 83 Iowa Law Review 569.

merely the case of filling a gap in the old law but also the rejection of existing law, and the creation of new law. For example, in its 2000 Report on Possible Future Work on Insolvency Law, the UNCITRAL Secretariat noted that an important justification for authorising the Working Group on Insolvency Law to begin its work on a Legislative Guide 'was to modernize insolvency practices and laws'.[80] Unlike the electronic commerce work in largely virgin territory, the Insolvency Legislative Guide sought to 'modernize insolvency practices and laws' by recommending to national actors that they reject their existing domestic insolvency laws in favour of more modern ones.

This form of modernisation represents a fairly acute form of incursion into the sovereignty of nation States and national legislatures. The existing efforts of at least some States are viewed as inadequate in the face of some modernist ideal hailing from outside. It may be that so-called 'modernisation' is really a euphemism for 'adaptation of a weaker country's laws in the direction of a powerful sovereign state or international organization which has the cultural authority to define the meaning of modern'.[81] It is also the case that modernisation might work against harmonisation or unification since 'modernisation' relates to a revision of the law to meet new exigencies; revisions that might not be consistent with existing national laws or global norms. Secured credit supplies a prime example of this. Most jurisdictions have laws that permit the taking of security in a variety of situations but these provisions are far from comprehensive and may impose onerous formality requirements. Hence advocates of secured credit see the need for 'modernisation' that would make security easier to take and to enforce. For instance, a 2000 UNCITRAL report authorised work on the Secured Transactions Legislative Guide on the basis that 'modernization and optimization of secured credit law can lead to expanded economic development and, therefore, promote the general welfare'.[82]

Chapter 2 considers in more detail the case for harmonisation and modernisation of the field of international commercial law and Chapter 3 turns the spotlight on secured credit law, but it is appropriate now to

---

[80] 'Possible Future Work on Insolvency Law' at p 3 produced by UNCITRAL Working Group on Insolvency Law, 22nd Session (6–17 December 1999), A/CN 9 WG V/WP 50.

[81] See S Block-Lieb and T Halliday above, note 76 at 477 fn 6, and see generally the discussion at 475–478. See also L LoPucki *Courting Failure: How Competition for Big Cases Is Corrupting the Bankruptcy Courts* (Ann Arbor, University of Michigan Press, 2006) at 231: 'Harmonization is a euphemism for forcing commercially less important countries to adopt the remedies and priorities of the commercially more important countries.'

[82] 'Security Interests: Current Activity and Possible Future Work: Report of the Secretary-General' – A/CN 9/475 (2000).

consider the instruments used to accomplish international harmonisation and modernisation.

WHAT INSTRUMENTS SHOULD BE USED TO ACHIEVE HARMONISATION AND/OR MODERNISATION?

The classic method of private law harmonisation is that of the Convention, and UNCITRAL's first international instruments directed to national actors are Conventions – namely, the 1978 Convention on Carriage of Goods by Sea[83] and the 1980 Convention on Contracts for the International Sale of Goods.[84] A Convention takes the form of a multilateral treaty with countries acceding to a single standard. The chief advantage of the Convention is that national actors are offered a single set of options around which to converge.[85] This unifying ideal suffers, however, from practical limitations. Conventions are not self-enforcing and they require States to sign, ratify and accede to the terms of the Convention. States face more or less the binary choice of acceding to the terms of the Convention in full, or failing to follow it at all. Ratification, in particular, is a difficult process since in many countries, including the UK, it requires the passage of national implementing legislation and countries may not alter any part of the Convention to suit domestic political or legal differences. Legislative timetables are often crowded, and implementing legislation often requires overcoming the opposition of a powerful pressure group. It may be politically expedient for a State to sign a Convention but then it is put on the back burner at the politically difficult stage of ratification. The willingness of delegates from States to sign up to a Convention does not guarantee that States will necessarily ratify that Convention.

Braithwaite and Drahos in their seminal text on *Global Business Regulation*[86] comment that Conventions as tools of private law harmonisation have not been particularly successful, with low ratification rates. Many such instruments remain 'little more than a dead letter'.[87] Even

---

83 United Nations Convention on the Carriage of Goods by Sea (1978) – the 'Hamburg Rules' – but see now the 2008 United Nations Convention on Contracts for the International Carriage of Goods Wholly or Partly by Sea – the 'Rotterdam Rules'.

84 United Nations Convention on Contracts for the International Sale of Goods (1980).

85 H Kronke 'International Uniform Commercial Law: Conventions, Advantages, Disadvantages, Criteria for Choice' (2000) 5 Uniform Law Review 13.

86 J Braithwaite and P Drahos *Global Business Regulation* (Cambridge, CUP, 2000).

87 See M Bonell 'Unification of Law by Non-Legislative Means: The UNIDROIT Draft Principles for International Commercial Contracts' (1992) 40 AJCL 617 at 617; R Goode in

getting to the stage of agreeing a Convention can be a fraught process. The Convention is essentially an 'all or nothing' instrument and requires zero-sum bargaining in order to reach agreement.[88] A Convention is also rather specific and fragmentary in character – in short, an island of uniformity in a sea of disharmony. The costs, in terms of time and inconvenience, of securing subsequent amendments of a Convention may also be prohibitive. Agreement has to be reached afresh among States on the terms of any modification of the Convention and then the process of ratification and implementation gone through again. In short, the process of formulation and implementation of a Convention is time consuming and the prospects of subsequent adaptation are prohibitive.

The Model Law, on the other hand, is a much more flexible instrument, being a legislative text that UNCITRAL recommends for enactment but States may be permitted to exclude, or modify, some provisions.[89] The Model Law sets a global standard, but it should be easier to achieve agreement on the text of a Model Law since it does not impose the same 'all or nothing' standard as a Convention. The conditions of implementation are also not as onerous, and essentially a Model Law acts as a spur to a reform-minded national legislature. Domestic law makers may take some or all of the provisions of the Model Law to update national legislation. As Roy Goode remarks:[90]

> A model law proposes, in more or less detailed provisions, a way of regulating a certain type of transaction (for example leasing) or a certain area of law (such as international commercial arbitration). National legislatures are then free to either not make use of the proposal at all, to take the model law as it is and transplant it into their domestic law, or, finally, to adopt in part and provide for amendments and variations required by or considered to be desirable in light of a specific domestic situation.

'International Restatements of Contract and English Contract Law' (1997) Uniform Law Review 231 at 232 comments that while 'many States participate in the work leading to a convention, for fear of losing the opportunity to influence its terms, most of them are likely to drag their feet for many years before ratifying the convention, if indeed, they ever get around to ratifying it at all'.

88 S Block-Lieb and T Halliday above, note 76 at 480.

89 See 'Possible Future Work on Insolvency Law' above, note 80 at p 42. See also the following comment by the Working Group at p 42: 'A model law is an appropriate vehicle for modernization and unification of national laws when it is expected that States will wish or need to make adjustments to the uniform text to accommodate local requirements that vary from system to system, or where strict uniformity is not necessary. . . . A model law would also be appropriate when the purpose of the uniform text is, on the one hand, to establish a standard of a modern law in an area where national systems are widely disparate, undeveloped or outdated and, on the other hand, to provide an incentive for a movement towards unification.'

90 R Goode et al. above, note 13 at 197.

While a Model Law may appear to be a less harmonising instrument than a Convention, the appearance does not necessarily square up to the reality. Its form may encourage both agreement on a wider set of provisions than can realistically be achieved through the mechanism of a Convention and also a higher take-up rate than could be accomplished with a Convention. Indeed, the Model Law technique has been described as 'breathtakingly successful in some instances'.[91] The usefulness of a Model Law is enhanced where it is coupled with a guide to enactment that explains its terms to national policy makers and advocates the enactment of implementing legislation. In general, guides to enactment set out background information including information on the different policy decisions; they explain decisions that have been reached in framing the relevant provisions and generally assist legislatures in arriving at coherent choices.[92] Model Laws do not necessarily contain a 'one size fits all' approach and UNCITRAL has increasingly recognised that domestic legislatures should be presented with a wider canvas of choices rather than only acceptance, or rejection, of the Model Law provisions in their entirety. A variety of legislative responses should be possible, and the emphasis placed on guides to enactment ties in with this recognition.

UNCITRAL has also distinguished between two types of Model Laws, with the Model Law on International Commercial Arbitration and the Model Law on Electronic Commerce being singled out as illustrating the flexibility of the form. The Model Law on Commercial Arbitration has been described as a procedural instrument, providing a discrete set of interdependent articles, and it was suggested that, in adopting the Model Law, very few amendments or changes were required. 'Deviations from the Model Law text have, as a rule, very rarely been made by countries adopting enacting legislation, suggesting that it has been widely accepted as a coherent model text.'[93] By contrast, the Model Law on Electronic Commerce has been described as more conceptual, establishing a set of model principles. These are drafted in the form of legislative provisions to facilitate consideration by legislatures and assist in the development

---

91 *Ibid* at 198.

92 See 'Possible Future Work on Insolvency Law' UNCITRAL Working Group on Insolvency Law, 22nd Session (6–17 December 1999), A/CN 9 WG V/WP 50, which adds at p 42: 'The guide might include, for example, information that would assist States in considering what, if any, provision of the model law might have to be varied to take into account particular national circumstances, as well as information relating to discussions in the Working Group on policy options and considerations. In addition, matters not addressed in the text of the model law may be included in the guide by way of further explanation and guidance to States enacting the model law.'

93 *Ibid* at 42.

of laws. It was suggested that legislation adopting the Model Law should largely reflect the principles of the text, but could depart from it in terms not only of drafting, but also in the combination of provisions proposed for adoption.[94]

The more 'conceptual' form of Model Law has the advantage that if a UNCITRAL Working Group cannot achieve consensus on some provisions, the complete project need not be abandoned in favour of a more limited set of prescriptions that do not cover the same field. Alternative provisions may be included in the Model Law with the choice left open to domestic legislatures, or the latter may be permitted to exclude certain provisions in deference to local social or cultural norms that may be at variance with the international norms of the Model Law.[95] In this scenario, guides to enactment can explain how the alternatives might work in practice as well as elaborate upon the competing policies and principles that are contained in the choices being offered. The existence of alternatives in the Model Law, as well as the possibility of exclusions, promotes a softer notion of harmonisation that is consistent with the reduction of differences over time.

The focus on 'modernisation' rather than 'harmonisation' has also encouraged a move away from rigid Conventions. There is a need for supple instruments that offer flexibility in reforming a broad range of laws, especially with the benefit of time and incremental progress. The rigidity and inflexibility of Conventions leads to the exclusion of issues where delegates cannot reach consensus or, worse still, agreement among delegates on a form of words but no agreement as to the meaning of those words. Such reliance on compromise language either leaves an issue unresolved or muddier than before. The changing context, and the development of the modernisation mission, has encouraged UNCITRAL to make use of new forms of modernising instruments that vindicate that mission. Uniformity may be unnecessary to the goal of modernisation and indeed may hinder it on occasion. Therefore, it is inappropriate for law reform projects with the modernisation mission in mind to rely on Conventions that are intended to produce a single, uniform legal standard.[96]

But even a Model Law may be insufficiently flexible to respond to the modernisation agenda. For instance, in 1981 the UNCITRAL Secretariat reported success on its initial 'four fields of interest: the law of international sales of goods, carriage of goods by sea, international

---

[94] See generally UNCITRAL Model Law on Electronic Commerce with Guide to Enactment (1996).

[95] S Block-Lieb and T Halliday above, note 76 at 495–496.

[96] *Ibid* at 478.

negotiable instruments and international commercial arbitration'.[97] In each of these fields, 'comprehensive texts' had been adopted but the Secretariat added that '[t]he subject matter of the Commission's new programme of work does not always require a comprehensive solution. . . .The difference in magnitude of the problems considered may have an impact on the final form which the Commission's work might take.' It was suggested that, if it was not feasible for UNCITRAL to suggest a text in a form that was suitable for adoption, then it might instead adopt a 'guidelines approach' on the basis that 'the development of guidelines or recommendations may be an appropriate first objective, leaving until later a decision as to whether further actions are desirable'.

A standalone Legislative Guide seems particularly appropriate when law reform seeks to reject law that is supposedly outmoded in favour of new, and more modern, principles.[98] Other international instruments are less well suited to this task. With Model Laws there is somewhat greater latitude in that domestic legislation may be enacted that adopts some, but not all, provisions of the Model Laws. One is stretching the concept of a Model Law very far however, if States are regarded as given a fairly free hand to choose among the provisions of a Model Law. For this reason, it is not altogether surprising that both the Insolvency and Secured Transactions Working Groups opted to work on Legislative Guides, rather than a Model Law or Convention.[99] The UNCITRAL Secretariat, in 'selling' to the Commission the task of taking on work in the insolvency and secured transactions fields, commended the flexibility of Legislative Guides as a form, particularly in light of the lack of global consensus on these issues. A propos insolvency, the Secretariat said:[100]

> It is not always possible to draft specific uniform provisions in a suitable form, such as a convention or a model law, for incorporation into national legal systems. One reason may be, for example, that national legal systems use widely disparate legislative techniques and approaches for solving a given issue, or that

---

[97] Report of the Secretariat of UNCITRAL, A/36/17, reprinted in UNCITRAL Yearbook Vol XII (1981) at 250, and available online at www.uncitral.org.

[98] See R Goode et al. above, note 13 at 200: 'Guides are truly educational exercises, the authors being the teachers and the government officials and parliamentarians being the pupils: a guide discusses in depth the structure of legal problems (for example, the taking of security in movables, the issues to be dealt with in the contract between franchisor and franchisee), including their economic, technical and other factual background, outlines possible solutions and explains the underlying legal concepts, and ideally concludes by making recommendations.'

[99] See the discussion in S Block-Lieb and T Halliday above, note 76 at 491–493.

[100] 'Working Paper Submitted to the Working Group on Insolvency Law on the Work of Its Twenty-second Session: Possible Future Work on Insolvency Law: Note by the Secretariat' A/CN 9/WG V/WP 5 (1999) at paras 167–168.

> States are not yet ready to agree on a common approach or a common rule. A further reason may be that not all States perceive a sufficiently urgent need to find a uniform solution to a particular issue. . . .[I]t may be appropriate not to attempt to elaborate a text in the form of a model statute, but to limit the action to a set of principles or legislative recommendations.

Similar sentiments were articulated within the Secured Transactions Working Group.[101] Before beginning the drafting exercise, the Working Group considered the merits of a 'convention unifying substantive rules governing security interests', a 'convention establishing uniform conflict rules', a 'convention or model law creating an international security interest', a 'statement of principles accompanied by a model law' or a 'statement of principles accompanied by a legal guide'. The Convention option was ruled out because national legal systems were considered to be too divergent and because a Convention would not be sufficiently flexible to take into account the diversity of circumstances across the world.[102] There was more support for the idea of a Model Law and it was suggested that a comprehensive Model Law had the potential to bring about the greatest possible benefit.[103] On the other hand, the UNCITRAL Secretariat hedged its bets, stating that 'to the extent that such a model law would need to reflect certain fundamental guiding principles that would not be common ground to all legal systems, it would represent a significant change from current law in many countries'. Therefore, it was cautious about the prospects of such a Model Law gaining general acceptance. While it ventured the view that a Model Law would be more desirable from the point of view of completeness and uniformity, it also observed that a set of key objectives and core principles along with a legislative guide 'would still be sufficiently useful to justify future work'.[104]

Legislative Guides are a malleable mechanism but the recommendations therein contained may be couched in a harder or softer form and they may reflect different orientations, whether pluralistic, or tending to mirror the norms of a hegemonic State. At the risk of over-simplification, the Insolvency Legislative Guide is more the former and the Secured Transactions Guide more the latter. The Insolvency Guide was a pragmatic response to address the diversity of insolvency laws among nation States and it was widely believed that policy differences were too deeply

---

[101] 'Security Interests: Current Activity and Possible Future Work: Report of the Secretary-General' – A/CN 9/475 (2000) and available online at http://www.uncitral.org/uncitral/en/commission/sessions/33rd.html.

[102] *Ibid* at para 46.

[103] *Ibid* at para 50.

[104] *Ibid* at para 62.

embedded in States to permit agreement on either a Convention or Model Law. Thus, the flexible alternative of a set of principles embodying legislative recommendations was seized upon. It was envisaged that these principles and recommendations would be of assistance in reviewing the adequacy of national laws and similar legislative texts in the insolvency field. They would set out a list of possible legislative solutions on certain issues, but not necessarily a single set of model prescriptions for the issues addressed.

The Insolvency Guide combined principles with recommendations, choices with justifications and options with explanations. The Insolvency Guide has been praised for employing a sophisticated repertoire of rules, organised in a hierarchy of specificity or generality that depends on the type of consensus that could be reached on a particular issue.[105] It is suggested that this array of rule-types contains ample flexibility to deal with cross-national variability on issues. For instance, where it did not seem possible to obtain consensus on the content of a particular rule, consensus could be achieved on the need for some sort of rule ('architectural' recommendations) coupled with acceptance of the principle that the rule should be clearly and expressly stated in the insolvency law. The Legislative Guide on Secured Transactions follows the same basic approach but is much more prescriptive in tone, leaving less leeway to national legislatures. Less use is made of so-called architectural recommendations and the Secured Transactions Guide also keeps very closely to the contours of American law, leaving less room for competing principles in other national legal systems to come into play.

CONCLUSION

UNCITRAL was established as a specialist organisation within the United Nations family to facilitate international trade. Its original mission was spoken of in terms of the progressive unification and harmonisation of the law of international trade. UNCITRAL has interpreted its mission flexibly by placing greater emphasis on modernisation rather than harmonisation. 'Modernisation' is interpreted as being within its remit on the basis that international trade is best facilitated by a modernised law. The international Convention is the classic vehicle by which international trade law is harmonised but UNCITRAL has made increasing use of Model Laws and Legislative Guides to keep pace with the modernising agenda.

---

105 S Block-Lieb and T Halliday above, note 76.

The Legislative Guide is a particularly flexible tool in that it contains policy prescriptions, recommendations and explanations for action rather than just a 'take it or leave it' diagnosis. Legislative Guides, however, come in different shapes and sizes and may be more or less imperative and prescriptive. They may also come with different biases and orientations. This chapter has outlined a difference in approach between the Insolvency Legislative Guide and the Secured Transactions Legislative Guide. This difference will be further considered and elaborated upon in subsequent chapters, but first it is necessary to address the case for modernising and harmonising international commercial law as the Secured Transactions Legislative Guide purports to do.

2. The case for harmonising and modernising the law of international trade

UNCITRAL's business is the harmonisation and modernisation of the law of international trade. This chapter considers the case for harmonisation and modernisation in this sphere and asks a number of subsidiary questions. The first part considers the justifications advanced for harmonisation and modernisation. The second part considers the objections raised against harmonisation and modernisation. The third part considers whether harmonisation/modernisation can be achieved in practice. The fourth part explains the concept of path dependency and how this may influence the harmonisation and modernisation agenda. The final part concludes and summarises the discussion.

WHY HARMONISATION AND MODERNISATION?

In the UNCITRAL Legislative Guide on Secured Transactions, harmonisation and modernisation are seen as working hand in glove. The Guide calls for the modernisation of secured credit law by the reform of rules that inhibit the taking of security either in whole or in part. The intention is that States across the world should subscribe to the same set of basic principles for the taking and enforcement of security. Jurisdictional diversity would be reduced, if not entirely eliminated, in favour of a common international set of 'modern' prescriptions. The modernisation script sees the substitution of restrictive national provisions by international provisions that facilitate rather than obstruct secured credit. As pointed out in the previous chapter, it is hard to be against modernisation since the corollary implies being outdated and old-fashioned. On the other hand, one might criticise the Guide on the basis firstly, that the modernising agenda it propounds in reality reflects a particular set of ideological values. Secondly, it could be argued that the Guide unduly mirrors the provisions of Article 9 of the American Uniform Commercial Guide and therefore it represents a further manifestation of US legal dominance. These criticisms will be addressed in later chapters but the work of this chapter is really to consider at a more basic level the justifications given for legal harmonisation, i.e. the displacement of national solutions in favour of some supranational modernist ideal from outside. The arguments usually given for harmonisation may be stated as follows:[1]

(1) Harmonisation reduces the operation of conflict-of-law rules. Such rules are often thought to be obscure and unsatisfactory, particularly by practitioners, and they often give rise to forum-shopping opportunities. Harmonisation does this by substituting a single law for a proliferation of national laws. It also fills a legal vacuum through the provision of rules in a field where national law was previously non-existent or obscure.

(2) Harmonisation also provides contracting parties with a neutral law and thereby eliminates the risks in having to choose the purely national law of one of the contracting parties.

(3) An international instrument that represents the outcome of a harmonisation process is more likely to achieve widespread international acceptance than the commercial law of another State no matter however powerful, or significant in terms of international trade, that other State may be. This reflects the pragmatic reality of a world where national pride still carries considerable weight. Even though suitable national provisions may be lacking, few States feel comfortable enough in their own sovereignty and national identity openly to embrace foreign commercial law, despite the fact that the foreign law may offer appropriate solutions to the legal problems at hand. Political reasons therefore militate against the open adoption of a foreign law although the search for an international instrument may obscure the influence of a foreign legal order or legal ideology.[2]

Law making, and the idea of law making, is closely related to issues of sovereignty and self-determination and this in turn encourages local law production rather than supply from a foreign source. The fact that an international instrument exists, on the other hand, provides the requisite degree of cover for States wishing to preserve the appearance at least of sovereign dignity and independence. Moreover, some foreign laws may have a bad smell in certain quarters, redolent of domination or legal imperialism, and States may be anxious to escape the odour. As Frederick Schauer has argued, factors other than the receiving nation's own evaluation of the worth of legal ideas, and other than an objective

---

[1] See also L Mistelis 'Is Harmonisation a Necessary Evil? The Future of Harmonisation and New Sources of International Trade Law' in I Fletcher, L Mistelis and M Cremona eds *Foundations of International Trade Law* (London, Sweet & Maxwell, 2001) at 20–21.

[2] See K Pistor 'The Standardisation of Law and Its Effect on Developing Economies' (2002) 50 AJCL 97 at 108.

assessment of the worth of legal ideas, are significant determinants of the patterns of legal globalisation.[3]

(4) Harmonisation produces a law that has been subject to the influence of many different jurisdictions and is therefore more likely to be in tune with the needs of international business relationships than national law, which is largely the product of domestic concerns and focuses on intra-State transactions. Put another way, while the unification process may sacrifice something in the way of accountability, it has at least the possibility of compensating through:

> exploiting technical expertise more fully than national law makers normally do. Unencumbered by petty political obstacles, experts engaged in the drafting of unified laws may have the freedom to develop sophisticated and well-balanced drafts that anticipate and resolve a wide range of potential problems. We should expect them to produce legislation that achieves both elegance and a certain scientific soundness.[4]

Shortly stated, the experts involved in the international harmonisation process work together to devise a draft that embodies what in their view are the best rules for international commerce. These technical experts should have a relatively free hand in trying to work out a common ground that can transcend differences in culture, history, levels of economic development, and social structure. 'While ideological and conceptual barriers may remain, the process should be free of less elevated distractions.'[5]

(5) Harmonisation is designed to reduce divergence across frontiers. This in turn may reduce legal risk and transaction costs thereby facilitating international business transactions. The expenses should be lower if the law applicable to all parts of the transaction is the same, irrespective of whether the relevant part is foreign or domestic.

(6) Harmonisation of law across frontiers breeds familiarity and enhances trade prospects. This in turn increases trust and understanding and serves to minimise the prospect of conflict. In short, the objective is to make peace through harmonised commercial law though this slogan does not trip off the tongue as easily as 'Make Love Not War'.

All these justifications for harmonisation, however, can be the subject of powerful counter-arguments. The first and second set of justifications

---

[3] See F Schauer 'The Politics and Incentives of Legal Transplantation' (2000) Center for International Development at Harvard Working Paper No 44 at p 24 – www.cid.harvard.edu/cidwp/044.htm.

[4] P Stephan 'The Futility of Unification and Harmonization in International Commercial Law' (1999) 39 Virginia Journal of International Law 743 at 753 but Stephan's general thesis is to suggest that UNCITRAL's quest for global harmonisation is mistaken.

[5] *Ibid* at 756.

are about eliminating obscure conflicts-of-law rules and introducing a neutral, unified law, but parties to a contract can always choose the law of a supposedly neutral third country. English law, New York law or Swiss law is often chosen for this reason by parties in different parts of the world. There may be additional costs and complexities caused by the introduction of a novel transnational law.[6] Parties may have to expend time and energy in coming to grips with the new transnational law as well as understanding and appreciating its effects. The transnational law may not have its roots in a particular national legal system and its proper interpretation may take some time, thus generating uncertainties. As Paul Stephan has presciently observed:[7]

> The persons to whom the rules will apply need to know how they work in practice, how decision makers fill in the inevitable gaps and react to particular fact patterns. They can acquire this information only by observing the system over time on the basis of many iterations of the dispute resolution process. . . . Any new internationally unified system . . . must involve a break with the past, and thus sacrifices density and stability.

Hugh Collins has remarked that the creation of another system of law, which the parties may select as their choice of law, does not reduce either uncertainty or ignorance: 'It has no benefits from a transaction cost point of view. Indeed, as is the case with any transnational and novel law, it is likely in fact to increase uncertainty, at least in the medium term, so that it would provoke increased transaction costs.[8]

The third and fourth justifications are that a harmonised product is more likely to be the product of many different influences and legal systems and is lacking the parochial instincts of national law. One could however turn this on its head and say that transnational law may end up as a mishmash lacking unity and coherence. International instruments may have a strong tendency either to further the cause of particular interest groups or to compromise legal certainty. In either of these scenarios, they do not seem to offer any additional benefits over and above rules

---

6 See H Collins 'Transaction Costs and Subsidiarity in European Contract Law' in S Grundmann and J Stuyck eds *An Academic Green Paper on European Contract Law* (The Hague, Kluwer Law International, 2002) 269 at 281: 'Transnational regulation can reduce transactions in commercial transactions only by becoming a compulsory uniform law, but the real benefits only emerge if the transnational regulation becomes reasonably certain or predictable.'

7 P Stephan above, note 4 at 792.

8 See H Collins 'Transaction Costs and Subsidiarity in European Contract law' above, note 6 at 277. See generally H Collins *The European Civil Code: The Way Forward* (Cambridge, CUP, 2008) chapter 3.

emanating from national legislatures. For example, Lord Hobhouse has remarked that conventions like the Vienna Sales Convention[9]

> are inevitably and confessedly drafted as multi-cultural compromises between different schemes of law. Consequently they will normally have less merit than most of the individual legal systems from which they have been derived. They lack coherence and consistency. They create problems about their scope. They introduce uncertainty where no uncertainty existed before. They probably deprive the law of those very features which enable it be an effective tool for the use of international commerce.

Advocates of harmonisation might respond that while there are examples of good and bad products of harmonisation there is no such thing as the perfect draft. It is easy to pick to pieces the open texture and verbal infelicities of international instruments but purely domestic law may suffer no less from obscurity, verbosity and general bad drafting.

The fifth factor is that harmonisation by reducing divergence can reduce legal risk and transaction costs.[10] On the one hand, while harmonisation may be desirable to the extent that it reduces legal risk, it ceases to be desirable with the imposition of so many highly developed and specific sets of rules that a substantial number of transactions require extensive individualised negotiations. Moreover, there is little empirical evidence that divergent national legal regimes present insuperable hindrances to international trade.[11] Most transactions today take place using law that has not been harmonised and this shows that harmonisation is not necessary for international trade and investment to take place.[12] It may be the case that international transactions are more expensive than purely domestic transactions in terms of transaction costs because of increased legal uncertainties, but these legal uncertainties can always be factored into the price and reflected in the terms of the agreement. A transnational uniform law may not actually achieve greater trade flows in that barriers to transacting

---

[9] JS Hobhouse 'International Conventions and Commercial Law: In Pursuit of Uniformity' (1990) 106 LQR 530 at 533.

[10] See P Stephan above, note 4 at 748.

[11] But see Ole Lando 'Why Does Europe Need a Civil Code' in S Grundmann and J Stuyck eds above, note 6 at 207: 'In Europe the existing variety of contract laws is a non-tariff barrier to the inter-Union trade. It is the aim of the Union to do away with restrictions of trade within the Communities, and therefore the differences of law that restrict this trade should be abolished.' See generally S Vogenauer and S Weatherill 'The European Community's Competence for a Comprehensive Harmonisation of Contract Law – an Empirical Analysis' [2005] European Law Review 821, and see now *Green Paper from the Commission on policy options for progress towards a European Contract Law for consumers and businesses* (Brussels, European Commission, July 2010) COM(2010)348 final.

[12] See K Pistor above, note 2.

across international frontiers are often psychological or social rather than merely legal. Non-legal considerations such as language barriers, lack of a common basis of trust and understanding, lack of local knowledge and lack of familiarity with local business practices are likely to loom larger in terms of impeding international trade.[13]

The final justification about international trade promoting peace and understanding is a bit like motherhood and apple pie. It is hard to be against peace and understanding but one can question whether trade does actually bring about increased peace and understanding. Can trade rivalries and battles for markets not lead to more disharmony and misunderstanding? Moreover, there is the potentially competing principle of national sovereignty that has to be brought into the equation. The establishment of UNCITRAL in 1966 was rooted in ethical considerations. It was argued that newly independent nations, who had just thrown off the yoke of colonialism, needed to be involved in the process of harmonising international trade law. But UNCITRAL drafts are much more likely to reflect the knowledge and experience of the developed world in general, and the US in particular. Others have spoken of a theory of imperial law,[14] of how the intellectual wind has changed, and how the imprint of the US, whether through 'prestige' or on supposed economic efficiency grounds, is likely to be deeply felt on 'harmonised' international commercial law.[15] As will become apparent later, this is particularly true with the UNCITRAL Legislative Guide on Secured Transactions.

THE CASE AGAINST HARMONISATION/ MODERNISATION

Loss of Sovereignty and Lack of Opportunities for Jurisdictional Competition

Objections to the word 'harmonised' are based upon an intricate interlinking of constitutional, economic and cultural considerations. In particular,

---

[13] See generally S Macaulay 'Non-contractual Relations in Business' (1963) 28 American Sociological Review 55; 'The Real and the Paper Deal: Empirical Pictures of Relationships, Complexity and the Urge for Transparent Principles' (2003) 66 MLR 44. See also J Michie and S Deakin *Contracts, Co-operation and Competition: Studies in Economics, Management and Law* (Oxford, OUP, 1997).

[14] See U Mattei 'A Theory of Imperial Law: A Study on U.S. Hegemony and the Latin Resistance' (2002) 10 Indiana Journal of Global Legal Studies 383.

[15] U Mattei 'Efficiency in Legal Transplants: An Essay in Comparative Law and Economics' (1994) 14 International Review of Law and Economics 3.

forms of harmonisation or modernisation that involve 'out with the old and in with the new' make deep inroads on the sovereignty and autonomy of nation States.[16] 'Unified' or even 'harmonised' transnational law suppresses national differences for the sake of uniformity and there is now little or no opportunity for national autonomy and divergence.[17] In short, jurisdictional diversity creates opportunities for competition between national legal orders whereas jurisdictional uniformity eliminates these opportunities.[18] The scope for innovation at the local level is reduced, if not entirely eliminated, and as a result there is less chance for initially unpromising, but ultimately beneficial ideas, to win through and gain general international acceptance. The creation of international uniformity can be stifling and can lead to economic sterility.[19] For instance, Lord Hobhouse has remarked that international commerce is best served 'by encouraging the development of the best schemes in a climate of free competition and choice'.[20] Where there is a plurality of approaches to commercial law making across countries, then so-called 'seeds of ingenuity' can be sown, tested and put into play at the local and national level and then reproduced across national frontiers if they turn out to be generally beneficial. A general 'harmonised' international legal order may submerge these potentially enriching seedbeds of dynamism and innovation in a sea of sterile uniformity.

This proposition builds upon a widely cited article by Charles Tiebout suggesting that a decentralised system of government, with horizontally arrayed municipalities competing to attract residents on the basis of differing tax and benefit structures, generates increased social welfare while not

---

[16] On nation-building and the idea of civil codes see generally W van Gerven 'Codifying European Private Law: Top Down and Bottom Up' in S Grundmann and J Stuyck eds above, note 6 at 405.

[17] See, for example, P Legrand 'On the Unbearable Localness of the Law: Academic Fallacies and Unseasonable Observations' [2002] European Review of Private Law 61; 'The Impossibility of Legal Transplants' (2003) 4 Maastricht Journal 111 and 'Antivonbar' (2006) 1 JCL 1 and for a slightly different perspective see B Markesinis 'Why a Code Is Not the Best Way to Advance the Cause of European Unity' [1997] European Review of Private Law 519.

[18] See Roger Van den Bergh 'Forced Harmonisation of Contract Law in Europe: Not to Be Continued' in S Grundmann and J Stuyck eds above, note 6 at 267: '[t]he advantages of competition between legal rules must not be underestimated: if rules differ, more preferences can be satisfied and learning processes remain possible.'

[19] See generally A Ogus 'Competition Between National Legal Systems: A Contribution of Economic Analysis to Comparative Law' (1999) 48 ICLQ 405, and see also U Mattei 'A Transaction Costs Approach to the European Civil Code' [1997] European Review of Private Law 537.

[20] J Hobhouse 'International Conventions and Commercial Law: In Pursuit of Uniformity' (1990) 106 LQR 530 at 535.

leaving anybody worse off as a result.[21] Frank Easterbrook has used this analysis to make the point that:[22] '[w]hen governments become sufficiently plentiful, and when the scope of laws matches the domain of their costs and benefits (that is, when costs and benefits are all felt within the jurisdiction enacting the laws), competitive forces should be as effective with governments as they are with private markets.' On this analysis, experimentation is best encouraged through the adoption of innovative rules at the national level and then permitting parties to select such rules to govern their relationships rather than by trying to achieve consensus in favour of innovation at the international level.

To the extent that innovation at the international level requires the exclusion of all other alternatives, securing consensus in favour of a novel legal rule would not be easy.[23] On the other hand, allowing individual States the opportunity to experiment instead of seeking out international uniformity means that many experiments may proceed at once. Not all innovations will turn out to be successful and the costs of wasted expenditure or unanticipated harm are reduced if the unsuccessful experiment is confined to a single jurisdiction or at least not reproduced across the whole international domain. Occasionally, a constellation of forces as well as institutional dynamics means that national legislation is captured by special interest groups, but there is no reason to suppose that such groups would be any less powerful at the international level. 'To guard against bad laws . . . we still should want a system with pluralism at the national level, albeit with less than complete freedom on the part of private parties to pick and choose among national laws.'[24]

The virtues of regulatory competition have been extolled in many fields, not least for providing the possibility of a more dynamic and innovative law-making process[25] though commentators have also drawn attention to the risk of 'social dumping'[26] and a so-called race to the

---

21 C Tiebout 'A Pure Theory of Local Expenditures' (1956) 64 Journal of Political Economy 416. Tiebout concedes however (at 424) his solution may not be perfect because of 'institutional rigidities' but he argues that it is 'the best that can be obtained given preferences and resource endowments'.

22 See F Easterbrook 'Federalism and European Business Law' (1994) 14 International Review of Law and Economics 125 at 127–128.

23 See P Stephan above, note 4 at 793.

24 *Ibid* at 796.

25 D Esty and D Geradin eds *Regulatory Competition and Economic Integration: Comparative Perspectives* (Oxford, OUP, 2001), and see generally F von Hayek 'Competition as a Discovery Procedure' (2002) 5(3) Quarterly Journal of Austrian Economics at 9.

26 In the context of employment law the European Court of Justice (ECJ) made specific reference to social dumping in Case 341/05 *Laval un Partneri Ptd v Svenska Byggnadsarbetareförbundet* [2007] ECR I-5751 at para 103. See also Case C-438/05

bottom.[27] In short, there is a lively debate about whether harmonisation or regulatory competition produces better rules from an economic efficiency point of view. The debate has spanned various branches of law, including the market for incorporations, and has proved particularly contentious in 'federal' systems such as the European Union where, for instance, a company may incorporate in one EU Member State but then carry on business in another. Advocates of regulatory competition argue that the result of harmonisation is suboptimal rules. The argument is that the process of selecting the harmonised rules will, or may, lead to the choice of the lowest common denominator instead of rules that pass muster on an efficiency criterion. Countries will be locked into suboptimal rules instead of being free to adopt better rules and respond to changing circumstances. Regulatory competition advocates suggest that competition between countries will lead to a race to the top and engender rule efficiency, because experience will teach them that in the long run they benefit from a high-quality and stable legal system.

Critics counter by referring to 'negative externalities' – the adverse impact of rules adopted in a particular jurisdiction on other jurisdictions. Countries, in an effort to attract foreign capital, may offer lax laws and lax standards of supervision in various spheres including tax, environmental protection and financial market regulation. In the EU context, financial institutions authorised in one jurisdiction are 'passported' to conduct business in other jurisdictions, and lax standards of regulation and supervision in the 'home' jurisdiction carry major dangers for the 'host' jurisdiction. Consequently, there is a strong argument in favour of minimum standards to prevent a race to the bottom between different jurisdictions.[28]

International Transport Workers' Federation, Finnish Seamen's Union v Viking Line ABP [2008] 1 CMLR 51.

[27] See generally J Dammann 'Freedom of Choice in European Company Law' (2004) 29 Yale Journal of International Law 477; J Armour 'Who Should Make Corporate Law? EC Legislation versus Regulatory Competition' (2005) 58 Current Legal Problems 369; and A Johnston 'EC Freedom of Establishment, Employee Participation in Corporate Governance and the Limits of Regulatory Competition' (2006) 6 Journal of Corporate Law Studies 71. See also C Barnard, 'Social Dumping and Race to the Bottom: Some Lessons for the EU from Delaware?' (2000) 25 EL Rev 57; L Enriques and M Gelter 'Regulatory Competition in European Company Law and Creditor Protection' (2006) 7 European Business Organization Law Review 417 and A Johnston and P Syrpis 'Regulatory Competition in European Company Law after Cartesio' [2009] EL Rev 378.

[28] The literature is voluminous, but for a sample in the area of corporate law see R Buxbaum and K Hopt eds *Legal Harmonization and the Business Enterprise* (Berlin, de Gruyter, 1988). See also R Romano *The Genius of American Corporate Law* (Washington, American Enterprise Institute, 1993); R Romano 'Law as a Product: Some Pieces of the Incorporation Puzzle' (1985) 1 Journal of Law, Economics and Organisations 225; L Bebchuk, 'Federalism and the Corporation: The Desirable Limits on State Competition in

Both harmonisation and regulatory competition can lead to suboptimal legal rules, though for different reasons. In respect of harmonisation, the pressure to compromise and achieve consensus can lead to imprecision and indeterminacies. But regulatory competition, apart from giving rise to the possibility of 'bottom scraping', may lead to an unequal allocation of benefits. Once the merits of a particular jurisdiction or regulatory regime have been established, that jurisdiction etc. has 'first mover' advantage and the advantages conferred by that status are not easily emulated by other jurisdictions.

Objections on Grounds of Legal Culture

On the cultural front, it can be argued that national law, even national commercial law, is closely connected with a country's history and development. For instance, Reinhard Zimmermann records that when the German Civil Code, the BGB, was enacted a leading German publication marked the occasion with a large front-page heading 'Ein Volk, Ein Reich, Ein Recht', which translates as One People, One Empire, One Law.[29] Historically, the 'law correlates with culture in the broadest sense' notion has been closely associated with Montesquieu, who declared that laws

> should be so closely tailored to the people for whom they are made, that it would be pure chance if the laws of one nation could meet the needs of another . . . They should be relative to the geography of the country; to its climate . . . to the quality of the land, its situation, and its extent; to the form of life of the people . . .; they should be relative to the degree of liberty that the constitution can tolerate; to the religion of the inhabitants, to their inclinations, wealth, number, commerce, customs, manners.[30]

It is certainly the case that the replacement of national provisions by supranational ones may involve casting aside a great deal of a country's historical legacy.[31] While not all aspects of a country's cultural and

---

Corporate Law' (1992) 105 Harvard Law Review 1435. See also more generally H Collins *The European Civil Code* above, note 8 at 10–12.

29 See R Zimmermann 'Civil Code and Civil Law, The "Europeanisation" of Private Law within the European Community and the Re-emergence of a European Legal Science' (1995) 1 Columbia Journal of European Law 63 at 65. See more generally H Collins 'European Private Law and Cultural Identity of States' [1995] European Review of Private Law 353; *The European Civil Code* above, note 8 chapters 5 and 6; C Twigg-Flesner *The Europeanisation of Contract Law* (Abingdon, Routledge-Cavendish, 2008).

30 Charles de Secondat Montesquieu (1748) *De l'esprit des lois*, book I, ch. 3 (Des lois positives). For statements by other leading thinkers on similar lines see A Watson *Society and Legal Change* (Edinburgh, Scottish Academic Press, 1977) at 3–4.

31 See S Weatherill 'Why Object to the Harmonization of Private Law by the EC' [2004] European Review of Private Law 633.

historical baggage are necessarily worth keeping, proponents of cultural diversity may consider that the large-scale submergence of national legal regimes in a supranational order is deeply troubling. In the European context Stephen Weatherill remarks:[32]

> This objection to harmonisation is driven by the perception that legal culture, represented in part by the shape of private law, has undergone a long-term, frequently unplanned evolution in the Member States, reflecting a range of influences. To confine such richness within the straitjacket of harmonization is to rob Europe of its past. . . . More broadly still . . . this dissenting vein is nurtured by the profound belief that Europe is strengthened by its diversity.

Roger Cotterrell has suggested that the dominant trend in modern comparative law scholarship has been to assume that unification or harmonisation of law is a primary objective of comparative legal studies.[33] Of the various reasons given for valuing the search for similarity in law, the main one has been to facilitate trade and transnational trade but Cotterrell points out that law is not merely valuable as a facilitator of contractual, commercial and corporate relationships. Law is also a protector and shaper of traditions, an expression of shared beliefs and ultimate values, and therefore, in much less definable ways, an expression of national expectations, allegiances and emotions. Put most imprecisely and mystically, law can be seen as embodying the spirit of a nation.

Traditionally differences between national legal orders have been seen as quite stark in relation to the common law/civil law divide. Lawyers respectively trained in the common law and in the civilian tradition are seen to approach legal issues in different ways.[34] They have different legal mindsets in that civilians tend to start off with statements of general principles while the common lawyer works more from the specific to the general. For the common lawyer, the facts of a specific situation come first and this leads through a process of analogy and induction to a statement of general principle. The civilian lawyer deduces the approach to be adopted in a

---

[32] *Ibid* at 647.

[33] See R Cotterrell 'Comparative Law and Legal Culture' in R Zimmermann and M Reimann eds *The Oxford Handbook of Comparative Law* (Oxford, OUP, 2006).

[34] See generally R Goode, H Kronke, and E McKendrick *Transnational Commercial Law* (Oxford, OUP, 2007) at 142: 'The common law gives a wide measure of freedom to the parties to a transaction, whether in relation to contractual rights and obligations or in relation to the organisation of property rights. The civil law adopts a more paternalistic, formal attitude which imposes constraints on what can be done. . . . Common law systems tend to be creditor oriented, civil law systems debtor oriented.'

particular case from an initial statement of general principle, thus working the other way around.[35] The differences can be exaggerated in that most areas of private law in the common law world are largely governed or, at the very least, deeply encrusted by statute.[36] But it remains the case that an appreciation of the effects of statute often requires an understanding of the common law backdrop since common law norms continue to apply in areas not regulated by the statute. Descriptions of cultural difference and their rootedness in legal constructs can become starker still when it comes to the contrast between Islamic systems of law and their Western counterparts. For instance, Islamic law embodies a proscription on 'Riba' or interest payments.[37]

The importance of difference has been forcefully expressed by Pierre Legrand, who cautions that the desire for sameness breeds the expectation of sameness which, in turn, begets the finding of sameness.[38] He criticises the 'scripts of underlying unity and transcendental universalism where particularism is assumed to be secondary and fated to play but a peripheral role in the future of human affairs'.[39] Legrand argues that '[c]omparison must not have a unifying, but multiplying effect. . . . It must avoid complicity in the disregard for different ways of doing things and the ensuring exclusion of alterity . . .'[40] Legrand suggests that the diversity of legal traditions, and the diversity of forms that these traditions embody, express the human capacity for choice and self-creation and play a constituting role in shaping cultural identity.

Legrand sees harmonisation endeavours, in part at least, as attempts to undermine national legal cultures. He also seeks to defend both 'culture' and 'legal culture' against claims that they are excessively inward-looking and nationalistic in nature. Culture is seen as 'a horizon of intelligibility' within which the 'effectuation of discriminations manifest themselves'. Legal culture is considered to be 'frameworks of intangibles within which

[35] *Ibid* at 142: 'common law judges are problem solvers rather than theoreticians, whereas the scientific formal approach of the civil law tends to impede effective problem solving', referring to JH Merryman *The Civil Law Tradition* (Stanford, Stanford University Press, 1969) at 71.

[36] See U Mattei *Comparative Law and Economics* (Ann Arbor, University of Michigan Press, 1997) at 79 and more generally L Del Duca 'Developing Global Transnational Harmonization Procedures for the Twenty-first Century: The Accelerating Pace of Common and Civil Law Convergence' (2007) 42 Texas International Law Journal 625.

[37] On Islamic finance see generally H Visser *Islamic Finance: Principles and Practice* (Cheltenham, UK and Northampton, MA, USA, Edward Elgar, 2008); R Ali *Islamic Finance: A Practical Guide* (London, Globe Law and Finance, 2008).

[38] P Legrand 'The Same and the Different' in P Legrand and R Munday eds *Comparative Legal Studies: Traditions and Transitions* (Cambridge, CUP, 2003) at 245.

[39] *Ibid* at 248.

[40] *Ibid* at 299.

interpretive legal communities operate and which have normative force for these communities'.[41] While the notion of culture may be abused by extreme actors, in Legrand's view it neither justifies the denigration of the term nor diminishes its intrinsic appeal. The fact that many concepts may be abused does not justify their jettisoning. Legrand argues that the apparent convergence of different legal systems is based on a misleading and distorted interpretation. In his opinion, legal systems will never converge in any meaningful sense because of fundamental differences between their underlying legal cultures.

Every culture however, including legal culture, is potentially open and dynamic rather than closed or static.[42] Legrand's description of legal systems tends to be grounded on a set of petrified stereotypes that place continuity, rather than change, on a pedestal. Moreover, it harks back to the Savigny–Thibault controversy of nineteenth-century Germany. The historical school of law represented by Savigny stressed the Volkgeist, or particular genius, of each people that was based on language, morals, habits, customs and law. Therefore, Savigny, in opposition to Thibault, was hostile to the projected codification of law in Germany on the basis that the law should arise slowly from the spirit of the people. He suggested that the codification exercise was artificial and constraining.[43]

Culture and tradition, however, as well as legal practices, are not rooted to a particular historical epoch. They cannot be tied down inexorably in a fixed and immovable pattern but instead, they can be transformed over time through absorbing different influences and developments. Sentiments and rhetoric about cultural difference can easily become overblown, ignoring the receptivity of particular legal systems to change.[44] Sources may oscillate and fragment within legal systems and there appear to be many instances of successful transplantation of legal concepts from one system to another, whether through imperial conquest, prestige, familiarity or some other factor. A standard example is Turkey

---

41 P Legrand 'European Legal Systems are Not Converging' (1996) 45 ICLQ 52 at 56.

42 See Mark Van Hoecke 'The Harmonisation of Private Law in Europe: Some Misunderstandings' in Mark Van Hoecke and Francois Ost eds *The Harmonisation of European Private Law* (Oxford, Hart Publishing, 2000) at 5.

43 For reference to this controversy see the review essay by David Gerber 'Idea-Systems in Law: Images of Nineteenth-Century Germany' (1992) 10 Law and History Review 153 and see also W van Gerven 'Codifying European Private Law' in M Van Hoecke ed *Epistemology and Methodology of Comparative Law* (Oxford, Hart Publishing, 2004) 137.

44 See A Chamboredon 'The Debate on a European Civil Code: For an "Open Texture"' in Mark Van Hoecke and Francois Ost eds above, note 42 at 66.

where a Civil Code founded on the Swiss Civil Code has been in force for over 80 years.[45]

Moroever, a stereotyped presentation that depicts the common law as based on case law and civil law as based on a Code does not necessarily tell us about the reality of the living law and, going further than that, points of similarity can be identified between the most superficially divergent systems. For instance, while Islamic law contains a prohibition on interest-bearing instruments, often the same economic result can be achieved by functionally equivalent legal devices such as Ijara and Mudaraba.[46] Ijara is similar to the finance lease, with an asset being leased for its effective economic life. Mudaraba is a form of agency sales financing, with a finance house purchasing assets on behalf of a client and then selling them to the client at a mark-up. Functional equivalents to Islamic finance instruments such as Ijara and Mudaraba exist, for instance, under English law. It has been remarked a propos English law that there 'are many ways of raising cash besides borrowing'.[47]

Many jurisdictions face a recharacterisation debate. In other words, the question is whether particular transactions, described by the parties in a certain way, should be seen or characterised by the law in a particular way. In Islamic jurisprudence the question may be whether a profit-sharing arrangement between a finance house supplying finance and a business entrepreneur in need of finance to expand business operations should be construed as a genuine partnership or instead as a credit transaction involving prohibited Riba. In the US, Article 9 of the Uniform Commercial Code, for the purpose of laying down registration requirements, adopts a broad functional definition of security interests that extends to any transaction, howsoever called, that secures the payment of money or the performance of any obligation. Some transactions are specifically identified as falling within the framework of security interests, including transactions such as retention of title which, in the eyes of English law and other European legal systems, would not be considered to constitute security. Moreover, in the US, outside the Article 9 context, the 'recharacterised' transactions would be viewed in a different light than standard transactions creating security interests.

---

45 See E Orucu 'Turkey: Change under Pressure' in E Orucu, S Attwool and S Coyle eds *Studies in Legal Systems: Mixed and Mixing* (London, Kluwer, 1996) at 89.

46 H Visser *Islamic Finance* above, note 37; R Ali *Islamic Finance* above note 37.

47 *Chow Yoong Hong v Choong Fah Rubber* [1962] AC 209 at 216. See also the comments of Lord Scarman in *Lloyds & Scottish Finance Ltd v Cyril Lord Carpet Sales Ltd* [1992] BCLC 609 at 618–619.

CAN HARMONISATION/MODERNISATION BE ACHIEVED IN PRACTICE?

Harmonisation endeavours are obviously futile if harmonisation or transplantation of legal ideas from one jurisdiction or legal culture to another is impossible to achieve in practice. At one end of this controversy lies Pierre Legrand who appears to argue that legal transplants are impossible, except perhaps to the most superficial degree.[48] At the other end lies a pioneer in the field, Alan Watson, suggesting that the transplant of legal rules is easy in a sense. Watson has argued that, irrespective of opposition from local lawyers etc., legal rules can move and be accepted into another legal system without too much difficulty, even where the rules originate in a very different kind of system. In his view, many legal rules make little impact on individuals, and while very often it is important that there should be a rule on a particular topic, the content of the rule may be of limited significance for general human happiness. Partly for this reason, he suggests that no area of private law can be regarded as extremely resistant to change from foreign influence.[49] In his view, transplants are the most fertile source of development and changes in most legal systems come about as the result of borrowing. This may be the best way of developing a particular system in terms of the economical use of resources and achievement of the most optimal rules.[50]

On certain occasions, Watson has been more modest in his assertions about transplants, and one sympathetic observer suggests that

> [t]wo souls dwell within his breast . . . Weak Watson and Strong Watson. Both Watsons argue against . . . the mirror theory of law, i.e., the theory that law is the mirror of some set of forces (social, political, economic, whatever) external to the law. Weak Watson opposes this theory weakly and cautiously; Strong Watson opposes it strongly and, I think, recklessly.[51]

---

[48] See also Ugo Mattei and Anna di Robilant 'The Art and Science of Critical Scholarship: Postmodernism and International Style in The Legal Architecture of Europe' (2001) 75 Tulane Law Review 1053 at 1073 criticising the 'absurd conclusion' of certain post-modern European scholars that 'legal transplants are impossible, that the importation of the concept of "good faith" into the arsenal of English judges is nothing more than an illusion, and that even the evidence of converging features in different legal systems is only a distorted interpretation due to a misunderstanding of modern hermeneutics'.

[49] A Watson *Legal Transplants: An Approach to Comparative Law* (Edinburgh, Scottish Academic Press, 1974) at 95.

[50] See A Watson *Society and Legal Change* above, note 30 at 141.

[51] W Ewald 'Comparative Jurisprudence (II): The Logic of Legal Transplants' (1995) 43 AJCL 489 at 491.

The 'weaker' Watson concedes that the extent of transplants depends on the receptivity of a system to a particular outside law and the variation in transplant bias is dependent on such factors as the existence of a shared linguistic tradition with a possible donor, the general prestige of the donor system and the accessibility of the latter through writings. Watson also concedes that jurists can at times exaggerate the extent of a transplant. The host system may have a similar rule and little of importance is received apart from the terminology, though the terminological change may guarantee the donor's continuing influence and the time of reception is when the provision can be looked at more closely and the law reformed or made more sophisticated. The 'weaker' Watson acknowledges that context is everything so that a rule, once transplanted, is different in its new home and that it is rules, institutions, legal concepts and structures that are borrowed and not the 'spirit' of a legal system.[52]

By way of summary on the feasibility of transplants, the available evidence would appear to contradict the extreme positions advocated by both Legrand and Watson, instead arriving at a position that is more in keeping with the 'weaker' Watson. It is undoubtedly the case that foreign models are often taken by law makers as valuable resources and tools for effecting change to their own system. In this sense, legal transplants are inevitable. Moreover, belief in convergence has also gained ground through the rise of supranational legal institutions, whether at the regional or global level. While there remain vocal advocates of the importance of difference, as von Mehren remarks 'the once predominant belief in uniqueness as a characteristic of legal systems has lost ground to the belief in convergence'.[53] But legal transplants are not just a recent phenomenon. The Turkish example illustrates this point. This is an extreme example and involves transplanting a considerable part of the legal system. Esin Örücü explains the wholescale reception of foreign laws in Turkey during the 1920s and 1930s as an integral part of President Ataturk's drive to create a 'Westernised', secular and modern society. As Örücü points out:[54]

> No single legal system served as the model. The choice was driven in some cases by the perceived prestige of the model, in some by efficiency and in others by

---

[52] See A Watson 'Legal Transplants and European Private Law (2000) 4 Electronic Journal of Comparative Law – http://www.ejcl.org/ejcl/44/44-2.html/ and see also A Watson *Law out of Context* (Athens GA, University of Georgia Press, 2000) at 1.

[53] See AT von Mehren 'The Rise of Transnational Legal Practice and the Task of Comparative Law' (2000) 75 Tulane Law Review 1215.

[54] See E Orucu *Critical Comparative Law: Considering Paradoxes for Legal Systems in Transition* (Deventer, Kluwer, 1999) 59 at 81 and available also at (2000) 4 Electronic Journal of Comparative Law text accompanying footnote 311 – see www.ejcl.org/41/abs41-1.html.

> chance. Choosing a number of different models may have given the borrowings 'cultural legitimacy' as the desire to modernise and westernise was not beholden to any one dominant culture. . . . It was . . . the civil law, the law of obligations and civil procedure from Switzerland, commercial law, maritime law and criminal procedure from Germany, criminal law from Italy and administrative law from France that were chosen, translated, adapted and adjusted to solve the social and legal problems of Turkey and to fit together.

On the other hand, there are some attempted transplants that seem to go too far. One can highlight the point by referring as an example to the Woody Allen film *Bananas*. In this film, the dictator of a small, fictional Latin American state, San Marcos, in attempting to modernise the country tried to change its language to Swedish. An equally outlandish example might be if one tried to transform Switzerland from a civil law into a common law system by the stroke of a pen.[55]

Turning from the hypothetical to the actual, transplanting 'modern' law into developing societies was one of the goals of the 1960s American 'law and development' movement, but this movement has generally been characterised as a failure – even by its early architects.[56] These architects saw development as a process

> by which 'traditional' or 'backwards' societies would transform along a host of dimensions to become 'modern.' Scholars from a range of disciplines shared the modernization ethos – indeed interdisciplinarity was fundamental to the goal of developing a total theory of society – so they naturally produced traditional-modern schemas based upon their disciplinary concerns.[57]

The architects shared a tacit set of assumptions about the relationship between law and development – a basic paradigm of 'liberal legalism' that was grounded in modernisation theory.[58] This theory suggested that law could be used as a means to promote economic growth. There

---

[55] This comparison was drawn by Ugo Mattei and Anna di Robilant above, note 48 at 1072.

[56] See D Trubek and M Galanter 'Scholars in Self-Estrangement: Some Reflections on the Crisis in Law and Development Studies in the United States' [1974] Wisconsin Law Review 1062 at 1063: 'Many scholars in the area have encountered difficulties defining the nature of their work or explaining its social utility.' See also J Gardner *Legal Imperialism: American Lawyers and Foreign Aid in Latin America* (Madison, University of Wisconsin Press, 1981); F Snyder 'Law and Development in the Light of Dependency Theory' (1980) 14 Law and Society Review 723.

[57] See J Ohnesorge 'Developing Development Theory: Law and Development Orthodoxies and the Northeast Asian Experience' (2007) 28 University of Pennsylvania Journal of International Economic Law 219 at 233 text accompanying footnote 43.

[58] See D Trubek and M Galanter 'Scholars in Self-Estrangement: Some Reflections on the Crisis in Law and Development Studies in the United States' [1974] Wisconsin Law Review 1062 at 1070.

was the perceived obstacle, however, that lawyers and legislators in the developing world held a set of culturally-driven attitudes, beliefs, and expectations about law that was marked by a high degree of formalism.[59] They were thought to make use of abstract and rigid legal rules that were out of touch with social needs and, therefore, often ignored. 'As first-wave law and development scholars perceived it, this state of affairs was paradigmatically not modern.'[60]

According to David Kennedy of Harvard: 'Blind rule following and unimaginative bureaucratic habits were preventing law in the books from realizing its potential in action. The solution was to build a more pragmatic and antiformalist local legal culture . . .'[61] The enthusiasms of the early law and development scholars largely evaporated, however, as their efforts failed to yield immediate fruit. Harsher realities intruded. As one commentator remarks: 'the broader modernization ethos succumbed to realities such as the Vietnam War and the extent to which "modern" Western societies did not themselves fit the model, and as funding for law and development activities dried up'.[62] First wave 'law and development' protagonists conceded in the early 1970s that the attempts to use Western law in the service of Third World development had not fared very well.[63]

Past failure, however, did not prevent the promotion of a largely similar strategy in the aftermath of the collapse of the Berlin Wall and the former Soviet Union. The fall of the former Socialist regimes saw a second wave of law and development initiatives, but this time associated with a neo-liberal rule of law orthodoxy and the so-called 'Washington Consensus'.[64] The Washington Consensus refers to a consensus between three Washington-headquartered institutions – the IMF, World Bank and US Treasury – about what policies were appropriate for developing

---

59 See D Trubek, 'The "Rule of Law" in Development Assistance: Past, Present, and Future' in D Trubek and A Santos eds *The New Law and Economic Development: A Critical Appraisal* (New York, CUP, 2006) at 74.

60 A Cohen 'Thinking with Culture in Law and Development' (2009) 57 Buffalo Law Review 511.

61 D Kennedy 'The "Rule of Law," Political Choices, and Development Common Sense' in D Trubek and A Santos eds above, note 59 at 112.

62 See J Ohnesorge 'Developing Development Theory' above, note 57 at 232.

63 See also J Merryman 'Comparative Law and Social Change: On the Origins, Style, Decline and Revival of the Law and Development Movement' (1977) 25 AJCL 457; F Snyder 'The Failure of Law and Development' [1982] Wisconsin Law Review 373.

64 See J Ohnesorge 'Developing Development Theory' above, note 57 at 243–252 and see also J Ohnesorge 'The Rule of Law, Economic Development, and the Developmental States of Northeast Asia' in C Antons ed *Law and Development in East and South East Asia* (London, RoutledgeCurzon, 2003), which examines the application of rule of law rhetoric in a study of north-east Asian economies.

countries.[65] The Washington Consensus has three pillars – fiscal austerity, privatisation and market liberalisation.[66]

The lessons of these second-wave initiatives are still being learnt, but some interesting findings have already come to light. The main point is that in considering harmonisation or transplantation, the political element cannot be ignored. This, however, is not a particularly new insight. For instance, Kahn-Freund remarked in the 1970s that anyone[67] contemplating the use of foreign legislation for law making in his country must ask himself: 'how far does this rule or institution owe its existence or its continued existence to the distribution of power in the foreign country which we do not share?' Kahn-Freund's theory is carefully nuanced and asks whether, and to what extent, legal institutions and doctrines are embedded in the life of a particular country. At one end of the spectrum they may be so deeply embedded that they are not easily transplantable to another jurisdiction, whereas at the opposite end their roots are much more superficial. Kahn-Freund moves on from Montesquieu[68] and moves on the metaphors by suggesting that in many cases the question is no longer how deeply a particular principle is embedded but rather who has planted the roots and who cultivates the garden.[69]

Analysing and evaluating the Eastern European experience, Berkowitz, Pistor and Richard use empirical evidence to demonstrate broadly this point.[70] Their study seeks to show various potential inefficiencies when law is transplanted into an 'alien' implementing or enforcing environment. Their view is that indigenous law making operates as a kind of focal point for cooperative law-making behaviour which then serves as the focal point for cooperative economic behaviour. They see institutions as being necessary for economic development and indigenous institutions functioning better than transplanted ones.[71] In consequence, attempts should be made to generate an internal process of legal development with a self-sustaining demand for legal innovation and change. While the possibility

---

65 See J Stiglitz *Globalisation and Its Discontents* (London, Penguin, 2002) at 16.

66 *Ibid* at 53–54.

67 O Kahn-Freund 'On Uses and Misuses of Comparative Law' (1974) 37 MLR 1 at 12.

68 Charles de Secondat Montesquieu (1748) *De l'esprit des lois*, book I, chapter 3 (Des lois positives) and see text accompanying note 30 above.

69 *Ibid* at 12–13 and for a response see A Watson 'Legal Transplants and Law Reform' (1976) 92 LQR 79.

70 See D Berkowitz, K Pistor and J-F Richard 'The Transplant Effect' (2003) 51 AJCL 163.

71 On these and related issues, see D North *Institutions, Institutional Change, and Economic Performance: The Political Economy of Institutions and Decisions* (Cambridge, CUP, 1990); R Posner, 'Creating a Legal Framework for Economic Development' (1998) 13 World Bank Research Observer, at 1–11.

of borrowing from other countries is not precluded, a good fit of foreign with domestic law is enhanced by meaningful adaptation of imported laws to local conditions.[72] In a related paper,[73] Pistor has argued on the basis of other empirical findings that laws, to be effective, need to have local constituencies with a strong interest and understanding of the laws.

CONVERGENCE AND PATH-DEPENDENT LEGAL DEVELOPMENTS

The process of legal change is path dependent, even legal change coming from outside. Pistor makes a valuable point about complementarity, suggesting that the interdependence of legal rules means that there are only a few rules that can be understood and applied without reference to other legal rules or concepts.[74] In her view, harmonisation may distort rather than improve the domestic legal framework unless there are complementarities between the new law and pre-existing legal institutions. Moreover, the notion that law is a cognitive institution means that for law to be effective and actually change behaviour, it must be fully understood and embraced by those using the law, i.e. 'customers' and legal intermediaries. The supply of 'better' law from an external source, although it may facilitate more radical change, insulates the law-making process from political and socioeconomic development and therefore distances it from the process of continuous adaptation and innovation.[75]

This line of reasoning ties in with another point about the role of organised pressure groups in channelling the desire and momentum in favour of legal change down a particular path. It is submitted that path-dependency is an important factor that helps to explain continued jurisdictional diversity even in the wake of determined international harmonisation efforts. The rival notions of global convergence and path-dependency have been contested in the secured credit context but the controversy has perhaps been even more acute in the closely aligned area of corporate

---

72 Referring to Cass Sunstein – 'the meaning of legal statements is a function of social norms, not of the speaker's intentions' – 'On the Expressive Function of Law' (1996) 144 University of Pennsylvania Law Review 2021 at 2050 and see also C Sunstein, 'Social Norms and Social Roles' (1996) 96 Columbia Law Review 903 at 925.

73 See generally K Pistor above, note 2 at 129.

74 *Ibid* at 98.

75 See also T Waelde and J Gunderson 'Legislative Reform in Transition Economies: Western Transplants – a Shortcut to Social Market Economy Status' (1994) 43 ICLQ 347; J deLisle 'Lex Americana? United States Legal Assistance, American Legal Models and Legal Change in the Post-Communist World and Beyond' (1999) 20 University of Pennsylvania Journal of International Economic Law 179.

governance.[76] For example, in this sphere Henry Hansmann and Reinier Kraakman have predicted the end of history for corporate law,[77] speaking of a widespread normative consensus that corporate managers should act exclusively in the interests of shareholders, including minority shareholders. In their view, while differences may persist as a result of institutional and historical contingencies, the bulk of legal development worldwide will be towards a standard model of the corporation. Others such as Klaus Hopt have acknowledged a greater role for path-dependent differences between corporate governance regimes that are deeply embedded in a country's tradition, history and culture but, at the same time, suggesting that market forces can be expected to be stronger in the long run.[78] In general, all proponents of convergence are committed to the idea that global competition is a strong enough force to bring about change in the laws. They assume that it is possible for a country to amend its existing legal norms to any degree that is desired or, in other words, that legal systems are free to choose from an open-ended menu of legal rules.[79]

Mark Roe has broken somewhat from this consensus, arguing that political forces cause legal systems to develop path-dependently.[80] It is submitted that Roe's work, while going some way to explain the persistence of divergence, fails to pay sufficient regard to the role of existing legal norms in shaping subsequent legal developments.[81] A distinction may be made between the factors that bring about changes in the law and the form in which the law absorbs the need for change. In short, politics, economics and culture as well as changing social and commercial norms can generate the need to alter legal rules but once such a need has emerged, the reform process has historically been shaped by legal doctrine. The

---

76 See generally P Hall and D Soskice *Varieties of Capitalism: The Institutional Foundations of Comparative Advantage* (New York, OUP, 2001).

77 H Hansmann and R Kraakman 'The End of History for Corporate Law' (2001) 89 Georgetown Law Journal 439. The title of this paper consciously and provocatively echoes Francis Fukuyama's *The End of History and the Last Man* (New York, Free Press, 1992).

78 See K Hopt 'Common Principles of Corporate Governance in Europe?' in J McCahery et al. *Corporate Governance Regimes, Convergence and Diversity* (Oxford, OUP, 2002) at 175.

79 For a somewhat different perspective see A Dignam and M Galanis 'Corporate Governance and the Importance of Macroeconomic Context' (2008) 28 OJLS 201 asserting the significance of trade and finance to corporate governance outcomes.

80 See M Roe *Political Determinants of Corporate Governance* (Oxford, OUP, 2003); M Roe 'Chaos and Evolution in Law and Economics' (1996) 109 Harvard Law Review 641; L Bebchuk and M Roe 'A Theory of Path Dependence in Corporate Ownership and Governance' (1999) 52 Stanford Law Review 127 and see generally P Gourevitch 'The Politics of Corporate Governance Regulation' (2003) 112 Yale LJ 1864.

81 See generally E Micheler *Property in Securities: A Comparative Study* (Cambridge, CUP, 2007) chapter 15 'Legal development as a path-dependent process' and see the statement at 228 'Legal doctrine causes the law to develop path-dependently'.

result of legal doctrine is to cause the law to develop in a path-dependent fashion. While the law will change and adapt to new demands and circumstances, the change is effected by adapting existing legal concepts rather than by introducing new ones. Legal systems are equipped with a certain limited set of doctrinal tools and these have a self-perpetuating effect. Legal problems are invariably solved by making use of existing concepts that are most developed and therefore safest to use. This is because legal concepts behave differently in different jurisdictions, and the importation of a concept may have unintended consequences for the rest of the body of law in the recipient jurisdiction.[82] Thus the law, and lawyers, tend to absorb change by digging deeper into existing soil, rather than by branching out into new fields. Political and other influences may trigger legal development and cause the law to produce certain outcomes, but the form that represents these outcomes is determined by the legal doctrine prevailing in the jurisdiction concerned. Legal doctrine is an independent factor that determines the form of future development.[83]

The institutions that prevail in a particular jurisdiction influence future developments and lawyers, by virtue of their role in shaping legal doctrine, are in a prime position to play an important role as a pressure group.[84] Their preference for certainty and predictability cause them to favour the use of familiar doctrinal tools rather than experiment with more straightforward, but to them unfamiliar and untested, legal techniques. The preference is for reform that requires little modification of existing rules over reform that requires significant change. Moreover, once a solution has been found to overcome what has been perceived to be a problem or an obstacle by the market, legal practice likes to stick to this solution even though a more straightforward solution may now appear on the horizon.

These points are well illustrated by the English experience of proposals for reform of secured credit law put forward by the Law Commission. The Law Commission advocated an American Article 9-type scheme for England but this endeavour has been resisted successfully thus far. At the forefront of resistance has been an influential lawyers' group that has essentially argued that any reform should occur within the existing legal

[82] See G Teubner 'Legal Irritants: Good Faith in British Law or How Unifying Law Ends up in New Divergences' (1998) 61 MLR 11, but see U Mattei and A di Robilant above, note 48 at 1073.

[83] See generally J Armour, S Deakin, P Lele and M Siems 'How Do Legal Rules Evolve? Evidence from a Cross-Country Comparison of Shareholder, Creditor and Worker Protection' (2009) 57 AJCL 579.

[84] This may be referred to as 'structure-driven path dependence' – see L Bebchuk and M Roe above, note 80.

landscape rather than by seeking a transformation exercise.[85] The English experience suggests that reform efforts are most likely to go down a path-dependent route. Market integration, technological innovation and economic imperatives may inspire reform initiatives in particular States, but the strength of legal doctrine and the influence of legal practice specific to the jurisdiction will shape what emerges at the end of the reform dialogue.

The crucial role of law and lawyers in shaping the reform agenda has been stressed the world over. Arguing from the perspective of law and development, particularly in Peru, Hernando De Soto suggests that no group – aside from terrorists – is in a better position than lawyers to sabotage capitalist expansion and, moreover, that lawyers know how to do it legally.[86] Lawyers are the professionals most involved in the day-to-day business of property, and any genuine change in the property regime and the capital formation process cannot take place without cooperation from at least some of them.

De Soto argues that lawyers are notorious for their reluctance to accept even the smallest changes in their traditional procedures and in his view, passive opposition may be even worse than active opposition. Passive opposition is more invidious for it can stultify progress whereas active opposition either triumphs or is overcome. He points to the fact that some

> statutes have withered on the vine after receiving a welcome from practitioners which proved to be merely lip service or even the kiss of death; other statutes have had built into them a procedure so long-term as to make progress almost imperceptible; such statutes certainly offer no dangers to established practice and so tend to be acceptable to the legal profession, but they do not really achieve the objective; they merely swell the list, if not of failures, at least of 'non-successes'.[87]

De Soto suggests that reformist politicians are at the mercy of legal technocrats who may pay lip service to reform while subverting it in the shadows.

Similar points have been picked up by Berkowitz, Pistor and Richard in their study of legal transition and economic development in Central/Eastern Europe and the former Soviet Union. Their basic proposition is

---

[85] See R Calnan 'The Reform of the Law of Security' [2004] Butterworths Journal of International Banking and Financial Law 88 at 92: 'The Law Commission's imperative seems to be to introduce a US-style functional system as a wholesale replacement for our current system. On a cost-benefit analysis, this seems difficult to justify. The implementation costs will be very large, and it is difficult to see what material benefits will result from it.'

[86] See H De Soto *The Mystery of Capital: Why Capitalism Triumphs in the West and Fails Everywhere Else* (London, Black Swan, 2008) at 209.

[87] *Ibid* at 211.

that for law to be effective, two conditions must be satisfied. Under these conditions they expect the legal order to function just as effectively as in the 'donor' country. The first requirement is that a demand for law must exist so that the law on the books will actually be used in practice, and the second requirement is that legal intermediaries responsible for developing the law are responsive to this demand.[88] They argue that if the transplant adapted the law to local conditions, or had a population that was already familiar with the basic legal principles of the transplanted law, then the expectation is that the law would be used and a strong public demand for enforcement institutions would follow. Legal intermediaries would be able to develop the imported law so as to match demand. The strong demand for law would provide resources for legal change.

On the other hand, they suggest that if the law was not adapted to local conditions, or the local populace was not familiar with the law, then there would be a weak demand for using these laws and legal intermediaries would have a difficult task. 'Countries that receive the law in this fashion are thus subject to the "transplant effect": their legal order would function less effectively than origins or transplants that either adapted the law to local conditions and/or had a population that was familiar with the transplanted law.'[89]

Berkowitz, Pistor and Richard acknowledge that legal transplantation has taken different forms in different countries, but their fundamental thesis is that a 'voluntary' transplant increases its own receptivity when it makes a significant adaptation of the foreign formal legal order to local conditions, in particular to the pre-existing formal and informal legal order. 'Changes in the transplanted rules of legal institutions indicate that the appropriateness of these rules has been considered and modifications were made to take into account domestic legal practice or other local conditions.'[90] They also recognise that a transplant is more likely to take root and flourish when the recipient country has a familiarity with the legal system that it uses as a model for legal borrowing. The implication is that transplants work best within legal families.[91]

This thesis has been expressly articulated by Holger Spamann,[92] who

---

88 See D Berkowitz, K Pistor and J-F Richard above, note 70.

89 *Ibid* at 168.

90 *Ibid* at 179.

91 *Ibid* and see also the statement at 181: 'From our discussion of law as a cognitive institution, it follows that the common history must still be recognizable in legal practice at the time when the foreign law is transplanted.'

92 H Spamann 'Contemporary Legal Transplants – Legal Families and the Diffusion of (Corporate) Law' [2009] Brigham Young University Law Review 1813. See also J Armour et al. above, note 83.

lends empirical support to the proposition that diffusion within legal families is the most successful case.[93] In other words, the degree of adaptability in transplant countries will in part depend on the closeness of ties with the mother country, particularly language.[94] According to Spamann, the choices of domestic actors are constrained by the available models, that models of one's own legal family are more available and hence more likely to be adopted than others, and that at least some of the differences between core models survive the transplantation to the periphery.[95] He states:[96]

> Transactional lawyers always start drafting from the template of a prior transaction. Given all the contingencies that need to be considered, starting from a blank page would probably be considered professional negligence. To be sure, the template (foreign model) will be adapted to the special circumstances of the transaction (recipient country), and drafters aspire to choose a suitable model. Still, there is good reason to think that some of the substance of the precedent (foreign model) will find its way into the final product (domestic law) even though the drafters would not have put it in had they started from scratch, or if they had perfect foresight and could draft a perfect contract (statute).

CONCLUSION

This chapter has rehearsed some of the often-stated justifications given for the harmonisation of commercial laws – increased trade and understanding, reducing transaction costs, provision of a neutral law to govern inter-State transactions. It concludes that on close analysis many of these justifications are less convincing than they might initially appear. International trade operates on a massive scale despite the lack of legal harmonisation in many areas. Nevertheless, having similar rules in different jurisdictions should increase the comfort factor for traders and investors and improve the propensity to trade or invest. The chapter also considered powerful objections raised against harmonisation; namely the limitation on the space available for jurisdictional competition and the threat posed to national legal cultures. While jurisdictional competition

---

93 See also W Twining 'Social Science and Diffusion of Law' (2005) 32 Journal of Law and Society 203 at 205; 'Diffusion of Law: A Global Perspective' (2005) 49 Journal of Legal Pluralism 1.

94 M Siems 'Shareholder Protection Around the World (Leximetrics II)' (2008) 33 Delaware Journal of Corporate Law 111 at 141–142.

95 H Spamann 'Contemporary Legal Transplants – Legal Families and the Diffusion of (Corporate) Law' [2009] Brigham Young University Law Review 1813 at 1822.

96 *Ibid* at 1857.

may increase the opportunities for experimentation and give rise to the possibility of desirable innovation, there is also the risk of a race to the bottom and the diminution of standards to the detriment of the vulnerable and poorly resourced. Homogenisation of law across international frontiers may pose something of a risk for national legal cultures but it should be remembered that legal systems are not rigid and inflexible over time. They are subject to a continual process of influence and development. Legal ideas are often imported from outside but they are most likely to need indigenous institutions to flourish and develop. Without such institutions imported ideas may wither on the vine. Successful transplants are most likely when the imported idea builds on existing institutions or legal principles in the receiving jurisdiction. In this respect, legal change is most likely to take place in a path-dependent way with transmission of legal standards and principles most successful within legal families rather than across such families.

The empirical findings, though based on corporate law and trade and investment law more generally rather than secured credit law more specifically, have important implications for the latter. The findings suggest that a harmonised international law of secured credit that is largely grounded on the law of one particular jurisdiction may not be the optimum method of legal change. The UNCITRAL Legislative Guide on Secured Transactions was clearly designed to bring about fundamental legal change. The Preamble talks about outdated laws in many jurisdictions restricting access to credit and the need to modernise such laws. The Guide clearly sees harmonisation and modernisation in the secured credit sphere going hand in hand – harmonising the law on a global basis that facilitates secured credit in all its guises. The assumptions that form the basis of the harmonising and modernising agenda underlying the Guide will be subject to detailed scrutiny in the next chapter.

3. Harmonising and modernising secured transactions law

The previous chapter looked at the harmonisation and modernisation of international private law in general. This chapter turns the spotlight more particularly on secured transactions, or secured credit law as it is variously called, and asks why harmonise and modernise in this area? In short, UNCITRAL's view is that this will aid in the cultivation and growth of individual businesses and also in general economic prosperity.[1] Harmonisation and 'modernisation' are assumed to equal 'liberal' security regimes and the facilitation of secured credit. In this chapter, the modernisation equals liberalisation agenda is subjected to greater scrutiny. The chapter begins by asking what is the effect of recognising security rights? In short, what do security rights do for you? The second part asks why harmonise the law of secured credit? The third part considers why 'liberal' secured credit regimes are considered to be beneficial. The fourth part considers critical perspectives on the international harmonisation and modernisation agenda. The final part summarises the discussion.

SECURITY RIGHTS

While there is probably no universally recognised definition of security rights, it is generally taken as meaning something equivalent to a right over property to ensure the payment of money or the performance of some other obligation. The property over which security is taken is referred to as 'secured' or 'collateralised'. The security taker has a superior claim to payment of the debt etc. out of the secured property than the generality of the debtor's creditors. The security taker will usually have access to speedier enforcement mechanisms as well. In the event that the secured debt is not repaid, the security taker will normally have a right of sale over the secured assets, whether unilaterally or by seeking the intervention of

[1] For the poverty reduction effect of the harmonised law of credit and security see B Kozolchyk, 'Secured Lending and Its Poverty Reduction Effect' (2007) 42 Texas International Law Journal 727.

an administrative mechanism or court. This provides the secured creditor with greater leverage than unsecured creditors through more control over the timing of the realisation of the secured assets. The debtor may also be more likely to pay the secured debt over unsecured debts since failure to pay can result in the loss of an asset that is crucial to the carrying on of the debtor's business. This gives the secured creditor a stronger hand in debt restructuring negotiations. Security also opens up the possibility of self-help remedies for the secured creditor, though self-help is a controversial concept in many jurisdictions, not least because it is seen to be possibly inconsistent with constitutional guarantees safeguarding peaceful possession of property.

Economists suggest that security plays a crucial role in lending decisions by addressing the problems of adverse selection, moral hazard and uninsurable risk.[2] The incentives of creditors and borrowers are aligned and a credible commitment added to the relationship. Security is seen as performing a disciplinary function and is a cornerstone of the theory of control rights and incomplete contracts that has been developed by Oliver Hart and others.[3]

Adverse selection refers to the fact that some borrowers may turn out to be untrustworthy or unreliable – knaves or fools. A lender cannot simply raise interest rates to screen out these borrowers because honest borrowers with sound projects will drop out of the picture as well. The potential pay-off from the project may not be enough to meet the borrowing costs. Where security is taken however, adverse selection problems are addressed more powerfully. The lender can back up its assessment of the character of the borrower and the soundness of the business plan with information on the value of the collateral. As well as the revenues generated from the project, the lender can look to the collateral for repayment. Moral hazard refers to the possibility that a borrower may abscond with the loan. The larger the loan, the greater the moral hazard, but if the borrower provides security, the lower are the lender's costs in monitoring moral hazard. One might say the borrower has given the lender a hostage against flight risk in the shape of security. Security reduces certain risks, i.e. the borrower not being able to repay due to loss of key customers, or losses on foreign exchange, that may not be easily insurable, or insurable at all. Uninsurable

---

[2] See generally J Stiglitz and A Weiss 'Credit Rationing in Markets with Imperfect Information' (1981) 71 American Economic Review 393. See also G Akerlof 'The Market for "Lemons": Qualitative Uncertainty and the Market Mechanism' (1970) 84 Quarterly Journal of Economics 488.

[3] See generally O Hart and J Moore 'Default and Renegotiation: A Dynamic Model of Debt' (1998) 113 Quarterly Journal of Economics 1.

risk is reduced in unsecured lending through 'spreading', i.e. through making smallish loans to a large number of borrowers. Security allows more concentrated lending and reduces uninsurable risk since the security serves as an alternative repayment mechanism.[4]

By way of summary, security rights provide the creditor with property rights which strengthen the creditor's contractual claims against the debtor in various ways. Firstly, the security taker should have priority over other creditors in the event of the debtor becoming insolvent. Secondly, the security taker should have a measure of control over the secured assets or at least share control with the debtor, thereby strengthening the debtor's hand in restructuring negotiations. Thirdly, the security taker should have easier enforcement mechanisms available to it than the generality of creditors, including a power of sale over the secured assets. Fourthly, the easier debt enforcement opportunities may include self-help measures such as sale of the secured assets through unilateral action by the creditor without having to seek the permission of a court or administrative agency. But not all these features are present in every jurisdiction. Not all jurisdictions, for instance, recognise the full priority of secured claims. A proportion of secured asset realisations may be carved out, or set aside, for the benefit of unsecured creditors. There may also be restrictions on the enforcement of security rights and in particular limitations, or indeed wholesale prohibition, on self-help enforcement. The overall effect, however, of recognising security rights is to improve a creditor's hand in dealing with adverse selection, moral hazard and uninsurable risk issues.

WHY HARMONISE THE LAW OF SECURED CREDIT?

In short, UNCITRAL has advocated harmonisation of the law of secured credit to make the law more liberal and facilitative of security and this in turn is seen as producing positive impacts in terms of economic growth.[5] UNCITRAL has suggested the removal of restrictions on the taking of security and increasing the range of assets that can be used as security. It has also suggested the introduction of mechanisms for the registration

---

[4] See H Fleisig 'The Economics of Collateral and Collateral Reform' in F Dahan and J Simpson eds *Secured Transactions Reform and Access to Credit* (Cheltenham, UK and Northampton, MA, USA, Edward Elgar, 2008) at 81.

[5] See, for example, 'Draft legislative guide on secured transactions – Report of the Secretary General' A/CN 9/WG VI/WP 2 (2002) at para 2.

of security rights thereby enhancing the amount of information that is available about such rights. In UNCITRAL's view:[6]

> The key to the effectiveness of secured credit is that it allows borrowers to use the value inherent in their assets as a means of reducing credit risk for the creditor. Risk is mitigated because loans secured by the property of a borrower give lenders recourse to the property in the event of non-payment. Studies have shown that as the risk of non-payment is reduced, the availability of credit increases and the cost of credit falls. Studies have also shown that in States where lenders perceive the risks associated with transactions to be high, the cost of credit increases as lenders require increased compensation to evaluate and assume the increased risk.

There is a suggestion that too many countries have too many restrictions on the taking of security and that countries with 'inadequate' secured transactions regimes have suffered significant losses in gross domestic product (GDP) in consequence. These studies suggest that gaps or weaknesses in collateral-based credit systems hinder financial and economic development.[7] Simply stated, banks and other financial institutions will not engage in large-scale lending activities if their position as secured creditors in the liquidation of their borrowers is not sufficiently certain, or sufficient means for the enforcement of security are not available. More controversially, it has also been suggested that businesses in less-developed financial systems and civil law countries substitute less efficient forms of external finance, trade credit and other sources of funds, for bank loans and equity.[8]

There are also sector-specific studies that purport to demonstrate the

---

6 *Ibid* at addendum 1 para 4 and see also the report by the Asian Development Bank *Secured Transactions Law Reform in Asia: Unleashing the Potential of Collateral* (Manila, Asian Development Bank, 2000). But for something of an alternative perspective see R Cranston 'Credit Security and Debt Recovery: Law's Role in Asia and the Pacific' in J Norton and M Andenas eds *Emerging Financial Markets and Secured Transactions* (London, Kluwer, 1998) at 219. See more generally A Perry-Kessaris 'Finding and Facing Facts about Legal Systems and Foreign Direct Investment in South Asia (2003) 23 Legal Studies 649; 'Recycle, Reduce and Reflect: Information Overload and Knowledge Deficit in the Field of Foreign Investment and the Law' (2008) 35 Journal of Law and Society 67.

7 See generally *Secured Transactions Systems and Collateral Registries* (Washington, DC, International Finance Corporation, 2010) at 6–13; H Fleisig 'Economic Functions of Security in a Market Economy' in J Norton and M Andenas eds above, note 6 at 15. See also D Arner *Financial Stability, Economic Growth and the Role of Law* (New York, CUP, 2007) at 112–114; D Arner, C Booth, P Lejot and B Hsu 'Property Rights, Collateral, Creditor Rights and Insolvency in East Asia' (2007) 42 Texas International Law Journal 515.

8 See the series of studies carried out by the so-called 'law matters' or 'legal origins' thesis, Rafael La Porta, Florencio Lopez de Silanes, Andrei Shleifer and Robert Vishny. Their work includes 'Legal Determinants of External Finance' (1997) Journal of Finance 1131 and 'Law and Finance' (1998) 106 Journal of Political Economy 1113.

value of particular types of collateral, and the economic impact of a stable legal environment for security creation and enforcement. One such study concerns the 2001 Cape Town Convention on International Interests in Mobile Equipment and the Protocol on Matters Specific to Aircraft Equipment.[9] It was estimated that savings to the aircraft industry from the creation of a sound international legal framework governing aircraft financing amounted to $4 billion a year in borrowing costs. Moreover, since 2003 the Export-Import Bank of the United States 'has offered a one-third reduction of its exposure fee on . . . financings of new U.S.-manufactured large commercial aircraft for buyers in countries that ratify . . . and implement the Cape Town [Convention]'.[10]

There is a consensus among international financial institutions that a 'liberal' secured credit regime is a general social and economic good. Three examples serve to highlight that consensus, Firstly, when the former socialist economies in Central and Eastern Europe were undergoing the transition to a more free market-oriented system, the task of reforming credit laws assumed a high priority on the legislative agenda.[11] Organisations like the European Bank for Reconstruction and Development (EBRD) considered that such laws impacted in a crucial way on the pace of private sector investment activity and were essential in fostering market-based decision making.[12] Consequently, the EBRD produced a Model Law on Secured Transactions to guide States in their reform efforts.[13]

---

[9] The Cape Town Treaty consists of a main Convention that sets out the general governing rules and a series of supplemental protocols that sets out specific rules for particular types of collateral (e.g. aircraft). See generally on the Convention R Goode 'Transcending the Boundaries of Earth and Space: The Preliminary Draft UNIDROIT Convention on International Interests in Mobile Equipment' (1998) 3 Uniform Law Review 52; I Davies 'The New Lex Mercatoria: International Interests in Mobile Equipment' (2003) 52 ICLQ 151.

[10] News Release, Cape Town Treaty on Cross-Border Financing of Aircraft, Helicopters and Aircraft Engines Takes Effect Today (March 1) (28 February 2006) http://www.exim.gov/pressrelease/, and see generally A Boss 'The Future of the Uniform Commercial Code Process in an Increasingly International World' (2007) 68 Ohio State Law Journal 349 at 386–389; R Goode, H Kronke and E McKendrick *Transnational Commercial Law* (Oxford, OUP, 2007) at 441: 'the international regime established by the Convention could reduce borrowing costs by several US$ billion a year'. See also V Linetsky *'Economic Benefits of the Cape Town* Treaty' (2009) – see www.awg.aero/pdf/CapeTownBenefitsAnalysis2009.pdf.

[11] See generally J-H Röver *Secured Lending in Eastern Europe: Comparative Law of Secured Transactions and the EBRD Model Law* (Oxford, OUP, 2007).

[12] See also D Berkowitz, K Pistor and J-F Richard 'The Transplant Effect' (2003) 51 AJCL 163 at 164 where it was stated that 'newly designed model laws for secured transactions marketed the value of Western law to their counterparts in the East, backing their campaign to transplant their home legal system with financial aid promises and/or the prospect of joining the European Union'.

[13] *Model Law on Secured Transactions* (London, EBRD, 1994); on which see J-H Röver above, note 11. There is also extensive discussion of the EBRD Model Law in J Norton and M Andenas eds above, note 6.

The second example comes from the late 1990s upheavals in the 'Tiger' economies of East Asia. An influential report on the financial crises highlighted the importance of debtor/creditor regimes and also articulated the features that ideally, in its view, should be contained in such regimes, stating:[14]

> The law should permit . . . all economically important assets to serve as collateral for a loan: and security interests in tangible property . . . and in intangible property . . . to be created. All economically important agents should be able to act as lenders and as borrowers in secured transactions and all economically important secured transactions should be permitted. The creation of security interests should be inexpensive relative to the amounts lent.

Thirdly, in the Latin American context[15] it has been argued that the lack of an effective framework for secured transactions has substantially limited economic growth, with legal restrictions on the use of collateral also reinforcing inequality in the distribution of wealth. This is because the laws and institutions that support the use of secured credit work well only for wealthy landowners who have clear title to their land. Such landowners have better access to credit allowing them to add more easily to their wealth whereas defects in the system hurt those who are already disadvantaged. Limitations on access to credit in Latin America are also seen in the high interest rate that borrowers must pay even when macroeconomic and country risk is taken into account.[16]

Heywood Fleisig of the Centre for the Economic Analysis of Law (CEAL) has generalised the same theme, suggesting that in most developing and transitional economies the generality of movable property cannot effectively function as collateral.[17] In his view, creating collateral over movable property is essential to growth since it amounts to a large proportion of the capital stock of enterprises, but obsolete laws and legal institutions sharply restrict collateralisation opportunities. The laws on the books may nominally permit taking of movable property as collateral but the procedures for doing so are very cumbersome, inefficient and awkward, such that collateral ceases to have much economic value

---

[14] *Report of the Working Group on International Financial Crises* (1988) at p 47 and available on the International Monetary Fund website – www.imf.org.

[15] N de la Pena 'Challenges in Implementing Secured Transactions Reform in Latin America' in F Dahan and J Simpson eds above, note 4 at 236, and also A Garro 'Difficulties in Obtaining Secured Lending in Latin America: Why Law Reform Really Matters' in J Norton and M Andenas eds above, note 7 at 251.

[16] See N de la Pena *ibid* at 241.

[17] See H Fleisig 'The Economics of Collateral and Collateral Reform' above, note 4 at 89–90.

in mitigating risk for lenders. This failure, in his view, stems from poorly designed laws and from badly run, badly designed legal institutions and from weak enforcement. Remedying this deficiency entails the reform of laws and institutions that govern the use of property as collateral for loans – a reform that costs little and can deliver large benefits.

WHY 'LIBERAL' SECURITY REGIMES ARE CONSIDERED TO BE BENEFICIAL

In short, liberal security regimes are considered to be beneficial because they are seen to promote economic growth. This is for two general reasons. Firstly, there is the contract/property rights argument, which goes along the lines that the secured creditor has bargained for rights of a proprietary nature. The law should respect this contractual bargain and the property rights that the secured creditor has thereby acquired in the debtor's assets. Recognition of property rights is good, so the argument goes, for economic growth. Secondly, security is a risk reduction device and therefore functions as a mechanism that both increases the availability and lowers the cost of credit. The effect of minimising risk is to encourage lenders to make loans that they would not otherwise make and also to reduce the risk premium that a lender might otherwise input into the interest rate calculations. The overall effect is to facilitate economic activity.

Taking the general value of property rights argument, scholars of new institutional economics, such as Douglass North, have suggested that financial sector development occurs best in a stable macroeconomic setting. This includes appropriate monetary, financial and fiscal policies and frameworks.[18] But they have also argued that financial systems require certain legal and institutional elements to be in place to function effectively. These include corporate law situated in a context that supports effective governance such as the enforcement of contracts and commercial dispute resolution mechanisms. The necessary legal and institutional elements also entail the recognition of property rights and the use of property to secure loans.

This 'property rights including security rights will produce economic

---

[18] North's theories are developed in *Institutions, Institutional Change and Economic Development* (Cambridge, CUP, 1990). See also C Goodhart 'Economics and the Law: Too Much One-Way Traffic?' (1997) 60 MLR 1 at 5 referring to Mancur Olson 'To realize all the gains from trade, then, there has to be a legal system and political order that enforces contracts, protects property rights, carries out mortgage agreements, provides for limited liability corporations, and facilitates a lasting and widely used capital market that makes the investments and loans more liquid than they would otherwise be.'

growth' argument has been reinforced by the 'legal origins' or 'law matters' thesis advanced by La Porta, Lopez de Silanes, Shleifer and Vishny.[19] It is also supported by an indirect offspring of La Porta – the series of *Doing Business* reports commissioned by the World Bank.[20] The thesis was first developed in the area of investor protection but also encompasses creditor rights and legal institutions more generally. The thesis says that 'law matters' in that legal institutions impact on economic growth.[21] But more controversially, the thesis also asserts that countries that adopted the common law perform better than those with a civil law origin. Legal families are evaluated on the basis of their economic performance and generally the common law comes out as superior. The alleged superiority of the common law is founded on two propositions. The first is that judges have greater independence in common law than in civil law systems, so that the government has less influence on market developments. The second is that the common law, being based on case law rather than on legislative codes, is more responsive to the changing conditions and requirements of society.

The legal origins literature has however been criticised for a US-centric approach.[22] The thesis suggests that US law is the benchmark, the goal of legal convergence, the end of (legal) history. The thesis has also been criticised as the work of a small group of economists whose knowledge of legal differences and cross-cultural legal comparisons displays deficiencies.[23] The civil/common law distinction is fundamental to the thesis with membership of a legal family seen as a cause for past and present economic development. But the way in which legal systems are assigned by proponents of the thesis to one or other legal family is crude. For example,

---

19 See R La Porta, F Lopez de Silanes, A Shleifer and R Vishny 'Legal Determinants of External Finance' (1997) 52 Journal of Finance 1131 and by the same authors 'Law and Finance' (1998) 106 Journal of Political Economy 113. The first three named authors refine the 'legal origins' thesis and defend it against criticisms in 'The Economic Consequences of Legal Origins' (2008) 46 Journal of Economic Literature 285.

20 The *Doing Business* reports are available at www.doingbusiness.org.

21 But see Mark Roe 'Legal Origin and Modern Stock Markets' (2006) 120 Harvard Law Review 460 who argues that politics instead of legal origins is a more relevant causal factor. In 'The Economic Consequences of Legal Origins' (2008) 46 Journal of Economic Literature 285 La Porta et al. above, note 19, use 'legal origins' as a sort of proxy for politics. They 'adopt a broad conception of legal origin as a style of social control of economic life (and maybe of other aspects of life as well). . . . [They] argue that common law stands for the strategy of social control that seeks to support private market outcomes, whereas civil law seeks to replace such outcomes with state-desired allocations'.

22 See generally R Michaels 'Comparative Law by Numbers? Legal Origins Thesis, Doing Business Reports and the Silence of Traditional Comparative Law' (2009) 57 AJCL 765 and the literature referred to therein. There is also a symposium on the legal origins thesis in the 2009 Brigham Young University Law Review.

23 See U Braendle 'Shareholder Protection in the USA and Germany: "Law and Finance" Revisited' (2006) 7 German Law Journal 257.

France is assigned to the same legal family as Lithuania but their economies (and their laws) are like apples and oranges in many other ways. All legal systems are mixed to a degree, and the civil law/common law divide seems especially irrelevant for the sphere of economic law covered by the legal origins literature. It may be argued that other aspects of a society, such as politics, culture or religion, and geographical position are much more likely to influence economic development than membership of a particular legal family.[24] Distinctions such as EU/non-EU, Eastern/Western Europe, and Baltic/non-Baltic countries seem far more salient than the legal origins scheme of classification which, e.g., places Latvia and Taiwan in one legal category and Lithuania and Syria in another.[25]

Despite the criticism, the legal origins literature has heavily influenced the *Doing Business* reports issued on an annual basis since 2004 by the International Finance Corporation (IFC), a member of the World Bank Group. These reports purport to measure and compare the 'ease of doing business' in more than 130 countries worldwide.[26] Indeed, the lead author of the earlier *Doing Business* reports is a frequent co-author with the originators of the 'legal origins' thesis.[27] While the reports purport to assess attractiveness for investors rather than economic performance per se, there are obvious linkages between the two. The reports have tended to show that credit bureaus, stronger creditor rights and simpler civil procedure rules have a significant impact on access to credit.[28] It is argued that strong creditor protection should lead to deeper credit markets and better financing for firms and individuals. The *Doing Business* reports have identified many laws, rules and institutions, grouped into four basic categories, that constitute the basis for private credit. These are: (1) mechanisms and procedures for the registration of property; (2) information-sharing

---

[24] See D Acemoglu, S Johnson and J Robinson 'The Colonial Origins of Comparative Development: An Empirical Investigation' (2001) 91 American Economic Review 1369; R Stulz and R Williamson 'Culture, Openness, and Finance' (2003) 70 Journal of Financial Economics 313; A Licht, C Goldschmidt and S Schwartz 'Culture, Law, and Corporate Governance' (2005) 25 International Review of Law and Economics 229.

[25] See M Siems 'Legal Origins: Reconciling Law and Finance and Comparative Law (2007) 52 McGill Law Journal 55 at 65. See also on legal origins P Wood *Law and Practice of International Finance* (London, Sweet & Maxwell, 2008) chapter 3.

[26] See www.doingbusiness.org.

[27] The reference is to Simeon Djankov, now Finance Minister and Deputy Prime Minister of Bulgaria and for co-authored publications see S Djankov, R La Porta, F López de Silanes and A Shleifer 'The Regulation of Entry' (2002) 117 Quarterly Journal of Economics 1; 'Courts' (2003) 118 Quarterly Journal of Economics 453 and also with Juan Botero 'The Regulation of Labor' (2004) 119 Quarterly Journal of Economics 1339.

[28] See F Lopez-de-Silanes chapter 1 'Turning the Key to Credit: Credit Access and Credit Institutions' in F Dahan and J Simpson eds *Secured Transactions Reform and Access to Credit* (Cheltenham, UK and Northampton, MA, USA, Edward Elgar, 2008).

arrangements or credit bureaus; (3) collateral rules and creditor rights; and (4) contract enforcement. The reports conclude that the wealth of a particular country is an important indicator of the effectiveness of institutions in that country that guarantee access to credit.[29] In the main, richer countries are said to have more expeditious procedures to register ownership of property; a higher presence of private credit bureaus; greater coverage and quality in terms of the information collected by information-sharing institutions; more extensive creditor rights and security rights, as well as better measures of contract enforcement.

The *Doing Business* reports have major resonance with national governments, which have often taken conscious steps to improve their country's rankings. This may not be a positive move however, not least because countries may be more inclined to improve their rankings by 'gaming' the system rather than taking the politically more problematic step of addressing actual problems that may be highlighted in the reports.[30] Otherwise the *Doing Business* reports may be subjected to similar criticism as the legal origins thesis; namely, faulty research, insufficient attention to detail, a common law bias (actual or perceived) and a preference for free market solutions and deregulation over other values such as solidarity and justice and the preservation of separate legal cultures.[31]

The deregulatory and free market agenda was quite explicit in the first *Doing Business* report in 2004, which purported to show that a 'heavy' regulatory regime produced the worst results in terms of economic outcomes because it was usually associated with inefficiency within public institutions, long delays in reaching decisions, high costs of administrative formalities, lengthy judicial proceedings, higher unemployment and more corruption, less productivity and lower investment.[32] The report also said 'Common law countries regulate the least. Countries in the French civil law tradition the most. However, heritage is not destiny.' The overall conclusion was a stark one, that 'one size can fit all' in respect of the legal regulation of business.

---

29 *Ibid* at 20.

30 R Michaels 'Comparative Law by Numbers? Legal Origins Thesis, Doing Business Reports and the Silence of Traditional Comparative Law' (2009) 57 American Journal of Comparative Law 765 at 772; B Arrunada 'Pitfalls to Avoid When Measuring Institutions: Is Doing Business Damaging Business?' (2007) 35 Journal of Comparative Economics 729.

31 See generally G Sarfaty 'Why Culture Matters in International Institutions: The Marginality of Human Rights at the World Bank' (2009) 103 American Journal of International Law 647.

32 See the 2004 *Doing Business* report at 83: 'Heavier regulation of business activities generally brings bad outcomes, while clearly defined and well-protected property rights enhance prosperity.'

There was some surprise and disappointment about the poor ranking given to the French legal system in the report, with France ranked 44th, behind countries such as Jamaica, Botswana and Tonga.[33] A variety of French institutions and commentators weighed in, severely criticising the 2004 report for an allegedly faulty understanding of French law and legal culture. For instance, the *Association of the Friends of French Legal Culture* published two critical commentaries.[34] A research institute was also established to demonstrate the attractiveness of French law.[35] The impact of these contributions in the international sphere was muted, if not largely nullified, however, by the fact that almost all of them were published in French.[36] But the French criticisms have been taken up to an extent by an Independent Evaluation Group within the World Bank, which in a 2008 critique of the *Doing Business* reports recommends greater transparency and some modifications to the methodology.[37] The critique also suggests that the focus on regulatory costs and burdens should only be one dimension of any overall reform of the investment climate in a particular country.

Essentially, the *Doing Business* reports use a creditor-centred approach with the highest grading given to countries that emphasise private contractual solutions rather than court-based ones. This approach appears one-dimensional and overly simplistic. It also ignores the recent economic success of countries such as China where many of the desiderata considered necessary by international financial institutions, such as strong property rights, are absent.[38]

In recent times, a popular exponent of the linkage between property

---

33 See B Fauvargue-Cosson and A-J Kerhuel 'Is Law an Economic Contest? French Reactions to the *Doing Business* World Bank Reports and Economic Analysis of the Law' (2009) 57 AJCL 811.

34 See Association Henri Capitant des amis de la culture juridique Francaise *Les droits de tradition civiliste en question. A propos des rapports Doing Business* (Paris, Société de Législation Comparée, 2006) and available at www.henricapitant.org.

35 Fondation pour le droit continental – see www.fondation-droitcontinental.org.

36 See the comment in R Michaels 'Comparative Law by Numbers? Legal Origins Thesis, Doing Business Reports and the Silence of Traditional Comparative Law' (2009) 57 AJCL 765 at 772: 'Somewhat typically, almost all of these contributions were published in French, leaving them with almost no impact in the international sphere.' There are however Russian and Chinese translations on the Henri Capitant website but none in English!

37 World Bank Independent Evaluation Group *Doing Business: an independant evaluation, Taking the measure of the World Bank-IFC doing Business indicators* (Washington, World Bank, 2008).

38 C Paulus 'Global Insolvency Law and the Role of Multinational Institutions' (2007) 32 Brooklyn International Law Journal 755 at 762. For somewhat varying views on the Chinese example see *Secured Transactions Systems and Collateral Registries* above, note 7 at 67 and 104.

rights and economic development has been Hernando De Soto.[39] In writings such as *The Mystery of Capital: Why Capitalism Triumphs in the West and Fails Everywhere Else*[40] De Soto argues that people in developing countries lack an integrated formal property system, and he contrasts this with the US where, in his view, a clear system of property rights was created early. De Soto suggests that the absence of such a system makes it impossible for the poor to leverage informal ownership into collateral for the extension of credit. In De Soto's view, property rights are not just privileges for the rich. The poor need them most of all, especially if they want to stop being poor. He argues that in developing countries the combined effect of bureaucracy and outdated legal systems is to drive economic activities underground with investment activity stifled. But property systems in the wealthy West allow assets, through ownership documentation, to lead an 'invisible, parallel life alongside their material existence'.[41] In developing countries, comparable means of documentation are lacking thereby creating 'dead capital'.

Formal property systems are said to produce six effects that facilitate the generation of capital. The first is fixing the economic potential of assets. De Soto uses the analogy of generating electric power from the energy in a mountain lake suggesting that the potential value locked up in real estate can be revealed, transformed and energised in the same way.[42] Where property rights are formalised and collateralised, there is the potential to produce surplus assets above and beyond the physical assets. The second effect is the integration of dispersed information into one system. The third is making people accountable – incorporation into a more integrated legal system facilitates individual accountability. The fourth effect is to put assets into a more accessible condition so that they can perform additional work. Assets become 'fungible' and can be fashioned to suit practically any transaction. Fifthly, increased fungibility in turn helps to network people and convert citizens into individually identifiable and accountable business agents. Increased information and integrated law makes risk more manageable not least by facilitating the pooling of assets to secure debts. The final effect is the protection of transactions. To sum

---

39 But see also G Hardin 'The Tragedy of the Commons' (1968) 162 Science 1243. For refinement and criticism of Hardin's work see *Governing the Commons: The Evolution of Institutions for Collective Action* (New York, CUP, 1990) by the winner of the 2009 Nobel Prize for Economics, Elinor Ostrom.

40 H De Soto *The Mystery of Capital* (London, Black Swan, 2008). For a much more nuanced analysis see R Ellickson 'Property in Land' (1992) 102 Yale LJ 1315 and in particular the conclusion at 1397.

41 H De Soto, *ibid* at 7.

42 *Ibid* at 47–61.

up, a documented system of ownership can 'provide a link to the owner's credit history, an accountable address for the collection of debts and taxes, the basis for creation of reliable public utilities, and a foundation for the creation of securities (like mortgage backed bonds) that can be rediscounted and sold in secondary markets'.[43]

De Soto argues that capitalism is the only game in town but that once the vast machine of capitalism was firmly in place, the question of how it came into being lost any sense of urgency in the developed world.

> Like people living in the rich and fertile delta of a long river, the advocates of capitalism had no pressing need to explore upstream for the source of their prosperity. . . . [T]he rest of the world turned to the West for help and was advised to imitate the conditions of life on the delta: stable currencies, open markets and private businesses. . . . Everyone forgot that the reason for the delta's rich life lay upriver, in its unexplored headwaters. Widely accessible legal property systems are the silt from upriver that permits modern capital to flourish.[44]

De Soto's work has been lavishly praised, with Bill Clinton, e.g., calling him the 'world's greatest living economist',[45] but the work has also attracted criticism on a number of grounds. Some have questioned the statistical validity of the claims about the size of the informal economy.[46] Others would argue that it is excessively narrow in its approach to economic development – basically a 'single bullet' approach. It is suggested that there should be a greater emphasis on culture, and how local conditions affect people's perceptions of their opportunities.[47] For instance, a study commissioned by the UK's Department for International Development has stressed the attention that must be paid to the local social context and noted many complications arising from the implementation of De Soto's policy recommendations.[48]

---

43 *Ibid* at 7.

44 *Ibid* at 66. For a parallel analysis see H Fleisig above, note 4 at 105 and see also M Safavian 'Firm-Level Evidence on Collateral and Access to Finance' in the same volume.

45 See the University of North Carolina at Chapel Hill News Release of 19 October 2004 available at http://www.unc.edu/news/archives/oct04/fpg_desoto101904.html, and see the praise for De Soto on the Cato Institute website from Richard Nixon and Ronald Reagan http://www.cato.org/special/friedman/desoto/praise.html (date last visited 15/10/2010).

46 See the review of De Soto's other famous book *El Otro Sendero* (The Other Path) by R Rossini and J Thomas (1990) 18 World Development 125.

47 See R Samuelson in 'The Spirit of Capitalism' in *Foreign Affairs* (Jan/Feb 2001) 'Unfortunately, de Soto strains too much. He wants to make property rights – or their absence – the center of everything.'

48 See E Daley and M Hobley *Land: Changing Contexts, Changing Relationships, Changing Rights* (September 2005). The paper was commissioned by DFID's Urban-Rural Change Team but views and opinions expressed in this report do not necessarily reflect those of DFID.

There are further empirical studies that take issue with the link between property registration mechanisms and the increase in credit to the poor.[49] Many micro businesses operate in the informal sector beneath the radar screen of the authorities.[50] They may not see the merit in availing of a reformed law if this means appearing on the official radar. They may not possess much conventional collateral, and reforming the law is unlikely to change that situation. In many countries, improved access to credit has only come about through the willingness of alternative financial institutions to look at cash flows rather than assets. Expanding the range of secured lending instruments is not a burning issue for the microfinance industry as several other bottlenecks are of greater relevance. Institutional capacity and operating costs remain big challenges and many rural areas are still stubbornly resistant to market penetration. Highlighting secured lending and collateral may put 'undue attention on an issue that the pioneer microfinance organizations and practitioners have worked very hard to reduce to a lower status'.[51]

There is also the experience in De Soto's native Peru which suggests that property registration, of itself, is unlikely to have much effect. To bring about concrete reform, it may have to be followed by more politically challenging steps such as improving the norms and efficiency of the judicial system as well as rewriting bankruptcy codes and restructuring financial market regulation. Reforms of this nature may entail much more difficult choices for policy makers.[52] Radical critiques suggest that one must look more to the current distribution of property rights rather than the formalisation of rights. Mattei, for instance, argues that the formalisation movement uses an illusory economic theory to justify the freezing and normalisation of the status quo. He suggests:[53]

---

49 See S Galliani and E Schargrodsky 'Property Rights for the Poor: Effects of Land Titling' Ronald Coase Institute Working Paper (January 2009) who conclude 'Our results suggest that land titling can be an important tool for poverty reduction, albeit not through the shortcut of credit access, but through the slow channel of increased physical and human capital investment, which should help to reduce poverty in the future generations.'

50 M Holtmann 'Use of Security in Challenging Environments: The Microfinance Perspective' in F Dahan and J Simpson eds above, note 4 at 159.

51 *Ibid* at 167.

52 See the review of *The Mystery of Capital* by C Woodruff in (2001) 39 Journal of Economic Literature 1215.

53 See U Mattei 'The Peruvian Civil Code: Property and Plunder. Time for a Latin American Alliance to Resist the Neo Liberal Order' (2005) 6 Global Jurist Topics text accompanying footnotes 18 and 19 and see also U Mattei and L Nader *Plunder: When the Rule of Law Is Illegal* (Oxford, Wiley-Blackwell, 2008).

> The Western path of economic development presents itself as a success story, while erasing the fact that imperial plunder has played a much more important role than domestic property law in Western capitalist development. Western capitalist development occurred because of Colonial exploitation, a system of global protracted illegality that paradoxically has used and continues to use the law as one of its most powerful ideological apparatuses.

Whatever the validity of the ideological criticism, certainly De Soto's rhetoric is overblown. 'Trifling details' such as significant differences between legal systems and property registration systems in developed countries simply do not concern him. According to De Soto,[54] in the West 'all the property records (titles, deeds, securities and contracts that describe the economically significant aspects of assets) are continually tracked and protected as they travel through time and space'. But registrationless regimes of personal property thrive in many parts of the developed world. It is almost as if De Soto is carried away by his own rhetoric and forgets the need for qualification, asserting that 'citizens in advanced nations can obtain descriptions of the economic and social qualities of any available asset without having to see the asset itself'.[55] As a bald, general statement this is simply not true, and casts doubt on the accuracy of De Soto's own research and his overall thesis about the role of registration of assets as a necessary concomitant of economic development.[56] De Soto also ignores the fact that Latin American countries, including Peru, have Civil Codes modelled on the Napoleonic Codes of France and Spain.[57] These Codes may not be the most 'efficient' and comprehensive in terms of protecting property rights, including the position of secured creditors, but they may not necessarily be any better or worse than the Codes in some modern European civilian jurisdictions. In short, De Soto's, and other theses, which suggest that the development of the West is explicable on the basis of a better formal structure of property rights which Western economies possess, and developing countries lack, seems much too pat, as well as being belied by the facts.

---

[54] H De Soto *The Mystery of Capital* above, note 40 at 60.

[55] *Ibid* at 53.

[56] See B Kozolchyk 'A Road Map to Economic Development through Law: Third Parties and Comparative Legal Culture' (2005) 23 Arizona Journal of International and Comparative Law 1 at 2–3: 'a merchant's inventory is nowhere represented by a "property document". . . The preceding objections are not intended as quibbles; they go to the heart of de Soto's argument.'

[57] See U Mattei 'The Peruvian Civil Code: Property and Plunder. Time for a Latin American Alliance to Resist the Neo Liberal Order' (2005) 6 Global Jurist Topics 'Latin American private law derives in large measure from Spanish and Portuguese law'.

Improving Credit Cost and Availability

Studies by various international financial institutions have suggested a correlation between enhanced security rights on the one hand, and greater access to, and cheaper, credit on the other.[58] This correlation has been borne out in an empirical study by Haselmann and Pistor examining the effect of legal change in respect of collateral rights on the lending behaviour of banks in twelve transition economies.[59] The study concludes that banks increase the supply of credit subsequent to legal change and that the ability to 'collateralise' or use assets as security seems to be an important determinant of credit supplied in the economy. It also finds that foreign-owned banks respond more strongly to legal change than incumbents. This is consistent with the proposition that especially in emerging and transition economies information asymmetries are of greater concern than in developed markets. Collateral rights tend to reduce information gaps between lenders and borrowers and, further, to even the playing field between foreign and domestic lenders and open up the credit market to new participants.

Where asset collateralisation is legally possible, it is argued that all but the largest borrowers should get better terms on a secured rather than an unsecured loan. Better terms can take the form of lower interest rates, larger loans relative to income and also more generous repayment periods. A more prosaic example has been cited in the case of a credit union for IMF and World Bank employees:[60]

> When the borrowers offer collateral for a loan instead of only a signature, the credit union offers better terms: it will lend at interest rates that are about half as high, make loans that are five to ten times larger relative to income and give the borrower as much as five times longer to repay.

In other cases, however, there may not be simple trade-off between interest rates and the cost of credit. For instance, sub-prime borrowers may be charged high interest rates and also required to provide security. With blue-chip borrowers, on the other hand, capacity to service the loan is not considered to be an issue. Security does not enter into the reckoning and the competition among lenders for a valuable source of business keeps interest rates low. Moreover, there are greater costs incurred in secured

---

[58] *Secured Transactions Systems and Collateral Registries* above, note 7 at 7–13.

[59] See R Haselmann and K Pistor 'How the Law Affects Lending' (2009) 23 Review of Financial Studies 549.

[60] See H Fleisig above, note 4 at 85.

as distinct from unsecured lending.[61] Secured loans are more expensive to set up since the expenses involved in arranging and documenting the transaction are higher. For this reason, it is not just loans to blue-chip borrowers but sometimes small loans, or loans to buyers with strong repayment records, that may be offered on an unsecured basis. While evidence suggests that between 60 and 65 per cent of loans to businesses in the United States are secured, the precise effect of security on credit cost and availability is very difficult, if not impossible, to verify empirically.[62]

CRITICAL PERSPECTIVES ON THE HARMONISATION AND MODERNISATION OF SECURED CREDIT LAW

In this section I consider three critical perspectives on the harmonisation and modernisation agenda of UNCITRAL in the secured credit sphere. The first considers general issues of fairness and, in particular, fairness to unsecured creditors from enhanced recognition of security rights. The second perspective looks at secured credit law reform as part of a neo-liberal economic agenda, pushed by international organisations, that also includes privatisation and marketisation of key sectors of a national economy. The third perspective considers secured credit reform as a possible instrument of American foreign policy and American economic interests.

Security and Fairness

The concept of security runs counter to instinctive conceptions of fairness in that it may involve one creditor being paid whereas other creditors remain unpaid.[63] In short, the idea of proportionate satisfaction of creditor claims, i.e. pari passu distribution, is disturbed. This concern can be met in various ways. For instance, one might argue that the general instrumentalist justifications for security override individual conceptions of fairness. In other words, increased credit creation and lower cost credit will help to stimulate economic activity and lead to better economic

---

[61] See generally R Mann 'Explaining the Pattern of Secured Credit' (1997) 110 Harvard Law Review 626.

[62] See F Lopez-de-Silanes 'Turning the Key to Credit: Credit Access and Credit Institutions' in F Dahan and J Simpson eds above, note 4, 3 at 10.

[63] For a strong critique of pari passu see generally R Mokal 'Priority as Pathology: The Pari Passu Myth' [2001] CLJ 581 and see also V Finch *Corporate Insolvency Law: Perspectives and Principles* (Cambridge, CUP, 2nd edn 2008) chapters 14 and 15.

conditions for all. Moreover, to the extent that security is seen as a fair exchange for the credit, the secured creditor has bargained for security and priority, whereas other creditors have not. Consequently, it does not seem unfair to privilege the secured creditor over other creditors who could equally have contracted for security but chose not to do so. On the other hand, there may be involuntary creditors, i.e. creditors not in a contractual relationship with the debtor, who are not in a position to bargain for security. Also there are other non-adjusting creditors, or poorly adjusting creditors, where it is unrealistic to suppose that they could bargain for security or where the transaction costs of doing so are too great. These creditors in a weak bargaining position are perhaps most likely to be the ones that will be hit hardest by the debtor's insolvency. The insolvency may impact disproportionately on them in that they are not very capable of sharing or passing on the costs of the loss. Large financial institutions most likely to take security are in a much better position to pass on losses.

Employees and small trade creditors are typically non-adjusting, or poorly-adjusting, creditors. Different jurisdictions may have different ways of protecting such creditors whether through social safety nets, or insurance schemes, or the like. Other possible approaches would be to impose restrictions on the taking of security thereby leaving a margin of unsecured assets that are available for payment of unsecured debts, or else to set aside a proportion of secured realisations for the benefit of unsecured creditors. The UNCITRAL Legislative Guide, however, follows the thread of Article 9 of the American Uniform Commercial Code and counsels against this, recognising the 'full' priority of security rights.

Secured Credit and 'Neo-Liberal' Economic Reforms

Secured credit law reform is generally promoted on the basis that it will foster market-based decision making on credit issues. Reform is often seen as part of an overall economic agenda – the so-called Washington Consensus – that includes privatisation and marketisation.[64] They may be viewed as interlinked ingredients in an overall growth and development strategy. In the early 1990s, international financial institutions pushed the advantage of a rapid privatisation process but, in many instances, this led to a massive transfer of state resources into the hands of privileged insiders, or the economically powerful. There is a growing recognition that

---

64 See J Stiglitz *Globalisation and Its Discontents* (London, Penguin, 2002) at 16 and 53–54.

rapid privatisation is not the best prescription for reform.[65] The Chinese experience indicates that a slower, more gradual process is more conducive to long-term economic stability.[66] A gradual process of privatisation allows the restructuring of large firms to take place before their move, in whole or in part, into the private sector.

One of the presumptions underpinning the Washington Consensus is that markets will intrinsically lead to efficient outcomes, but the recent global financial crisis has instead highlighted the possibility of desirable government intervention that can guide economic growth, and make everyone better off. Commentators such as Joseph Stiglitz have also criticised the focus of the Washington Consensus on GDP, which is seen as the be-all and end-all of development. He argues that[67]

> because GDP is relatively easy to measure, it has become a fixation of economists. The trouble with this is that we measure what we strive for. Sometimes, increases in GDP are associated with poverty reduction, as was the case in East Asia. But that was not an accident: governments designed policies to make sure that the poor shared in the benefits. Elsewhere, growth has often been accompanied by increased poverty and sometimes even lower income levels for individuals in the middle.

It is submitted that this is a valuable insight and that the merits of secured credit reform should be disaggregated from wider notions about the alleged efficacy of market-based decision making, and the implementation of a privatisation agenda.

The Legislative Guide as an Instrument of American Economic Power

The previous chapter considered in general terms the role of transplants in the legal harmonisation process. It is the case that a variety of factors drive countries to adopt legal transplants from other jurisdictions, and models of greater, or lesser, sophistication have been used to explain the typology of transplants. Alan Watson, e.g., has acknowledged that reception and

---

65 *Ibid* at 6: 'countries were told by the West that the new economic system would bring them unprecedented prosperity. Instead, it brought unprecedented poverty. . . . The contrast between Russia's transition, as engineered by the international economic institutions, and that of China, designed by itself, could not be greater . . .'.

66 See J Ohnesorge 'Developing Development Theory: Law and Development Orthodoxies and the North East Asian Experience' (2007) 28 University of Pennsylvania Journal of International Economic Law 219 and see also J Ohnesorge 'The Rule of Law, Economic Development, and the Developmental States of Northeast Asia' in C Antons ed *Law and Development in East and South East Asia* (London, RoutledgeCurzon, 2003).

67 See J Stiglitz above, note 64 at 45.

transplants come in all shapes and sizes, speaking of an imposed reception, solicited imposition, penetration, infiltration, crypto-reception, inoculation and so on.[68] Another approach is to propound a straightforward distinction between coercive transplants and voluntary receptions. The notion of 'coercive' transplants can be used to explain the relationship between the mother country and its overseas colonies whereby the law of the mother country is imposed on its 'foreign' possessions and territories as part of the project of imperial governance. The concept of 'voluntary' reception explains situations where the aura, or prestige, of a particular jurisdiction persuades other countries to adopt its laws.[69]

The sufficiency of this basic taxonomy has been challenged. In particular, the distinction between imperialistic and non-imperialistic transplants could be seen as a matter only of degree, and not of kind. There is not a straightforward dichotomy between 'free' or 'coercive' transplants of a foreign model. This is so because law is a detailed and complex machinery of social control that cannot effectively function without some cooperation from local officials. These local officials usually consist of a professional elite possibly created by the imperial power. This elite provides the degree of consent to the reception of foreign legal ideas that is necessary for any transplant to occur.[70] In this connection, one might also make use of the notion of reflexive law, thereby acknowledging that the influence exerted by exporting or 'hegemonic' jurisdictions is most likely to be effective when it seeks to achieve its ends not by direct prescription but by inducing second order effects on the part of social actors in the receiving State.[71] There is likely to be a lively debate and dialogue between consent and dissent, and between 'hegemonic' and 'counter-hegemonic' forces. One may also tie in the concept of path dependency.[72] The law, and lawyers, tend to absorb change by digging deeper into existing soil, rather than branching out into new fields. Political and other influences may trigger legal development and cause the law to produce certain outcomes,

---

68 A Watson *Legal Transplants: An Approach to Comparative Law* (Edinburgh, Scottish Academic Press, 1974) at 30.

69 See U Mattei 'A Theory of Imperial Law: A Study on U.S. Hegemony and the Latin Resistance' (2002) 10 Indiana Journal of Global Legal Studies 383 at 385.

70 See D Berkowitz, K Pistor and J-F Richard 'The Transplant Effect' (2003) 51 AJCL 163 who suggest that indigenous law making operates as a kind of focal point for cooperative law-making behaviour which then serves as the focal point for cooperative economic behaviour. See also G Teubner 'Legal Irritants: Good Faith in British Law or How Unifying Law Ends up in New Divergences' (1998) 61 MLR 11.

71 See generally G Teubner 'Substantive and Reflexive Elements in Modern Law' (1983) 17 Law and Society Review 239.

72 L Bebchuk and M Roe 'A Theory of Path Dependence in Corporate Ownership and Governance' (1999) 52 Stanford Law Review 127.

but the form that represents these outcomes is determined by the legal doctrine prevailing in the jurisdiction concerned.[73] In short, the law develops in a path-dependent fashion.

Another commentator, Ugo Mattei, has sought to explain transplants on the basis of prestige or efficiency.[74] While acknowledging that each single legal transplant has its own peculiarities that make it different from every other, Mattei deploys economic analysis to explain the perceived convergence of modern legal systems as a movement towards efficiency, despite the large variety of institutional backgrounds. A synergy is also said to exist between 'efficiency' and 'prestige', with the most efficient models being seen as the more prestigious. The 'efficiency' notion links up with concepts of regulatory competition. This implies convergence around a single, efficient system which wins out through the competitive process. But the evidence about regulatory competition suggests that it may produce rules that are far from optimal from the viewpoint of economic theory.[75] There is also the risk of 'social dumping'[76] and a so-called 'race to the bottom'.[77] Proponents of the 'efficiency' thesis then have to fall back on arguments about the long-term benefits of market solutions.

In some cases, the idea of co-evolution may better explain the process whereby countries observe and sometimes emulate practices in jurisdictions to which they are closely related by trade and institutional connections. The co-evolution concept assumes that a variety of diverse systems may exist side by side with each one retaining its viability. More fundamentally, a recent empirical study of private credit in more than 100 countries over 25 years has amassed evidence contradicting the hypothesis

---

[73] See generally Eva Micheler *Property in Securities: A Comparative Study* (Cambridge, CUP, 2007) chapter 15 'Legal development as a path-dependent process' and see the statement at 228 'Legal doctrine causes the law to develop path-dependently'. See also H Spamann 'Contemporary Legal Transplants – Legal Families and the Diffusion of (Corporate) Law' [2009] Brigham Young University Law Review 1813; J Armour, S Deakin, P Lele, and M Siems 'How Do Legal Rules Evolve? Evidence from a Cross-Country Comparison of Shareholder, Creditor and Worker Protection' (2009) 57 AJCL 579.

[74] U Mattei 'Efficiency in Legal Transplants: An Essay in Comparative Law and Economics' (1994) 14 International Review of Law and Economics 3. See also A Ogus 'Competition Between National Legal Systems: A Contribution of Economic Analysis to Comparative Law' (1999) 48 ICLQ 405 and see generally F von Hayek 'Competition as a Discovery Procedure' (2002) 5(3) Quarterly Journal of Austrian Economics at 9.

[75] See D Esty and D Geradin eds *Regulatory Competition and Economic Integration: Comparative Perspectives* (Oxford, OUP, 2001).

[76] In the context of EC employment law the ECJ made specific reference to social dumping in Case 341/05 *Laval un Partneri Ptd v Svenska* 2007 ECR I-5751 at para 103.

[77] See generally C Barnard 'Social Dumping and Race to the Bottom: Some Lessons for the EU from Delaware?' (2000) 25 EL Rev 57; L Enriques and M Gelter 'Regulatory Competition in European Company Law and Creditor Protection' (2006) 7 European Business Organization Law Review 417.

that legal institutions converge towards the more successful ones over time.[78] In addition, the study suggests that since credit institutions vary so much across countries and legal origins, the evidence is also inconsistent with the 'functional convergence' hypothesis holding that institutions in different countries, while distinct on the surface, functionally converge to accomplish the same goals.

But evidence of a lack of a convergence is not necessarily inconsistent with the proposition that certain legal systems may hold an appeal on prestige or other grounds. John Braithwaite and Peter Drahos, in their seminal book *Global Business Regulation*,[79] have spoken of how models are adopted 'when they appeal to identities that we hold dear. An identity that is particularly crucial in this regard is that of being successful, modern, civilised, advanced. The periphery models the centre in the world system because of this pursuit of modernity in identity (or postmodernity, for the truly avant-garde).' The French economist Michel Albert has spoken of the irresistible force of US legal expansionism.[80] US legal paradigms gain a competitive advantage from the political and ideological sway exercised by the United States. Alternative approaches are overwhelmed by American political and cultural influences. Albert explains the spread of American influences using notions of seductiveness and appeal. In his view, the intrinsic characteristics of the neo-American model exalt the success of risk-taking, gambling and 'glittery' behaviour. In the same vein, another commentator has talked about how the European Community method of rational planning, bureaucratic solutions, suppression of political passion and a steady incrementalism is incapable of igniting the popular emotions in a way that would allow Europe to mount a true global challenge to the US.[81]

Mattei has now moved away from his earlier reliance on 'prestige' or 'efficiency' to propound a theory of 'imperial law':[82]

---

78 See S Djankov, C McLiesh and A Shleifer 'Private Credit in 129 Countries' (2007) 84 Journal of Financial Economics 299.

79 J Braithwaite and P Drahos *Global Business Regulation* (Cambridge, CUP, 2000) at 591.

80 M Albert *Capitalism Against Capitalism: How America's Obsession with Individual Achievement and Short-term Profit Has Led It to the Brink of Economic Collapse* (London, Whurr, 1993).

81 See S Dillon 'Looking for the Progressive Empire: Where Is the European Union's Foreign Policy?' (2004) 19 Connecticut Journal of International Law 275 at 278.

82 See U Mattei 'A Theory of Imperial Law: A Study on U.S. Hegemony and the Latin Resistance' (2002) 10 Indiana Journal of Global Legal Studies 383. See also J Gardner *Legal Imperialism, American Lawyers and Foreign Aid in Latin America* (Madison, University of Wisconsin Press, 1981).

> Imperial law is produced, in the interest of international capital, by a variety of both public and private institutions, all sharing a gap in legitimacy, sometimes called the 'democratic deficit'. Imperial law is shaped by a spectacular process of exaggeration, aimed at building consent for the purpose of hegemonic domination. Imperial law subordinates local legal arrangements world-wide, reproducing on the global scale the same phenomenon of legal dualism that thus far has characterised the law of developing countries. Predatory economic globalization is the vehicle, the all-mighty ally, and the beneficiary of imperial law.

In the realm of literary and cultural discourse, notions of imperialism and American hegemony have been advanced by Edward Said.[83] He talks about American culture's phenomenally incorporative capacity and a system of pressures and constraints which induces other States to follow the essentially imperial identity and direction of US norms.[84] In his view, the pressures are subtle, and generally indirect.[85] Said makes the point that[86]

> American attitudes to American greatness, to hierarchies of race, to the perils of other revolutions (the American revolution being considered unique and somehow unrepeatable anywhere else in the world) have remained constant, have dictated, have obscured the realities of empire, while apologists for overseas American interests have insisted on American innocence, doing good, fighting for freedom.

Said also links his theory of imperialism with a law-making creed that suggests it is the goal of US foreign policy to bring about a world increasingly subject to the rule of law, as defined in US terms.

In the sphere of secured credit, the UNCITRAL Guide can be seen as an instrument by which the norms postulated in Article 9 of the American Commercial Code are writ large across the globe. The Guide reproduces the key features of Article 9, emphasising the removal of restrictions on the taking of security, all-assets security, notice filing of security interests on American lines, and the full priority of security rights. US private and public interests combined and collaborated in the formulation and development of the Guide. It is hardly surprising that agencies of the US government, as well as US private interests, should act to defend what they consider to be US business interests.[87] First World nations, including

---

[83] E Said *Culture and Imperialism* (London, Chatto & Windus, 1993). See also M Hardt and A Negri *Empire* (Cambridge MA, Harvard University Press, 2000).

[84] *Ibid* at 392.

[85] *Ibid* at 401.

[86] *Ibid* at 7.

[87] See the following statement by the Commercial Finance Association (CFA) General Counsel – (UN Press Release ECO/56 L/3061 – 29/03/2010) 'CFA members, which include

the US, 'have a collective interest in promoting generalized dependency and reverence from the periphery'. But as one US commentator remarks 'efforts to export U.S. legal models are more likely to succeed if they eschew detailed, distinctively U.S.-derived prescriptions in favor of presenting advice or exemplars in terms of more 'general' standards, 'international' norms, 'universal' principles . . .'.[88] Best international practice is considered to be represented by the work of bodies such as UNCITRAL.[89] The US, by virtue of its economic power, and the associated prestige of its economic and legal models, heavily influences the work of such bodies.[90] In simple terms, what is considered to be good for the US is also considered to be good for the world.[91] Of course, others may disagree in the assessment of what is good, both for the US and for the world.

CONCLUSION

Security rights give the credit provider property rights, normally in the debtor's assets. The whole harmonisation and modernisation agenda appears to be driven largely by a desire to remove restrictions on the taking of security. This is because of a widespread belief that a 'liberal' secured transactions regime promotes economic growth. In many World Bank and other studies, the availability of credit has been identified as one of the key factors driving economic growth. Lack of access to credit, and in particular low-cost credit, is seen as a major constraint on economic development. While economic and other factors may hamper access to credit,

large United States banks but also smaller lenders, often make loans to companies located in other countries supported by collateral. The guide will help countries to modernize their laws, so that lenders who are interested in making loans in other countries will know with certainty and predictability what their rights and obligations are.'

88 See J deLisle 'Lex Americana? United States Legal Assistance, American Legal Models and Legal Change in the Post-Communist World and Beyond' (1999) 20 University of Pennsylvania Journal of International Economic Law 179 at 269 and see also his comment at 202 about the US government promoting the indirect export of US models through multilateral organisations that shape international standards.

89 See generally K Pistor 'The Standardization of Law and Its Effect on Developing Economies' (2002) 50 AJCL 97.

90 For a discussion of UNCITRAL working methods referring to earlier controversies see 'UNCITRAL rules of procedure and methods of work: Note by the Secretariat' A/CN 9/676 (March 2009) and A/CN 9/697 (2010). Note too UN General Assembly Official Records Sixty-fifth session, Supplement No 17 (A/65/17) Annex 111. The controversies covered the role and status of non-State actors, primarily American-based organisations, in UNCITRAL deliberations. See also C Kelly (2009) 'The Politics of International Economic Law: Legitimacy and the UNCITRAL Working Methods' ExpressO available at: http://works.bepress.com/claire_kelly/15.

91 See J Braithwaite and P Drahos above, note 79 at 587.

legal, regulatory and institutional frameworks are also seen significantly to contribute to this problem. In many jurisdictions, the laws relating to secured transactions are fragmented and antiquated. Businesses may be unable to utilise the full value of their assets or, if they try to do so, they are strait-jacketed down a particular and restrictive path. Unlocking the value of collateral to serve as security is seen as a highly important task.

But the harmonisation and modernisation agenda also has its critics. The law of secured finance is often perceived to embody cultural attitudes and public policy choices that vary greatly among States. In this area, more than in other areas of commercial law, sovereignty issues remain central since many of the rules governing enforcement of security rights reflect policy interests that are external to the credit relationship itself. An agreement between debtor and creditor cannot regulate completely the operation of the resulting security right against third parties. In the event of debtor insolvency, there is an additional layer of policy issues to be considered. The rules governing the distribution of the debtor's assets may reflect local social goals.

Changes to law and legal doctrine in a particular jurisdiction often mirror, to a greater or lesser extent, changes that have taken place in other jurisdictions. The desire for change may stem from societal developments or from a desire to promote the social and economic infrastructure of a particular country. In the previous chapter, Turkey was highlighted to exemplify a country that set out on a path of modernity as a result of top-down political leadership and then consciously borrowed laws and legal institutions from other jurisdictions that were considered to offer a superior product. Changes may also to a greater extent be coerced. In decades and centuries past, England exported the common law to its overseas territories and possessions, and generally these former colonies persisted with the common law as they gained political independence and cut away the apron strings of the mother country in other respects. The French Napoleonic Code found its way to Spain as a result of military conquest and from there it passed to the Hispanic world of Central and South America. In recent times, coercion has come in more subtle forms, perhaps through conditions attached to international loans to developing countries from the World Bank and International Monetary Fund (IMF).

The US strongly influences if not entirely controls the workings of these international financial institutions, in particular the IMF. World Bank and IMF conditionality may require economic austerity measures, and also changes to the economic structures of the country concerned, including privatisation and restructuring of State-owned enterprises and strengthening the role of the private sector. The conditions may also require changes to corporate law, as well as the enactment of measures to enhance the availability of credit by means of a modern secured transactions regime. Prescriptions in this regard are most unlikely to be expressed as crudely as 'Enact Article 9 of the American Uniform Commercial Code'. Instead, they are more likely to call for progress and advancement in line with best international practice. Best international practice is considered to be represented by the work of organisations such as UNCITRAL. The US, by virtue of its economic power, and the associated prestige of its economic and legal models, heavily influences the work of UNCITRAL and analogous bodies. Critical commentators have therefore spoken of a process of imperialism and imperialist law.

4. National models and replication across international frontiers – Article 9 of the American Uniform Commercial Law and the English common law

The previous chapters have reported a widespread view, reflected in the work of international organisations, that a modern and efficient secured credit law should liberalise restrictions on the taking of security thereby making it freely available. Article 9 of the United States Uniform Commercial Code is often seen as a beacon for law reformers worldwide in this regard.[1] It has been described as the 'most modernised, rational and comprehensive system of security interests in the present world'.[2] Article 9 has certainly been a major influence in other common law jurisdictions and the common law provinces of Canada, New Zealand and Australia have now enacted Personal Property Security Acts that are modelled along American Article 9 lines. This chapter begins by looking at the main features of Article 9. Secondly, it considers the influence of Article 9 on other common law jurisdictions. Thirdly, it considers the English common law approach towards security rights. Fourthly, it provides a comparative international perspective. The conclusion then summarises the discussion.

---

[1] Article 9 was first promulgated in the 1950s by two sponsoring organisations, the American Law Institute (ALI) and the National Conference of Commissioners on Uniform State Laws (NCCUSL). It has been revised on many occasions with the most recent revision coming into force in 2001. It has been adopted by all 50 States in the United States including Louisiana with its mixed civil law/common law inheritance. See generally the ALI and NCCUSL websites – www.ali.org and www.nccusl.org. It should be noted that on the recommendation of the Permanent Editorial Board for the UCC, a joint review committee was formed in spring 2008 to examine the operation of Article 9 in practice and to identify any issues that should be addressed. The committee is instructed not to reconsider policy decisions made during the drafting of Article 9, except as may be necessary to address any provisions that are creating significant problems in practice.

[2] Ulrich Drobnig – see (1977) volume 8 UNCITRAL Yearbook at 171 but for criticism of Article 9 from a distinguished practitioner see P Wood *Law and Practice of International Finance* (London, Sweet & Maxwell, 2008), who suggests it is based on the obsolete notion of trying to thwart the appearance of false wealth.

ARTICLE 9 OF THE UNITED STATES UNIFORM COMMERCIAL CODE

Article 9 applies to all security interests, regardless of whether the security provider is a business entity or an individual. Article 9 abandons old distinctions between creating security over an asset and the use of absolute title to achieve the same economic objective. Article 9 adopts the universal, generic concept of a security interest, and all the old terminology of the law such as pledge, mortgage, conditional sale, trust receipt etc. has been replaced by the unitary concept of a security interest. Article 9 does not make any distinction between legal and equitable security interests nor between fixed and floating security interests.

Article 9-109 applies Article 9 to any transaction, regardless of its form, that creates a contractual security interest in personal property and, more specifically, to a sale of accounts, chattel paper, payment intangibles or promissory notes.[3] 'Accounts' is basically Article 9-speak for receivables. 'Security interest' is defined in Article 1-201(37) of the Uniform Commercial Code as meaning an interest in personal property or fixtures that secures either payment or else the performance of an obligation. The term also includes any interest of a buyer of accounts etc. The special property interest of a buyer of goods on identification of those goods to a contract for sale[4] is not characterised as a 'security interest', but a seller may acquire a security interest by complying with Article 9. In other words, even a 'simple' retention of title clause, by which a seller of goods retains ownership of the goods until it has paid for them, is transformed by statutory language into the reservation of a security interest.[5] Article 9 applies irrespective of whether title to the collateral is in the secured party or the debtor, though there are special rules, e.g. applicable to the sales of accounts.[6]

On the other hand, Article 9, and other national systems based upon it, does not apply to security over land or to security over certain types of property that may be registrable in specialist property registers, e.g.

---

3 Article 9, however, does not apply to a sale of accounts, chattel paper, payment intangibles or promissory notes as part of a sale of the business out of which they arose or to an assignment of the same which is for the purpose of collection only. Neither does it apply to an assignment of a right to payment under a contract to an assignee that is also obligated to perform under the contract nor to an assignment of a single account, payment intangible or promissory note to an assignee in full or partial satisfaction of a pre-existing indebtedness.

4 See Section 2-401 of the Uniform Commercial Code.

5 For a description of the different forms of retention of title clause see G McCormack *Reservation of Title* (London, Sweet & Maxwell, 2nd edn 1995) at 2.

6 A payment intangible is defined in Article 9-102(61) as meaning a general intangible under which the account debtor's principal obligation is a monetary obligation. General intangibles are the residual category of personal property.

security over intellectual property rights and ship and aircraft mortgages. These exclusions are difficult to justify rationally.[7] Pressure group politics and lobbying by vested interest groups undoubtedly has a part to play as well. They may also be explained on the basis in particular that land tends to have its own distinctive legal regime. Also in federal jurisdictions, land law is often considered to be a matter within the exclusive competence of the State or provincial legislature, as distinct from chattel mortgage law that has a more cross-territorial reach.

Article 9 – Creating a Security Interest and Making It Effective Against Third Parties

The central concepts of Article 9 are attachment and perfection. A security interest is said to attach when it becomes enforceable between creditor and debtor, i.e. it creates an obligation.[8] Article 9-203 lays down that a security agreement attaches if value has been given, the debtor has rights in the collateral, or the power to transfer rights in the collateral to a secured party and one of a number of other alternative conditions are fulfilled, including that the debtor has authenticated a security agreement that provides a description of the collateral. The parties, however, may agree to postpone the time for attachment, in which case the security interest attaches at the agreed time. It is specifically stated in Article 9-204 that a security agreement may cover after-acquired property but, of course, the security agreement will not attach unless and until the debtor 'has rights in the collateral'. The concept of 'rights in the collateral' is not free from controversy though it clearly connotes something less than full ownership.

Perfection, on the other hand, refers to the process whereby the security interest becomes effective against third parties.[9] Perfection generally occurs through filing and the date of filing is the reference point for settling the order of priorities between competing security interests in the same collateral. Article 9-308 states that a security interest is perfected (a) when it has attached and (b) when all the steps required for its perfection have been complied with. A security interest is perfected when it attaches if the applicable requirements are satisfied before the security interest attaches.[10] The filing of a financing statement is the standard way

---

[7] For example, the European Bank for Reconstruction and Development (EBRD) Core Principles for a Mortgage Law have been directly inspired by EBRD's Core Principles for a Secured Transactions Law with the language adapted to refer specifically to mortgages – see www.ebrd.com.

[8] Articles 9-203(f) and 9-315.

[9] See generally Article 9-308.

[10] Article 9-308(a).

of perfecting a security interest but three other methods of perfection are permissible in certain circumstances.[11] Firstly, perfection by possession is allowed thereby validating the equivalent of a common law pledge. Secondly, security over certain property including investment property may be perfected by the secured party taking control of the collateral. In the case of intermediated securities, this will occur if the securities intermediary agrees to respond to instructions from the secured party rather than from the debtor. Finally, certain security interests are perfected automatically upon attachment.[12]

Article 9-style Notice Filing

Under Article 9 in the main, public notice of a security interest is given through filing. The security agreement itself, however, is not filed but is rather a simple record – a financing statement – that provides a limited amount of information.[13] The financing statement may be filed either before or after the security agreement has been drawn up. The filed notice merely indicates that a person may have a security interest in the collateral (property) concerned, but to ascertain the complete state of affairs it would be necessary to make further inquiry from the parties. There is a statutory procedure under Article 9-210 whereby a secured party, at the debtor's request, may be required to make disclosure. In many cases however, the debtor or another prospective financier may be able to obtain the requisite information without the need to invoke the compulsory features of Article 9-210.

Notice filing under an Article 9 regime removes the need to make a number of repeated filings where there is a series of transactions between the parties.[14] The financing statement is effective to cover transactions under a security agreement that was not in existence and not even contemplated by the parties at the time that the financing statement was filed, provided that the indication of collateral in the financing statement is sufficiently broad to cover the collateral concerned. Similarly, a financing statement is effective to cover after-acquired property of the type indicated and to perfect future advances under security agreements, irrespective of whether after-acquired property or future advances are mentioned in the financing statement and even though they may not have been in the

---

11 Article 9-310.

12 Article 9-309. These exceptions appear to be essentially pragmatic; based on industry need or lobbying by pressure groups.

13 Article 9-502.

14 See generally Article 9-502 Official Comment.

contemplation of the parties at the time that the financing statement was drawn up.[15]

In simple terms, a financing statement may cover the entire credit relationship of the parties. Therefore, a seller who is contemplating the supply of goods to a buyer over an extended period of time may take a security interest in all the supplies by filing a simple financing statement instead of having to register each contract of sale separately. The creditor may state simply that it is taking security in certain collateral to cover advances made to the debtor, including future advances, irrespective of whether or not there is any commitment on the part of the creditor to make the advance.[16] There are simple, formal requirements for an effective financing statement; namely, the debtor's name, the name of a secured party or representative of the secured party, and an indication of the collateral. A financing statement must reasonably identify the collateral or alternatively it is permissible to state that the financing statement covers all assets or all personal property.[17] A broad statement of this kind (e.g. all debtor's personal property) would not, however, be a sufficient description for the purposes of a security agreement.[18] Article 9, in fact, lays down fairly strict requirements for the description of collateral in the security agreement. In Article 9-108 it calls for a description of the collateral by specific listing, category, quantity, computational or allocational formula or procedure or any other method if the identity of the collateral is objectively determinable. These requirements are stricter than for the description of property in an English-style floating charge.

Article 9-506 provides that a financing statement substantially satisfying the formal requirements is effective, even if it has minor errors or omissions, unless the errors or omissions make the financing statement seriously misleading.[19] Records filed in the filing office do not require signatures for their effectiveness, though there is a requirement that the debtor authorises the filing in an authenticated record.[20] A person who files an unauthorised record is liable for damages.[21] Article 9-516 provides that communication of a record to a filing office and tender of the filing fee or acceptance of the record by the filing office constitutes filing.

[15] Article 9-204.

[16] Article 9-323.

[17] Article 9-504.

[18] Article 9-504 Official Comment and Article 9-108(c).

[19] Article 9-506(c). In an English-style registration system the certificate of due registration issued by the registrar means that the registration can be accepted as valid even though the particulars registered were not an accurate description of the charge.

[20] Article 9-509.

[21] Article 9-625.

In the United States, the complete divorce between security agreement and financing statement means that there is no scope for the filing office to verify any correspondence between the two. A financing statement may be filed long before a security agreement is executed and also may be intended to cover more than one security agreement. The filing office performs a purely ministerial function and has no role in checking the accuracy of the information provided:[22] 'A filing office may not reject . . . an initial financing statement indicating that the debtor is a State A corporation and providing a three-digit organizational identification number, even if all State A organizational identification numbers contain at least five digits and two letters.' Article 9-516 provides an exhaustive list of grounds upon which the filing office may reject a record. Some of these are grounds that have the effect of rendering the financing statement itself ineffective but some grounds are not ones that would have this effect. The latter includes the failure to provide a name and mailing address for the secured party of record. If the filing office improperly rejects a financing statement that complies with all the requirements of Article 9, then the financing statement is still regarded as effective[23] except as against a purchaser of the collateral which gives value in reasonable reliance upon the absence of the record from the files.

Priorities under Article 9

Article 9-322 determines priorities among conflicting security interests in the same collateral and applies a basic principle that the first secured party to file a financing statement should have priority over competing security interests in the same collateral. The revised version of Article 9 that came into force in 2001 introduces additional variants on the basic priority position. This is done most notably by permitting perfection by control and providing this method of perfection with a status superior to that of perfection by filing.

Under the primary rule, priority dates from the earliest time that a security interest is first perfected, provided that the security interest does not become unperfected at any stage thereafter. A perfected security interest

---

22 See Article 9-516 Official Comment.

23 Article 9-516(d). The effect is somewhat similar in an English-style registration system though in the latter there is no protection for purchasers who acquire property in the reasonable though mistaken belief that the property is unsecured. The crucial issue is whether or not the particulars have been delivered to the registrar of companies within the prescribed period and not whether or not the particulars appear on the register during that period or even at all.

has priority over a competing unperfected security interest.[24] The first security interest to attach has priority if competing security interests are unperfected.[25] Article 9, however, does not preclude a secured party from voluntarily giving up priority.[26]

The central importance of the 'first-to-file-or-perfect' priority rule should be emphasised. The secured party who first registers a financing statement obtains priority even though it is not the first in terms of executing a security agreement with a debtor or indeed acquiring an attached security interest in the collateral. Consequently:[27]

> Once a financing statement is registered any person who is planning to deal with someone named as debtor in the financing statement has the ability to determine whether or not the interest he intends to acquire will be subject to a security interest having a prior status. If such a person goes ahead and acquires an interest in the personal property described in the financing statement without making some accommodation with a registering party or without obtaining a discharge of the financing statement, there is no reason to give his interest priority over a subsequent security interest acquired by the registered party.

There is an exception to the general priority rule in the case of purchase money security interests (PMSIs),[28] which will rank ahead of a prior security interest containing an after-acquired property clause. The PMSI favours creditors who extend credit on the understanding that the debtor will use it to acquire collateral,[29] and there is a complex definition in Article 9-103 which requires a close nexus between the acquisition of the collateral and the security interest. What is required is the giving of value that enables the debtor to acquire rights in, or the use of, the collateral, if the value is in fact so used.

Article 9 distinguishes between PMSIs and general security interests, awarding the PMSI a kind of super-priority status that has traditionally been enjoyed by retention of title claimants. The possibility of enjoy-

---

24 Article 9-322(a)(2).

25 Article 9-322(a)(3).

26 Article 9-339. The Official Comment makes it clear that a person's rights cannot be adversely affected by an agreement to which the person is not a party. On debt-subordination agreements under English law see *Re Maxwell Communications Corp (No 2)* [1993] 1 WLR 1402; *Re British & Commonwealth Holdings plc (No 3)* [1992] 1 WLR 672.

27 See R Cuming and R Wood 'Compatibility of Federal and Provincial Personal Property Security Law' (1986) 65 Canadian Bar Review 267 at 285.

28 Article 9-324 deals with the priority of purchase money security interests.

29 One of the justifications given for recognising purchase money super-priority is that whereas a general financier takes account of average risk, the PMSI lender may have particular skills and is able to lend on particularly advantageous terms because of its special knowledge of the collateral – see generally A Schwartz 'The Continuing Puzzle of Secured Debt' (1984) 37 Vanderbilt Law Review 1051.

ing super-priority status has been extended to other financiers in certain circumstances. If a debtor has granted an all-assets security interest that extends over future property then, notwithstanding the general first-to-perfect priority rule, a creditor whose advances funded the acquisition of 'new property' in the debtor's hands outranks the earlier financier in respect of this property.[30]

PMSI super-priority may be justified on the basis that the release of funds by the creditor increases the debtor's total pool of assets. The debtor is enabled to acquire new assets as distinct from merely rolling over existing debt with the debt representing the purchase price of the assets being offset by the additional property. If the new property helped the debtor's business to earn extra profits, it may even improve the position of existing creditors by swelling their security interest. Further, if an earlier creditor could rely on an after-acquired property clause to the detriment of a PMSI holder, the earlier creditor would obtain an unjustified windfall at the expense of the PMSI holder whose advance facilitated the acquisition of the property.[31] On the other hand, according super-priority privileges to the PMSI carries the assumption that the provision of funds tied to the acquisition of 'new' assets is more beneficial in a business sense than more general loans that can be used to pay the wages of employees.[32] One advance may not necessarily carry any greater social benefit than the other.

It is necessary to comply with special requirements, however, to obtain super-priority status. Article 9-324, for instance, distinguishes between inventory and other goods such as capital equipment and a claim to PMSI status in inventory is more difficult to establish.[33] Before a security interest

---

30 Under Article 9-324(g) the holder of a purchase money security interest that secures the unpaid purchase price of collateral will prevail over the holder of a conflicting purchase money security interest that enables the collateral to be acquired. This means that a retention-of-title seller has priority over a lender that makes an enabling loan. There is some possible inconsistency with Article 9-328 which deals with investment property. Priority in investment property is given to the secured party who has control. Article 9-328(2) provides that if two or more secured parties have control, priority is determined by who obtained control first.

31 For a law and economics perspective on this view see H Kanda and S Levmore 'Explaining Creditor Priorities' (1994) 80 Virginia Law Review 2103 at 2138–2141.

32 See the comments in WJ Gough *Company Charges* (London, Butterworths, 2nd edn, 1996) at 436: 'It assumes that financial accommodation for the purpose of, for example, paying wages and salaries through cheques drawn on an overdrawn account is less important than for the purchase of stocks or plant and equipment. This is not a real world distinction. Credit, as a matter of business need, is indivisible in the sense that all business inputs, including wages, overheads, equipment and supplies are all vital to an ongoing business.'

33 For the definition of 'inventory' see Article 9-102.

in inventory can qualify as a PMSI the secured party must, before the debtor receives possession of the inventory, give notice in writing to every other secured party who has already registered a financing statement over the same collateral. The notice is required to state that the person has, or expects to acquire, a PMSI in inventory of the debtor and also to describe the inventory.[34]

In the case of capital equipment rather than inventory, the qualifications necessary for obtaining PMSI status are somewhat less demanding. Automatic super-priority over prior secured lenders is gained if the PMSI is registered within 20 days of the debtor acquiring possession of the collateral.[35] 'The rules intimate that the acquisition of new inventory and its associated debt is more threatening to earlier creditors than the debt-financing of new equipment but that debt tied to new inventory is still less threatening than new money unlinked to particular assets.'[36]

INFLUENCE OF ARTICLE 9 ON OTHER COMMON LAW JURISDICTIONS

The American Article 9 has been used as a model for Personal Property Security Acts in Canada, New Zealand and recently Australia.[37] While there are some differences of detail, typically this legislation applies to a broad range of transactions including transactions traditionally not thought of as creating security interests such as debt factoring and simple retention of title arrangements.[38] The legislation applies irrespective of the

---

[34] Article 9-324 Official Comment explains the purpose of the notification requirement as being to protect a non-purchase money inventory secured party which, under an arrangement with the debtor, is typically required to make periodic advances against incoming inventory or periodic releases of old inventory as new inventory is received. If the inventory secured party receives notice it may not make an advance. While the notification requirement is not the same as imposing a consent requirement before a PMSI over inventory can take priority, through the mechanism of an inventory secured party exerting pressure on the debtor it may function in roughly the same way.

[35] Article 9-324(a).

[36] See H Kanda and S Levmore 'Explaining Creditor Priorities' (1994) 80 Virginia Law Review 2103 at 2139.

[37] See generally R Cuming 'Article 9 North of 49: The Canadian Personal Property Security Acts and the Quebec Civil Code' (1996) 29 Loyola LA Law Rev 971.

[38] Iacobucci J said in the Supreme Court of Canada in *Re Giffen* (1998) 155 DLR (4th) 332 at 344 quoting T Buckwold and R Cuming 'The Personal Property Security Act and the Bankruptcy and Insolvency Act, Two Solitudes or Complementary Systems' (1997) 12 Banking and Finance Law Review 467 at 469–470: 'Simply put, the property rights of persons . . . are what the legislature determines them to be . . . The rights of parties to a transaction that create a security interest are explicitly not dependent upon either the form of the transaction or upon traditional questions of title. Rather, they are defined by the Act itself.'

location of title, i.e. it does not matter whether the debtor or the secured party has title to the secured property.[39]

The statutes create a comprehensive registration obligation but registration is based on notice filing, i.e. the creditor files a notice that it intends to take a security interest in the debtor's property and the notice describes the intended subject matter of the security interest. It is possible to file a notice either before or after the execution of a security agreement and it is possible for a single notice to relate to more than one security agreement.

The legislation also contains a first-to-file or perfect priority principle, i.e. the first secured party to file a financing statement has priority over competing security interest holders claiming the same collateral.[40] If, however, a security interest is perfected by taking possession of the collateral rather than by filing, then priority will generally be determined by the date of possession. The 'first-to-file or perfect has priority' principle is subject to an exception for purchase money security interests (PMSIs), i.e. where a lender extends credit to enable the debtor to acquire rights in the collateral and the credit is so used, then the lender will have super-priority in the collateral.[41] In other words, the purchase money lender will outrank earlier general creditors who are claiming the collateral as after-acquired property. The statutes also contain special priority rules to accommodate chattel paper and certain forms of intangible property such as investment securities and negotiable instruments.[42]

The statutes treat all security interests as one for priority purposes.[43] Under pre-Article 9 US law it was regarded as being incompatible with the nature of a security interest that the debtor should have dominion over the assets and the freedom to dispose of the assets in the ordinary course of business.[44] A multitude of avoidance techniques developed to circumvent this ruling, and Article 9 simplified the position by validating what is

---

39 See s 24 of the New Zealand PPSA, but for criticisms of this general approach of purporting to render questions of title irrelevant see T Plank 'Sacred Cows and Workhorses: The Sale of Accounts and Chattel Paper under the UCC and the Effects of Violating a Fundamental Drafting Principle' (1994) 26 Conn L Rev 397.

40 See s 66 of the New Zealand PPSA.

41 For purchase money super-priority see sections 73–77 of the New Zealand PPSA. The priority of purchase money security interests is discussed generally by T Jackson and A Kronman 'Secured Financing and Priorities among Creditors' (1979) 88 Yale LJ at 1171–1178. Jackson and Kronman suggest that the purchase money super-priority is best thought of as a device for alleviating the situational monopoly created by an after-acquired property clause.

42 See sections 96–99 of the New Zealand PPSA.

43 See s 40(4) of the New Zealand PPSA which stipulates that a reference in a security agreement to a floating charge is not an agreement that the security interest created by the floating charge attaches at a later time than would otherwise be the case.

44 *Benedict v Ratner* (1925) 268 US 353. The inspiration behind Article 9, Grant Gilmore has argued, is that if floating charges had been accepted in the US, then some of the pressure

termed 'a floating lien on shifting collateral'.[45] Unlike in the United States, the floating charge was recognised in common law Canada and New Zealand before the reform statutes. The Canadian Supreme Court has declared that the effect of PPSA legislation is to sweep away the distinction between fixed and floating charges as well as between legal and equitable security interests, notwithstanding the fact that the security agreement used by the parties may have employed the old floating charge terminology.[46] The court referred to an implicit legislative declaration that, as a matter of public policy, there was nothing objectionable about having a fixed charge on stock-in-trade of a debtor coupled with a licence to deal with the collateral in the ordinary course of business. The New Zealand PPSA mandates a similar result. Lord Millett presciently remarked in *Agnew v Commissioner of Inland Revenue*:[47] 'A curiosity of the case is that the distinction between fixed and floating charges, which is of great commercial importance in the United Kingdom, seems likely to disappear from the law of New Zealand when the Personal Property Securities Act 1999 comes into force.'

Variants on the Article 9 Position – Invalidation of Unregistered Securities

The North American precedents invalidate an unregistered security interest in the event of a debtor's insolvency. The New Zealand PPSA does not follow this approach and an unregistered, but registrable, security interest is still enforceable as against the liquidator or bankruptcy trustee. Proponents argue that invalidation of unregistered securities gives unsecured creditors an undeserved windfall in liquidation. Liquidators are given a perverse incentive to litigate the issue of registration and to point to possible errors in the registration process whereas, in fact, nobody has been misled.[48] It has also been argued that the invalidation policy rests on an outdated conception of how business

for change which brought about Article 9 would have been absent – see *Security Interests in Personal Property* (Boston, Little Brown, 1965) at 359–361.

45 According to Grant Gilmore in 'Security Law, Formalism and Article 9' (1968) 47 Nebraska LR 659 at 672: 'Article 9 draftsmen argued from the premise that, under existing security law, a lender could take an enforceable interest in all of a debtor's present and future personal property to the conclusion that the new statute should provide for the accomplishment of this result in the simplest possible fashion.'

46 *Royal Bank of Canada v Sparrow Electric Corp* (1997) 143 DLR (4th) 385.

47 [2001] 2 AC 710 at 716.

48 See the statement by J McCoid 'Bankruptcy, the Avoiding Powers, and Unperfected Security Interests' (1985) 59 American Bankruptcy Law Journal 175 at 190.

is actually conducted.[49] The fact that a debtor happens to be in possession of assets does not provide the appearance of ostensible ownership to anybody. An unsecured creditor does not in practice check the register before extending credit for, even if a check had been conducted, the unsecured creditor would still have his interest primed by a security interest granted and registered the day after the registry search.

One might question, however, the wisdom of the policy choices reflected in the legislation.[50] It may be suggested that invalidating unregistered securities promotes a general reliance interest. Although an unsecured creditor may not actively seek a proprietary right against the company, the register provides important information about the existence of creditors who possess such rights.[51] The general credit assessment of a company would involve the receipt and analysis of such information. The fact that a particular individual unsecured creditor may not have relied on the register in this way is irrelevant.[52] It may be difficult to show on a purely factual level whether a particular unsecured creditor did or did not rely on the state of the register. Having a general invalidating principle may be seen as capable of being cost-effective because it removes the need to conduct potentially complex factual inquiries. Overall the effect of secured transactions reforms is to extend and strengthen the rights of secured creditors, and registration may be seen as a small price to pay for these enhancements.[53] Moreover, the absence of any invalidation principle marginalises even more the position of the unsecured creditor.[54]

---

49 See DF Dugdale 'The Proposed PPSA' [2000] New Zealand Law Journal 383 at 384.

50 See generally J Ziegel 'Canadian Perspectives on the New Zealand Chattel Securities Act' (2001) 7 New Zealand Business Law Quarterly 118.

51 See J De Lacy 'Ambit and Reform of Part 12 of the Companies Act 1985 and the Doctrine of Constructive Notice' in J De Lacy ed *The Reform of UK Company Law* (London, Cavendish, 2002) 333 at 362–363 but see also D Baird 'Notice Filing and the Problem of Ostensible Ownership' (1983) 12 J Legal Stud 53 at 60.

52 'Ambit and Reform of Part 12 of the Companies Act 1985 and the Doctrine of Constructive Notice' in J De Lacy ed *ibid* at 356–357. De Lacy refers in this connection to the observations of Lord Wilberforce in *Midland Bank Trust Co Ltd v Green* [1981] AC 513 at 530.

53 See, for instance, D McLauchlan 'Unperfected Securities under the PPSA' [1999] NZLJ 55 who argues that if the policy objective of adherence to the perfection requirement is to be achieved then failure to perfect should have the meaningful penalty of defeating the security interest on the insolvency of the debtor. In McLauchlan's view this is a bare minimum step that the law should take in redressing the balance somewhat in favour of unsecured creditors.

54 For a discussion of the pros and cons of the position reflected in the New Zealand legislation see P Wood above, note 2 at 268–269.

SECURED CREDIT UNDER THE ENGLISH COMMON LAW

Unlike the position in the US under Article 9 of the Uniform Commercial Code, in England there is no comprehensive statutory code on secured transactions.[55] This makes it difficult to 'sell' English law to international audiences as a model to draw upon.[56] The present law on security interests in England is contained in a multitude of sources. Case law defines a security right or interest as basically a right over property to ensure the payment of money or the performance of some other obligation.[57] The security giver may itself have secured the obligation or it may be that it is the interest of some third party that is secured. Property law determines the kinds of security right that may be created and there are four types of security right known to English law – mortgages, charges (fixed and floating), pledges and liens. Mortgages and charges are both non-possessory consensual rights. They are created by agreement between security giver and security taker. Moreover, the security giver retains possession of the property that serves as security. In *NatWest Bank plc v Spectrum Plus Ltd*,[58] Lord Scott suggested that the essential characteristic of a floating charge that distinguishes it from a fixed charge is that the 'asset subject to the charge is not finally appropriated as a security for the payment of the debt until the occurrence of some future event. In the meantime, the charge giver was left free to use the charged asset and to remove it from the security.'

Sometimes, the expression 'mortgage' and 'charge' (meaning a fixed charge) are used interchangeably.[59] On other occasions, however, the

---

55 See generally on the presentational difficulties caused by this, M Bridge 'The Law Commission's Proposals for the Reform of Corporate Security Interests' in J Getzler and J Payne eds *Company Charges: Spectrum and Beyond* (Oxford, OUP, 2006) 267 at 289. See also Roy Goode 'Insularity or Leadership? The Role of the United Kingdom in the Harmonisation of Commercial Law' (2001) 50 ICLQ 751.

56 Scottish law is different, still displaying features of Scotland's civil law heritage, though the floating charge was introduced to Scotland by statute in 1961 – see Companies (Floating Charges) (Scotland) Act 1961 and now Bankruptcy and Diligence etc (Scotland) Act 2007 and see generally D Cabrelli 'The Case Against the Floating Charge in Scotland' (2005) 9 Edinburgh Law Review 407.

57 *Re Paramount Airways Ltd* [1990] BCC 130 at 149 per Browne-Wilkinson VC; see also the statement of Lord Scott in *Smith v Bridgend County Borough Council* [2002] 1 AC 336 at p 355 that a 'contractual right enabling a creditor to sell his debtor's goods and apply the proceeds in or towards satisfaction of the debt is a right of a security character'.

58 [2005] 2 AC 680 at para 111.

59 The Law of Property Act 1925 s 205(1)(xvi) states that 'mortgage' includes any charge or lien on any property for securing money or money's worth and see also Insolvency Act 1986, s 248.

expression 'charge' may be used as a general umbrella concept that also embraces mortgages.[60] The pledge is also created by agreement between security giver and security taker, but it differs from the mortgage or charge in that actual or constructive possession of the property serving as security, or documents representing the same,[61] is handed over to the security taker.[62] A lien can take at least two forms.[63] The common law lien is perhaps the most straightforward and gives the lien holder the right to retain possession of items originally delivered for some other purpose until some outstanding indebtedness is discharged.[64] The lien holder has a passive power to retain possession, and no power of sale over the assets, though statute sometimes brings into existence such a power of sale.[65] The equitable lien, on the other hand, is essentially an equitable charge over property, arising by operation of law, rather than by agreement between the parties.[66]

Whereas property law serves to determine what security rights may be created, contract law sets out the formalities for the creation of consensual security rights. These requirements are not onerous. In the generality of cases, a simple oral contract is all that is required though, in practice, there will be writing in considerable and expensive detail. For security interests relating to land the writing requirement is mandatory under the Law of

---

60 The Companies Act 1985 s 396(4) provides that 'charge' includes 'mortgage'; see now to the same effect Companies Act 2006, s 861(5).

61 See *Harrold v Plenty* [1901] 2 Ch 314.

62 The Privy Council explained the nature of a pledge in *Official Assignee of Madras v Mercantile Bank of India Ltd* [1935] AC 53 at 58–59: 'At common law a pledge could not be created except by a delivery of possession of the thing pledged, actual or constructive. It involved a bailment. If the pledgor had the actual goods in his physical possession, he could effect the pledge by physical delivery; in other cases he could give possession by some symbolic act, such as handing over the key of the store in which they were held. If, however, the goods were in the custody of a third person, who held for the bailor so that in law his possession was that of the bailor, the pledge could be effected by a change of the possesion of the third party, that is by an order to him from the pledgor to hold for the pledgee, the change being perfected by the third party attorning to the pledgee, that is acknowledging that he thereupon held for him; there was thus a change of possession and a constructive delivery and the goods in the hands of the third party became by this process in the possession constructively of the pledgee.'

63 In *Re Cosslett (Contractors) Ltd* [1998] Ch 495 at 508 Millett LJ referred to a contractual lien and distinguished it from a pledge stating that, in the case of a pledge, the owner delivers possession to the creditor as security, whereas, in the case of a lien, the creditor retains possession of goods previously delivered to him for some other purpose. It should be noted that under the draft Company Security Regulations 2006 published as an appendix to the Law Commission Final Report, a contractual lien is considered to be a pledge.

64 See *Tappenden v Artus* [1964] 2 QB 185.

65 See *Bristol Airport plc v Powdrill* [1990] Ch 744.

66 For descriptions of equitable liens see *Re Bond Worth Ltd* [1980] Ch 228 at 251 and *Re Bernstein* [1925] Ch 12 at 17–18.

Property (Miscellaneous Provisions) Act 1989 and, before that, the Statute of Frauds 1677.

Registration of Security Interests under English Law

Once a security right has been created then it is good not only as between the security giver and the security taker, but also with respect to third parties. Chapter 25 of the Companies Act 2006 lays down, however, that particulars of certain types of charge created by a company, along with the original instrument of charge, must be delivered to Companies House within 21 days of the date of creation of the charge. If this is not done, then the charge is invalid in the event of the corporate charge giver going into liquidation or administration. Registration requirements apply to the most common types of charge, including floating charges and fixed charges over land, goods, debts, ships, aircraft and intellectual property rights. The list of registrable charges is set out in section 860(7) Companies Act 2006 and only if a charge is on the list is it registrable. To use American Article 9 legal jargon, the requirement of registration is a 'perfection' requirement. Another way of putting it is to say that Part 25 Companies Act 2006 must be complied with before the enumerated categories of charge become effective against certain parties, i.e. companies in administration or liquidation.

While there have been variations in procedure, the essential features of the registration scheme have remained the same for over a hundred years.[67] Certain particulars of the charge such as to date of creation, amount secured, property charged and persons entitled thereto, together with the instrument of charge, must be delivered to the companies registrar within 21 days from the date of creation of the charge. The registrar compares the instrument of charge with the filed particulars and, once satisfied that everything is in order, issues a certificate of due registration which is stated by statute to be conclusive evidence that all the requirements as to registration have been complied with. There is a procedure whereby a charge may be registered out of time but this requires a court application.[68]

---

[67] For a detailed historical account of the development of the company charge registration provisions see De Lacy 'Reflections on the Ambit and Reform of Part 12 of the Companies Act 1985 and the Doctrine of Constructive Notice' in J De Lacy ed above, note 51. For possible reform of English law along American Article 9 lines see J De Lacy ed *The Reform of UK Personal Property Security Law: Comparative Perspectives* (Abingdon, Routledge-Cavendish, 2010).

[68] In 2010 the relevant government department in the UK produced a consultation paper canvassing views on a variety of proposals for reforming the UK registration procedure. The topics for consideration include the introduction of electronic registration, what

Many common law countries still follow the broad outlines of the English approach towards registration of company charges including Ireland, Singapore and Hong Kong. There are however some differences in detail. For instance, in Ireland and in Singapore there is no obligation to submit the instrument of charge along with the prescribed particulars to the registrar of companies.[69] Because of the absence of the instrument of charge itself, the registrar does not, as a matter of course, check whether the particulars are a full and accurate description of the charge. Nevertheless, in both countries the registrar is still required to issue a certificate of due registration.

The company charge registration system does not apply to security agreements executed by individuals but there is a parallel system in place, namely the Bills of Sale Acts. Basically this legislation requires that chattel mortgages and other similar security agreements created by individuals should be in a particular statutory form and also registered in court offices. Failure to comply with the statutory requirements results in invalidity of the security. In fact, the requirements are so cumbersome and difficult to comply with that the Bills of Sale Acts are effectively bypassed in practice. Consumer purchases in England are often funded through hire-purchase agreements which technically speaking are an agreement for the hire of goods coupled with an option to purchase the goods at the end of the hire period.

The Bills of Sale Acts have a consumer protection aspect to them albeit one which is imperfectly and inappropriately realised. The company charge registration system has a different orientation however. Its main rationale is the provision of information for persons such as credit reference agencies and prospective charge holders who wish to assess the creditworthiness of the company. For instance, prospective charge holders are able to ascertain from the register whether or not security has already been created over the assets of the company. In consequence, they are better informed about making a lending decision and structuring the terms of any loan.

The English system is essentially a transaction-based system of

---

charges should be registrable, whether there should be a time limit for registration, and the consequences of both registration and of the failure to register – see Department for Business, Innovation and Skills 'Registration of Charges Created by Companies and Limited Liability Partnerships' (London, March 2010) and the revised proposals in the response to the consultation (December 2010).

[69] For the position in Ireland see s 99 Irish Companies Act 1963 and for the Singaporean position see sections 131–133 Singapore Companies Act 1994 and see generally Yock Lin Tan 'Personal Property Security Interests in Singapore' in J De Lacy ed above, note 51 at 387.

registration and this should be contrasted with the notice filing system under Article 9 and the PPSAs:[70]

> The most characteristic difference between notice filing and traditional systems of registration is that notice filing is parties-specific rather than transaction-specific. What is filed are not the details of a particular security but notice that certain parties have entered into, or may in future enter into, a secured transaction in relation to specified property. This approach has certain implications. A notice may be filed in advance of the transaction and the proposed transaction may never take place. The same notice may serve a series of connected transactions. And the information given on the register is necessarily rather general in character, being an invitation to further inquiry rather than a full account of the right in security.

The main points of comparison between the English system and Article 9/ PPSA regimes can be tabulated as follows (see Table 4.1):

Priorities under the English Regime

The main purpose behind the English registration regime appears to be the provision of information and prevention of the implication of false wealth.[71] It also, however, has an incidental effect in determining priorities, for an unregistered, though registrable, charge is void in a company's liquidation or administration. According to Lord Hoffmann in *Smith v Bridgend County Borough Council*: 'The plain intention of the legislature was that property subject to a registrable but unregistered charge should be available to the general body of creditors (or a secured creditor ranking after the unregistered charge) as if no such charge existed.'[72]

But registration has no comprehensive role in determining priorities. Priority between competing security interests in the same property turns on a number of factors as well as registration, such as the order of creation of the respective security interests, whether the security interest in question is a fixed or floating charge, and whether one security interest holder had notice of another earlier security interest before taking its later

---

[70] Scottish Law Commission discussion paper *Registration of Rights in Security by Companies* (October 2002) at p 8.

[71] According to the DTI 'Regulatory Impact Assessment on Proposals for the Registration of Companies' Security Interests' (London, DTI, July 2005) at para 2.7 'The system for registration of company charges is needed to address the following risks: the concealment of secured credit with markets being misled by the apparent unencumbered ownership by companies of assets which in fact are encumbered in favour of prior creditors, uncertainty over the rights of secured parties in the event of the borrower's insolvency, uncertainty over the rights of those who buy assets that are subject to security interests.'

[72] [2002] 1 AC 336 at para 68.

Table 4.1 Main points of comparison between the English system and Article 9/PPSA regimes

Features	English-style registration	US-style notice filing
What is registrable/ fileable?	• certain categories of charges • grantor – companies	• transactions that are security in a functional sense (save certain excepted ones) • grantor – not limited to companies
Obligation	On the chargor	Not an obligation but an available means of perfection
Priorities	Strictly no but failure to register means charge holder loses priority	Date of filing is reference point for settling order of priorities
Non-registration	Void against liquidator and other creditors	May lose priority Can also be avoided by a company's trustee in bankruptcy (equivalent to an English liquidator)
Timing	• Prescribed time to register • *After* creation of charge • Extension by court	• No prescribed time • May be filed in advance of transaction
Particulars filed	• Details of transaction • Particulars such as date of creation of charge, amount secured, property charged, names of charge holders • Instrument of charge but does not appear on register	• Financing statement with name of debtor and secured party and indication of collateral • May cover a series of connected transactions • Security agreement not filed
Certificate of due registration	• Issued by registrar • Conclusive evidence that statutory requirements met	• None – filing office does not check accuracy of information

security interest. Where the security interests are charges the order of priority is roughly as follows: assuming that all the charges have been duly registered, fixed charges run ahead of floating charges irrespective of the order of creation unless the floating charge contains a restrictive or negative pledge that forbids the creation of subsequent fixed charges having priority and the fixed charge has actual notice, not just constructive notice, of the restrictive clause.[73]

The basic priority position is complicated further by the freedom of contract principles that underlie English law. Security interest holders are free to alter the order of priority amongst each other by contractual provision.[74] Moreover, while there is a finite list of security interests, parties can often achieve the functional equivalent of security through other legal strategies. The retention of title by the seller of goods pending payment of the purchase price serves the same legal effect as a loan of money on the security of goods. In the same way, the assignment of debts owing to a company to a finance house will provide the company with immediate funds to the same extent as a loan of money on the security of the debts. Both these kinds of transaction are referred to as 'quasi-security', i.e. functionally equivalent legal devices to security rights strictly so-called. Moreover, quasi-security rights are generally stronger than security rights since the holder of the quasi-security right has ownership of the asset in question.[75]

A COMPARATIVE INTERNATIONAL PERSPECTIVE

In the secured transactions field, the common law/civil law divide has often been spoken of as a factor accounting for legal splintering and division. In general, the civil law calls for greater specificity in collateral descriptions; certain kinds of property may not be collateralised and there is a reluctance to embrace the concept of all-assets security with distinct collateral regimes persisting for different types of property. The common law is said to be more flexible when it comes to the requirements for the creation and enforcement of security; the kinds of property that may be collateralised and the kinds of debt that may be secured are both broadly understood and there is a greater tolerance of all-assets security. This, however, is a generalisation and, like all generalisations, there is a risk

---

[73] See generally *G & T Earle Ltd v Hemsworth Rural District Council* (1928) 44 TLR 605; *Re Standard Machine Co Ltd* (1906) 95 LT 829, *Wilson v Kelland* [1910] 2 Ch 306; and for possible circularity problems see *Re Portbase Clothing Ltd* [1993] Ch 388 and *Re Woodroffes (Musical Instruments) Ltd* [1986] Ch 366.

[74] See *Cheah v Equiticorp Finance Group Ltd* [1991] 4 All ER 989; *Re Maxwell Communications Corp (No 2)* [1993] 1 WLR 1402; *Re British & Commonwealth Holdings plc (No 3)* [1992] 1 AC 472. See generally E Ferran 'Subordination of Secured and Unsecured Debt' in *Company Law and Corporate Finance* (Oxford, OUP, 1999) chapter 16; R Nolan 'Less Equal than Others' [1995] JBL 485.

[75] For a defence of the English priority position see P Wood above, note 2 at 278.

of over-simplification. The American common law, for instance, had a multiplicity of separate security devices and this state of affairs was only rectified and rationalised by the promulgation of Article 9 of the Uniform Commercial Code in the 1950s.

Article 9 has now gone through various incarnations, each progressively more complex, but nevertheless is often held up as a beacon of light and progress for law reformers throughout the world. It has directly influenced Personal Property Security statutes in Canada, New Zealand and now Australia. The English law of security interests is less easily marketable internationally in that it is not written down in a single code or statute. Nevertheless, it has held traditional sway in other common law jurisdictions and, while this influence is being displaced in favour of Article 9 in certain countries, its dominance still continues in important emerging economies like Singapore and Hong Kong.[76]

Both US and English law exemplify 'liberal' secured credit regimes facilitating the creation and recognition of security interests in almost all kinds of collateral. This is seen if one measures the law in each country against a World Bank 'scorecard'. In the *Doing Business* reports prepared on behalf of the World Bank the credit and security law in a particular jurisdiction is given a positive grading if it contains certain specified features.[77] A mark of '1' is given for each of the features that the law contains, and obviously the more of the features embodied in the law the greater the grade. The features are as follows: (1) General rather than specific description of debt is permitted in collateral agreements; (2) General rather than specific description of collateral is permitted in collateral agreements; (3) Any legal or natural person may grant or take security in the property; (4) A unified registry operates that includes charges over movable property; (5) Secured creditors have priority outside of bankruptcy; (6) Secured creditors, rather than other parties such as government or workers, are paid first out of the proceeds from liquidating a bankrupt firm; (7) Secured creditors are able to seize their collateral when a debtor enters reorganisation; there is no automatic stay or asset freeze imposed by the court.[78]

---

[76] See also *ibid* at 315–316.

[77] See F Lopez-de-Silanes 'Turning the Key to Credit: Credit Access and Credit Institutions' in F Dahan and J Simpson eds *Secured Transactions Reform and Access to Credit* (Cheltenham, UK and Northampton, MA, USA, Edward Elgar, 2008) 3 at 49 and S Djankov, C McLiesh and A Shleifer 'Private Credit in 129 Countries' (2007) 84 Journal of Financial Economics 299. See more generally R La Porta, F Lopez de Silanes, A Shleifer and R Vishny 'Legal Determinants of External Finance' (1997) 52 Journal of Finance 265.

[78] The methodology employed in the 'Doing Business' reports issued annually since 2004 by the World Bank Group has been refined slightly over the years. In the 2010 *Doing Business* report the 'getting credit' indicator includes a 'legal rights' index that purports to measure

The US and England score highly on the first four measures. Almost any kind of obligation may be secured over almost any type of property in favour of almost any creditor. The fourth measure is slightly more problematic in that the registration regime contains gaps in both countries but it certainly does cover security over movable property. Secured credit law in both countries must yield however to bankruptcy and restructuring law.[79] In general, US bankruptcy law does enforce the full priority of secured claims in bankruptcy proceedings and secured claims take priority over governmental or employee claims.[80] In England, though, there are some limited exceptions with respect to the floating charge. A limited category of preferential creditors, primarily certain tax claims below certain monetary limits, take priority over claims secured by a floating charge.[81] There is also a limited set-aside of realisations under a floating charge for the benefit of unsecured creditors, though this is subject to strict percentage and monetary bounds.[82]

The main departure from the World Bank *Doing Business* report scorecard comes with respect to the enforcement of collateral during restructuring proceedings. Under US bankruptcy law, claims by secured creditors to enforce collateral are subject to an automatic stay or freeze during bankruptcy proceedings.[83] The secured creditor may apply to have the stay lifted and the court should lift the stay in question if the property is not needed for a corporate reorganisation that is effectively in prospect.[84] In England the stay operates in administration but not liquidation proceedings. Administration is a procedure with the legislative objective of rescuing all or part of the business of a company, though it can also be used to achieve a more advantageous realisation of company assets than could be accomplished in a winding up.[85] In liquidation there is no automatic stay on enforcement procedures by secured creditors. In administration such a stay operates but can be lifted on the authorisation of either the court or the administrator. The court and administrator are obliged to conduct a

---

eight features of collateral law and two aspects of bankruptcy law – see www.doingbusiness.org and the discussion in the concluding chapter of this book.

79 See generally G McCormack *Corporate Rescue Law: An Anglo-American Perspective* (Cheltenham, UK and Northampton, MA, USA, Edward Elgar, 2008).

80 See sections 506 and 507 of the US Bankruptcy Code.

81 Sections 40 and 175 and Schedule 6 Insolvency Act 1986.

82 Section 176A Insolvency Act 1986 and Insolvency Act 1986 (Prescribed Part) Order 2003 (SI No 2003/2097).

83 Section 362 US Bankruptcy Code.

84 See *United Timbers Association of Texas v Timbers of Inwood Forest Associates Ltd* (1988) 484 US 365.

85 Para 3(1) Schedule B1 Insolvency Act 1986.

balancing exercise between the property rights of the secured creditor and the need to accomplish the statutory objectives of administration.[86]

CONCLUSION

Article 9 has often been held out as 'state of the art' by secured credit reformers worldwide. Certainly, it has proved a lasting monument for the largest economy in the world and it has been tried and tested in mercantile practice and judicial interpretation. Its basic philosophy facilitates access to credit in terms of easy-to-comply-with rules for the creation of security interests and making those rules effective against third parties. Moreover, almost all kinds of assets may be collateralised. It has, however, to be viewed against the backdrop of US bankruptcy law, which reins in the enforcement of security during bankruptcy and restructuring proceedings. One of the main selling points of Article 9 is its track record of keeping the credit markets unlocked, and partly for this reason it has been indirectly copied in Canada, New Zealand and Australia. Even more indirectly, its ideas and substance have been reflected in the contents of Model Laws and Guiding Principles from international organisations including UNCITRAL.

But even if one accepts that a liberal security regime like Article 9 facilitates the availability of credit in general, and low-cost credit in particular, there are other exemplars that may be drawn upon at the international level. The English common law is less easily saleable because, unlike Article 9, the law is not contained in a single source but nevertheless may be inherently more flexible and malleable. Moreover, it does not have the complex conceptual superstructure of Article 9. The English common law has certainly influenced the shape and content of the EBRD Model Law on Secured Transactions and its later Guiding Principles for an effective law. Civil law concepts have also imprinted themselves on the EBRD Model Law. The next chapter will consider the EBRD Model Law as well as other international initiatives in the field of secured transactions that predate the UNCITRAL Legislative Guide.

---

86 See Para 43 Schedule B1 Insolvency Act 1986 and, inter alia, the following cases *Bristol Airport plc v Powdrill* [1990] Ch 744 and *Re Atlantic Computer Systems* [1992] Ch 505 but compare *Goldacre (Offices) Ltd v Nortel Networks UK Ltd* [2010] 3 WLR 171.

5. International harmonisation efforts before the UNCITRAL Legislative Guide

UNCITRAL's efforts to promote harmonisation in the sphere of secured transactions have been preceded by other international initiatives both at the global and at the regional level. This chapter will assess previous harmonisation efforts and set them against the background of the UNCITRAL Legislative Guide. The focus will be on two particular instruments – the European Bank for Reconstruction and Development (EBRD) Model Law on Secured Transactions and the Organisation of American States (OAS) Model Law. These are both general instruments applying in principle to all types of collateral and can be considered as precursors of the Legislative Guide, but before considering the two instruments in detail it is useful to address the issue of global versus regional harmonisation as well as touching upon the merits of collateral-specific instruments.

LAYERS OF HARMONISATION

Loukas Mistelis has spoken of at least two competing strategies in the harmonisation of international commercial law on a worldwide basis: firstly, the global conventions/model laws etc. proposed by international organisations and secondly, the regional agreements drafted by regional organisations. 'The goals of such regional conventions may derive from quite different motivations, but often they produce agreements that concern the same subject matter as the global conventions.'[1]

Others such as Spiros Bazinas, Senior Legal Officer at UNCITRAL, see global and regional harmonisation as more complementary than competitive processes. In his view, regional harmonisation promotes regional

[1] L Mistelis 'Regulatory Aspects: Globalization, Harmonization, Legal Transplants and Law Reform – Some Fundamental Observations' (2000) 34 International Lawyer 1055 at 1062–1063.

trade and facilitates international harmonisation at least to the extent that it enhances certainty, helps to reduce the number of legal systems and provides a basis for international harmonisation. For these reasons, one of UNCITRAL's professed aims from its inception has been to encourage unification and harmonisation efforts at the national or regional level.[2] Ulrich Drobnig, whose work has been very influential in this area, points out that given different degrees of economic development throughout the world, the need for credit may not be as pressing in all countries as it is in certain financially developed countries.[3] Moreover, 'national and regional legislators may place different degrees of emphasis on the protection of the secured creditor . . . and . . . of the debtor's unsecured creditors. . .'.[4] In addition, because there are fewer legal systems at the regional level than at the global level and because the legal systems within any given region are less diverse, it may be possible to tackle a problem in greater depth at the regional level than at the global level.[5] But of course achieving consensus at the regional level may exhaust the appetite for international harmonisation in that there is now no longer the energy to pursue another layer of agreements and compromises at the global level.

Along with regional harmonisation efforts,[6] there have also been initiatives by international organisations including UNCITRAL as well as UNIDROIT, the International Institute for the Unification of Private Law, to promote consensus in relation to particular types of collateral. One can mention in this regard the UNIDROIT Conventions on International Factoring and International Financial Leasing, the UNCITRAL Convention on the Assignment of Receivables in International Trade, the Cape Town Convention on Aircraft Financing and various maritime Conventions.[7] These sector-specific instruments are by definition limited to transactions that involve certain categories of

---

2 S Bazinas 'Harmonisation of International and Regional Trade Law: The UNICTRAL Experience' (2003) 8 Uniform Law Review 53 at 54. See also A Garro, 'Harmonization of Personal Property Security Law: National, Regional and Global Initiatives' (2003) 8 Uniform Law Review 357; J Basedow 'Worldwide Harmonisation of Private Law and Regional Economic Integration – General Report' (2003) 8 Uniform Law Review 31.

3 U Drobnig 'Brief Considerations on Co-ordinating Developments in the Field of Secured Transactions Law' (2003) 8 Uniform Law Review 353 at 354.

4 *Ibid.*

5 See C Vazquez 'Regionalism versus Globalism: A View from the Americas' (2003) 8 Uniform Law Review 63 at 66–67.

6 For other regional harmonisation efforts see the OHADA Model Law 'Acte uniforme adopte le 17 avril 1997, portant organisation des sûretés' designed originally for the Francophone countries of West Africa and which is available on the OHADA website: www.ohada.com. See also the work of the Asian Development Bank – www.adb.org – including the production of a 'Guide to Movables Registries' (2002).

7 On the work of UNIDROIT see its website: www.unidroit.org.

collateral and, even within the relevant categories, the Conventions are often limited in scope. Certain types of transactions are often excluded, including consumer transactions and transactions that involve intellectual property rights or interests in securities. For some instruments there is an internationality requirement that has to be satisfied before the instrument applies, so that domestic transactions are excluded from their reach. Others such as the Receivables Convention relate primarily to inter-party contractual arrangements and the possible effects on third parties are limited to setting out conflict-of-law rules. In the negotiations leading up to the Receivables Convention no consensus could be reached on substantive priority rules.

Sector-specific agreements may respond to the concerns of particular industry groups. The 2001 Cape Town Convention on International Interests in Mobile Equipment and the Protocol on Matters Specific to Aircraft Equipment can be singled out in this regard. This Convention was designed to reduce the risks faced by creditors in financing aircraft transactions and was described as providing tremendous economic opportunities to its adherents.[8] It seems that the airline industry had a prominent role in the drafting of the Convention and actively sought its ratification in the United States.[9]

It could be argued that these sector-specific agreements have contributed to the creation of a shared vocabulary and a shared knowledge base about the various techniques that facilitate secured lending.[10] While not present in all of the accords, there is now more widespread acceptance of non-possessory security interests, after-acquired property clauses, the use of intangibles as collateral and, though more controversial, the use of publicly accessible registries for notifying the existence of security interests as well as determining their priority. Roy Goode has also drawn the analogy of the field of security rights being carved up slice by slice like a salami, and when enough slices have been processed they can be reassembled to

---

[8] See generally J Wool 'The Case for a Commercial Orientation to the Proposed Unidroit Convention as Applied to Aircraft Equipment' (1999) 4 Uniform Law Review 289 and also J Wool and J Pritchard 'Secured Financing and Leasing of Aircraft under the Cape Town Convention: Breaking Ground' *Law in Transition 2010* (London, EBRD, 2010) 88.

[9] But see C Paulus 'Global Insolvency Law and the Role of Multinational Institutions' (2007) 32 Brooklyn International Law Journal 755 at 766, criticising the super-priority for certain collateral in all insolvency laws – 'global rules shall be set in force which overthrow the application of local laws for the benefit of global players with effective lobbyists' – and arguing that the success of attempts to create such rules will undermine any broad-based economic justification for harmonisation.

[10] See H Buxbaum 'Unification of the Law Governing Secured Transactions: Progress and Prospects for Reform' (2003) 8 Uniform Law Review 321 at 339.

provide a body of law covering the field as a whole.[11] On the other hand, it is probably unlikely that a slow accumulation of different accords would ever be able to cover the field entirely. The piecemeal, pragmatic, approach can result in problematic overlaps among sector-specific accords and hence the need for more general harmonisation instruments such as the European Bank for Reconstruction and Development (EBRD) Model Law on Secured Transactions, which will now be considered.

THE EBRD MODEL LAW ON SECURED TRANSACTIONS AND LATER GUIDING PRINCIPLES

The EBRD has addressed reform of the law of secured credit from the early stages of its existence and this attention has continued to the present day.[12] The EBRD was established in 1991 to assist the former Communist States of Eastern Europe and the Soviet Union with the transition to a market economy. In its own words, EBRD seeks to foster the transition to open market-oriented economies and to promote private and entrepreneurial initiative in its countries of operation.[13] The transition from a command economy to a market economy is a process that is both complex and poorly understood. When the countries of the former Communist bloc began to undertake the process, a number of them adopted the 'shock therapy' approach of privatising enterprises on a massive scale and attempting to liberalise the economy. But it came to be generally recognised that this approach alone was unable to provide the momentum for sustained economic growth. The latter was more directly dependent on the ability to develop enterprises that could function effectively in a market economy and privatisation alone did not provide any guarantees about the efficiency, competitiveness and consumer attractiveness of the enterprises being privatised: 'Responding to the new opportunities created by market liberalisation requires of the enterprises which emerged from

---

11 See R Goode 'The Protection of Interests in Movables in Transnational Commercial Law' (1998) 3 Uniform Law Review 453 at 460.

12 See generally the EBRD website – www.ebrd.com and the 'secured transactions' section of the website.

13 See the Foreword by EBRD General Counsel E Maurice in J-H Röver *Secured Lending in Eastern Europe: Comparative Law of Secured Transactions and the EBRD Model Law* (Oxford, OUP, 2007) at v: 'EBRD has a special role amongst international financial institutions, because of the unique nature of its region, because of the emphasis placed on promoting the private sector, and because of widespread expectation that countries in the region should catch up rapidly with their western neighbours.'

the command economy the ability and the incentive to adapt to the new economic environment.'[14]

EBRD has tried to achieve its general objectives in two distinct, but complementary, ways. Firstly, it provides direct financing for private sector activities such as restructuring and privatisation as well as funding for the infrastructure that supports these activities. Its investments also help to build and strengthen private sector institutions. The financing may take various forms, such as loans to private sector enterprises or State-owned enterprises operating competitively, equity investments in private sector enterprises, and facilitating access to domestic and international capital markets through services such as guarantees and financial advice. In this regard, EBRD operates as a commercial bank. Its interest rates are almost as high and it follows the same banking and investment principles. The EBRD is, however, restricted from undertaking any function where a borrower would be able to obtain sufficient financing and facilities elsewhere and this distinguishes it from commercial banks.

Secondly, EBRD promotes private sector activity, the strengthening of financial institutions and legal systems in its client States, and the development of the infrastructure needed to support the private sector.[15] In this sense, EBRD acts as a catalyst for change in the region by facilitating credit for other investors.[16] The technical assistance it provides includes legal assistance. The legal transition programme has three main objectives: (i) to improve the investment climate through the promotion of effective and enforceable laws; (ii) to increase bankable transactions for the bank and other investors by tackling legal 'bottlenecks' and (iii) to enhance respect for the rule of law in economic development.

EBRD's law reform activities have been significantly directed towards secured transactions. In 1992, the Secured Transactions Project was established within the Office of the General Counsel, leading in 1994 to a

---

14 *Transition Report 1997 Enterprise Performance and Growth* (London, EBRD, 1997) at iv.

15 The EBRD website (date last visited 29/9/2010) describes its mission as follows: 'The EBRD is an international financial institution that supports projects from central Europe to central Asia. Investing primarily in private sector clients whose needs cannot be fully met by the market, the Bank fosters transition towards open and democratic market economies. In all our operations we follow the highest standards of corporate governance and sustainable development.'

16 J Simpson and J-H Röver, 'An Introduction to the European Bank's Model Law on Secured Transactions' in J Norton and M Andenas eds *Emerging Financial Markets and the Role of International Financial Organisations* (London, Kluwer, 1998) 165. The Secured Transaction Project is now incorporated within the Legal Transition programme.

Model Law on Secured Transactions.[17] EBRD's role did not end there and since then the bank has provided direct legal assistance in the drafting and implementation of secured transactions laws to a number of countries in which it operates. Moreover, in the course of individual projects, inconsistencies or deficiencies in the laws of client States have been revealed and the countries concerned have been encouraged to seek assistance from EBRD in addressing these deficiencies.

The 1994 Model Law is stated to result from a comparative survey of various laws on secured transactions, not only in Europe but elsewhere in the world, and drawing from both common law and civil law systems. The guiding principle behind its drafting was to produce a text compatible with the civil law concepts upon which many Central and Eastern European legal systems are based,[18] while at the same time borrowing from common law systems which 'have developed many useful solutions to accommodate modern financing techniques'.[19] The Model Law consists of 35 articles accompanied by a very detailed article-by-article commentary, plus a Schedule consisting of a model charging instrument and registration statement. The Model Law does not purport to be a complete set of rules but 'a basic system on which more sophisticated rules can be developed'. The Model Law has no legal force as such but is intended to be used as a skeleton for the legislators of the region to flesh out by drafting their own domestic laws.[20]

Key Features of the Model Law

The Model Law is less comprehensive than the US Article 9. Essentially, it implements five key elements for a modern secured transactions law that

---

17 *Model Law on Secured Transactions* (London, EBRD, 1994); on which see J-H Röver above, note 13. There is extensive discussion of the EBRD Model Law in the edited volume by Joseph Norton and Mads Andenas in J Norton and M Andenas eds *Emerging Financial Markets and Financial Transactions* (London, Kluwer, 1998) and see also D Fairgrieve 'Reforming Secured Transactions Laws in Central and Eastern Europe' [1998] European Business Law Review 245; G McCormack and F Dahan 'The EBRD Model Law on Secured Transactions: Comparisons and Convergence' [1989] *Company, Financial and Insolvency Law Review* 65; L Mistelis 'The EBRD Model Law on Secured Transactions and Its Impact on Collateral Law Reform in Central and Eastern Europe and the Former Soviet Union' (1998) 5 Parker School Journal of East European Law 455.

18 Introduction, see *Model Law*, above, note 17 at p v.

19 *Ibid.*

20 It was hoped that the Model Law could have a wider impact with even an official Japanese translation produced – see T Akahane 'The EBRD's Model Law on Secured Transactions: New Developments' in *Law in Transition* (Newsletter on Legal Co-operation & Training from the European Bank for Reconstruction and Development, Autumn/Winter 1997) at 12.

EBRD has later articulated and refined: (1) the security right must adhere to the essential qualities of a property right; (2) the law should provide for the granting of security in the widest possible range of circumstances; (3) the existence of security over property must be effectively publicised; (4) there should be a rapid and cost-effective means of recovering the debt from the secured asset; and (5) the cost of creating, maintaining and exercising the right should be kept at a reasonable level. These principles shine through the Model Law.

The Model Law is based on the concept of a single security right that is capable of having proprietary force with respect to all types of assets and choses in action. A 'charge' under the Model Law is a property right and not a mere obligation. There are flexible definitions of the key concepts of 'debtor', 'secured debt' and 'charged property'. The Model Law, however, is limited to loans that secure business credits since this was considered to be the most pressing area for transitional economies. EBRD also took the view that extensive security rights in consumer transactions should be accompanied by developed consumer protection regimes and not all transitional economies had such laws in place.[21]

The publicity principle is also enshrined in the Model Law so that a business which uses its assets to secure loan transactions should not give the impression of false wealth. This is considered detrimental to other creditors and to the credit system in general. A further feature is a broad right of enforcement: the charge holder is given the right to sell the charged property in whatever way it considers most appropriate. Finally, the Model Law is grounded on the principle of minimum restrictions. The parties to the loan transaction are given maximum flexibility to arrange their relationship in a manner that best suits their particular needs.

The Model Law recognises three types of security interest. The first is the registered charge, which is by far the most important. The second is the possessory charge broadly equivalent to a common law pledge and valid without registration. The third is the unpaid vendor's charge, which is valid for six months without registration. In effect, this is like a simple reservation-of-title clause securing the unpaid purchase price of goods supplied. If the debt remains outstanding for more than six months then the supplier loses the benefit of its provision retaining ownership of the goods. Property in the goods is deemed to have passed to the buyer. The

---

[21] This view has been criticised on the basis that pledge law could in fact be a vehicle for development of the consumer finance market which may in turn cause the enactment of consumer protection rules – see generally E Summers 'Recent Secured Transactions Law Reform in the Newly Independent States and Central and Eastern Europe' (1997) 23 Review of Central and East European Law 17.

supplier must obtain a registered charge if its interest in the goods is to survive longer than six months.

Part I of the Model Law lays down the fundamental principle that the charged property used as collateral may comprise anything capable of being owned, whether tangible or intangible, presently owned or to be acquired in the future. The secured debt may be conditional or future. For example, a bank taking a charge in return for a loan may provide that the charge also covers subsequent advances after the making of the loan agreement. The Model Law provides that a charge may cover all the assets of an enterprise, in which case it is referred to as an enterprise charge.[22] The idea of the enterprise charge closely resembles the English floating charge or the floating lien over shifting collateral under US Article 9.

Problems of Terminology

One of the most innovative features of the US Article 9 is the idea of a unitary security device. In pre-Article 9 days, the lawyer had to work with a variety of security devices, each governed by its own law. In place of the plethora of devices (e.g. pledge, chattel mortgage, and conditional sale) and in place of the jargon itself, Article 9 substitutes one device and one set of terms: 'secured party', 'debtor', 'collateral', and 'security interest'. There is no official name for the device itself, only names for its components, so the device is often referred to simply as 'the Article 9 security interest' though the pre-Article 9 expression 'lien' is also used. The EBRD Model Law uses the terminology of the charge. According to the Model Law Article 1, things and rights may be encumbered by the owner with a security right (called a charge) in order to grant security for a debt. The commentary adds that the term 'charge' has been used because it is probably the most general and neutral expression in the English language.[23]

It appears, however, that legislators in Central and Eastern Europe have preferred use of the term 'pledge' and later EBRD documents in fact use the term 'pledge' instead of charge.[24] The expression 'pledge' is used

---

22 Article 5.6 of the Model Law.

23 See also J-H Röver above, note 13 at 76: 'The term "charge" is . . . only a linguistic borrowing from the English language. The security established by the Model Law is subject to the rules of the Model Law and has little in common with the English charge. The word "security", on the other hand, was not used for the right created by the Model Law because it can be, and often is, confused with "securities" in the sense of negotiable instruments.'

24 See the following statement on the EBRD website: www.ebrd.com/country/sector/law/st/facts/method.htm when visited on 17/03/11: 'The terminology used in the English language when discussing secured transactions laws is confusing. Some of the key terms have several quite distinct meanings (security and charge, for examples). Even within the secured transactions context the same expression may be used by different people in quite different ways. . . .

therein in a sense that is far wider than the narrow English concept. As we have seen in the previous chapter, the concept of pledge in English law has a narrow technical ambit, basically signifying the actual or constructive delivery of possession of an asset to a creditor by way of security. The requirement of delivery means that the category of assets which may form the subject-matter of a pledge is fairly circumscribed, being essentially confined to goods and documentary intangibles. In many Continental European jurisdictions, however, the term 'pledge' is used to cover situations that in English law would be encompassed by the expression 'charge'. Under French law, for example, the terms for a pledge, '*gage*' or '*nantissement*', apply to various situations: although originally requiring dispossession of a tangible asset so as to secure the creditor, the term has gradually become used to denote a security interest over assets of various kinds including intangible assets. In some cases, a fictitious dispossession is deemed by statute to have taken place.[25]

Obviously, no language is completely neutral and all interested parties, including foreign lenders and their advisers, should be aware of possible discrepancies that may exist between the meaning of a term as used in a security agreement, Model Law or international instrument and the meaning they usually associate with it. It is certainly the case, however, that using a technical expression in a non-technical way or vice versa can lead to serious misunderstandings, exacerbated by the difficulties of translation. For example, the Czech Civil Code does not use the term *hypoteka* 'mortgage' in its provisions on security instruments but instead uses a term that has been translated into English as 'lien'.[26] This expression encompasses security interests over both movable and immovable assets.[27] Polish law uses the term '*zastaw*', literally 'pledge'.[28] Moreover, there is no distinction

---

The general word we use for the right of security is charge. Although it has connotations of English law, which are obviously irrelevant when referring to the law of another jurisdiction, it has the advantage of being a generic term, even as a matter of English law there are no firm rules as to what is, and what is not, a charge. It therefore is used to convey the broad meaning of proprietary security without implying a specific type of transaction. The word pledge is often used, especially by translators, to refer to both possessory and non-possessory security.'

[25] See Marie-Elodie Ancel 'Recent Reform in France: The Renaissance of a Civilian Collateral Regime?' in F Dahan and J Simpson eds *Secured Transactions Reform and Access to Credit* (Cheltenham, UK and Northampton, MA, USA, Edward Elgar, 2008) 259.

[26] See the translation of Article 152 of the Czech Civil Code on the EBRD website (date last visited 29/09/2010).

[27] *Ibid* Article 153 and see generally BW Roelvink 'Security Interests in the Czech Republic' in G Ginsburg et al. eds *The Revival of Private Law in Central and Eastern Europe* (The Hague, Kluwer, 1996) at 557; R Drake 'Legal Aspects of Financing in Czechoslovakia, Hungary and Poland' (1992) 26 International Lawyer 505.

[28] See the translation of Article 306 of the Polish Civil Code on the EBRD website (date last visited 29/09/2010).

made between the terms used to refer to a possessory, a non-possessory or even a statutory pledge. The same term '*zastaw*' covers all situations.[29]

Creation and Registration of Security Interests

The Model Law goes into some detail regarding the formalities for the creation and registration of charges. Two documents are required: a charging instrument and a registration statement. The charging instrument must be dated and is required to identify the chargor, the charge holder, and the secured debt as well as the charged property. In the case of a registered charge, a registration statement must be presented at the charges' registry within 30 days of the execution of the charging instrument. This statement must identify the chargor, the secured debt, the maximum amount secured, the charged property and, in the case of an enterprise charge statement, the fact that the charge is an enterprise charge. The 30-day registration time limit is designed to avoid the creation of 'secret' charges where the charge holder takes a charge but does not register the charge until it becomes expedient to do so. An unregistered charge is invalid not only against third parties who choose to rely upon the fact of non-registration but also against the whole world. This may represent the influence of the civil law tradition of 'notarisation' upon the Model Law. The registration of contracts continues to be a requirement for validity in many post-communist legal systems.[30] Under US Article 9, on the other hand, as well as under the English regime, filing or registration serves exclusively the goal of third party notice. It is not required for the effectiveness of the security interest vis-à-vis the debtor.

Enforcement of Security

It is clear that the manner in which a security right can be exercised and enforced by the creditor is one of the prime factors in determining its economic value. Generally speaking, a charge becomes immediately enforceable if there is failure to pay the secured debt and enforcement proceedings are commenced by the delivery of an enforcement notice. Upon delivery of such a notice, the charge holder has the right to possession of the charged property, where this consists of movable objects. The preference under the Model law is for self-help enforcement of security and under Article 24 the

---

[29] See generally T Stawecki 'Secured Transactions in Poland: Coping with the Traditional Thinking and the New Challenges for Central and Eastern Europe' (1999) 32 Uniform Commercial Code Law Journal 25.

[30] See generally E Summers above, note 21.

charge holder has the right to sell the charged property without judicial intervention or authorisation, provided that 60 days have elapsed since the delivery of the enforcement notice to the chargor. During that 60-day period the charge holder may take protective measures under Article 23 to ensure that the property remains available for sale. These protective measures may involve taking possession or, where the taking of possession is impracticable, such steps as are necessary to immobilise the charged property so as to prevent the chargor or a third party using it and to prevent the chargor transferring title to it. The idea of self-help enforcement is a particularly sensitive one, and not only for the countries of Central and Eastern Europe where there is often considerable reluctance about reducing the role of the judiciary in the enforcement process. In many other jurisdictions there is also the concern that allowing the creditor itself to realise the security may endanger the debtor's 'equity' and the interests of other creditors. Control by the courts is often thought to provide an appropriate safeguard.[31]

The Model Law contains special provisions designed to cover the situation where a charge covers the entirety of an enterprise. The creditor is empowered to appoint an enterprise administrator whose functions are very similar to those of an English administrative receiver appointed by the holder of a floating charge which covers the whole, or substantially the whole, of the assets of a business.[32] While the basic function of an administrative receiver is to realise the assets of the company for the benefit of the charge holder, the receiver also has extensive powers to manage the affairs of the company.[33] Pursuant to the Model Law, the enterprise administrator's appointment is registered at the charges' registry at the same time as the enforcement notice. Upon delivery of the enforcement notice, the

---

[31] See J-H Röver above, note 13 at 84: 'the Model Law does not try to promote single-sidedly the interests of the chargeholder. It seeks to strike a balance between interests of both chargor and chargeholder. . . . Also the interests of other parties with rights in the charged property cannot be ignored. Where protections lead to a loss of efficiency in the security regime this is counter-balanced by a gain in social peace.'

[32] Section 29(2) Insolvency Act 1986. It should be noted, however, that the Enterprise Act 2002 has abolished the right on the part of a general floating charge holder to appoint an administrative receiver in the generality of cases.

[33] Schedule 1, Insolvency Act 1986 confers various implied powers on an administrative receiver. Moreover, he has the power, with leave of the court, to dispose of property subject to a prior or equal security interest. An administrative receiver is required to be a qualified insolvency practitioner. In the UK, the Enterprise Act 2002 abolished the right to appoint an administrative receiver in most cases, replacing it with a right to appoint an administrator out-of-court. The administrator has wider duties than an administrative receiver and is statutorily obliged to consider corporate rescue as distinct from merely paying back the secured debt. See generally G McCormack *Corporate Rescue Law: An Anglo-American Perspective* (Cheltenham, UK and Northampton, MA, USA, Edward Elgar, 2008).

enterprise administrator immediately displaces the directors, or other persons previously empowered to run the enterprise, assuming all their powers. The purpose of enterprise administration is to sell the enterprise as a going concern.

Evaluating the EBRD Model Law

The EBRD Model Law has attracted both plaudits and brickbats though not necessarily in equal measure.[34] Some of the criticism has come from American observers who find it wanting in at least five respects: the concept of the unpaid vendor's lien; the blurring of the distinction between creation and registration of security interests; the non-recognition of purchase money security interests; the lack of treatment of quasi-security; and finally, what is perceived to be a cumbersome enforcement machinery.[35]

On the first, the validation in the Model Law of unpaid vendors' liens undoubtedly constitutes a form of security without registration, and this is anathema to those who hail filing as an almost exclusive touchstone of third party effectiveness of security interests. On the other hand, there are at least three doctrines under current US bankruptcy law that produce almost an equivalent effect. First in bankruptcy restructuring proceedings under Chapter 11 of the US Bankruptcy Code, it is common for a debtor company to seek judicial authority to pay the outstanding unsecured claims of so-called 'critical' vendors – first day orders. These may be suppliers whose goodwill and continuity of supply is essential to the company remaining in business.[36] On occasions, the critical vendor doctrine has attracted criticism. Most notably, this occurred in *Re Kmart*[37] where the amount of the payments was particularly large – $290m. Other courts have adopted a more sympathetic approach authorising critical vendor payments on the basis of a value maximising test. In *Re CoServ LLC*[38] it was said that the corporate debtor must demonstrate three things:

> First, it must be critical that the debtor deal with the claimant. Second, unless it deals with the claimant, the debtor risks the probability of harm, or,

---

34 See generally J Simpson 'Ten Years of Secured Transactions Reform' [2001] Butterworths Journal of International Banking and Financial Law 5.

35 See J Spanogle 'A Functional Analysis of the EBRD Model Law on Secured Transactions' in J Norton and M Andenas eds above, note 16 at 157 and also G McCormack and F Dahan above, note 17.

36 See generally A Resnick 'The Future of the Doctrine of Necessity and Critical-Vendor Payments in Chapter 11 Cases' (2005) 47 Boston College Law Review 183.

37 (2004) 359 F 3d 866.

38 (2002) 273 Bankr Rep 487 at 498–499.

alternatively, loss of economic advantage to the estate or the debtor's going concern value, which is disproportionate to the amount of the claimant's pre-petition claim. Third, there is no practical or legal alternative by which the debtor can deal with the claimant other than by payment of the claim.

Secondly, under amendments to the Bankruptcy Code effected by the Bankruptcy Abuse Prevention and Consumer Protection Act 2005 ('BAPCPA'), sellers, who have sold goods to the company, in the ordinary course of the sellers' business, within 45 days prior to the commencement of the bankruptcy, may reclaim these goods if their company was insolvent at the time of receipt.[39] This provision effectively invests sellers with the right to reclaim goods sold on credit and received 45 days before formal bankruptcy proceedings provided that their company was insolvent when it received the goods – a condition that is normally satisfied. Thirdly, s 503 of the Bankruptcy Code confers administrative expense status in respect of 'the value of any goods received by the debtor within 20 days' before the date of commencement of a bankruptcy case.[40] The provision is quite broad and, somewhat anomalously, gives suppliers of goods a priority that is denied to suppliers of services or lenders who extended value to the debtor company during the 20-day period. This provision departs quite radically from the general rule that only expenses incurred after the filing of a bankruptcy petition are given administrative priority.[41]

On the blurring of the distinction between creation and registration of security interests it is undoubtedly the case that the perfection/attachment distinction found in US Article 9 does not exist under the EBRD Model Law. An 'EBRD' security interest, apart from the unpaid vendor's lien, only comes into existence when it is publicised, normally by registration. This however, is not a matter of great consequence and in any event the policy reflected in the Model Law is in conformity with the general American philosophy deprecating 'secret' security interests.

On the third issue, while the EBRD Model Law does not recognise the concept of a purchase money security interest as such, security interest holders are free to alter the priority position by an agreement, though such an agreement must not impair the interests of any third party without the latter's consent. Some advocates of purchase money super-priority claim that in reality it benefits existing lenders whose security interests are primed, in that the new finance released by the purchase money security makes it more likely that the debtor's business will grow and develop and

39 See now s 546(c) of the Bankruptcy Code.

40 Section 503(b)(9).

41 See A Resnick above, note 36 at 204.

pay back earlier loans. But if this benefit to earlier lenders really accrues, surely the earlier lenders should be given the opportunity of authorising the super-priority new loan? This is effectively what the EBRD Model Law does.

On the fourth point, the EBRD Model Law is limited in that it does not purport to deal with quasi-security, leaving it to be regulated by other legal provisions and legal regimes. But not all legal systems follow the approach of Article 9 in recharacterising quasi-security and assimilating its treatment to that of security interests strictly so-called. Not all lawyers – even sophisticated financial lawyers – accept the Article 9 approach. For instance, a very influential group representing lawyers in the City of London have argued strongly that there was no material benefit to be obtained from treating quasi-security in this way 'both because of the very material uncertainty which will result and because the requirement to recharacterise quasi-security will unnecessarily interfere with the ability of the parties to structure their business transactions as they wish'. The group has argued that parties in international financial transactions, including sale and repurchase agreements (repos), choose English law precisely because of their confidence that the English courts will not generally engage in a recharacterisation exercise.[42] In its view, there was a fundamental distinction between a company granting an interest over its own asset and a company obtaining limited rights in someone else's assets. This was not an arcane legal concept which served to obscure the reality of the transaction but, instead, was the reality of the transaction. In the second scenario, the company never owned the asset and so could not grant security over it. The inclusion of quasi-security in a security-style legislative regime would alter these fundamental legal conceptions.[43]

On the final point however, one can concede that the enforcement machinery provided for under the EBRD Model Law is cumbersome. In particular the 60-day notice period before enforcement action can be taken seems to give debtors ample time to dissipate valuable assets or spirit them away. The anti-evasion provisions contained in the Model Law may not be much of an obstacle to this happening.

Nevertheless, despite its limitations, the EBRD Model Law has proved to be an invaluable tool for legislators in Central and Eastern Europe and their foreign advisors, whether from EBRD itself or elsewhere. It

---

42 See R Calnan [2005] BJIBFL 25 at 28.

43 See *ibid* at 29. For a different perspective see J Ziegel 'The Travails of English Chattel Security Law Reform – a Transatlantic View' [2006] LMCLQ 110 at 116: 'a conditional sale agreement is only a short form of chattel mortgage and that in each case the seller or mortgagee merely retains or obtains title as security for performance of the buyer's obligation'.

serves as a signpost for countries in the region, which can 'pick and mix' from the Model Law whatever provisions appear appropriate to their needs, bearing in mind their legal traditions and existing legal provisions. Directly through the work of the EBRD's Legal Transition Team, or indirectly via the reference material used by other organisations, the Model Law has been widely advertised to reform-minded legislators. It has been used as a starting point when the various legislatures, some of whom were assisted by Western advisors, sat down to draft new provisions but many concepts have been left to one side or used in radically different ways, to the point where the system that is implemented bears little resemblance to the Model Law. This should not matter, however, since the Model Law was intended to serve only as a guide for drafters, providing them with an example of legislation to address the needs of domestic and international investors.

EBRD has not been the only body advising on secured transactions law reform in Eastern Europe. Several American organisations have also been involved such as IRIS (Institutional Reform and the Informal Sector).[44] IRIS was launched in 1990 with initial funding from the US Agency for International Development (USAID) and helps to promote reforms relating to property and contract rights as well as in the general area of 'good government'. It also serves as a key resource for USAID in the restructuring of market institutions through the provision of advisory and implementation services. IRIS has been particularly active in the secured transactions sphere. In Poland, e.g., the Ministry of Justice established a Civil Law Reform Commission in 1990 including a small working group concerned with secured transactions and USAID entered into an agreement with IRIS to conduct research on the topic.[45] IRIS has also undertaken extensive work in Albania as well as conducting a general survey of asset-based lending in Central and Eastern Europe[46] designed to ascertain the effectiveness of the laws of these countries on non-possessory pledges over movable property.

The American Bar Association (ABA) has also played an important role in the region, particularly with its Central European and Eurasian Law Initiative (CEELI).[47] CEELI's legal assistance programmes began in

44 See its website: http://www.iris.umd.edu.

45 On the Polish law see generally F Dahan and G McCormack 'International Influences and the Polish Law on Secured Transactions: Harmonisation, Unification or What?' (2002) 7 Uniform Law Review 713; T Stawecki above, note 29 and see also the EBRD website: www.ebrd.com/pages/sector/legal/secured/facts/poland.shtml (date last visited 29/09/2010).

46 'Special Supplement (September)' (1995) 10 Butterworths Journal of International Banking and Financial Law.

47 See its website: www.abanet.org/ceeli.

1990 in Central and Eastern Europe and in 1992 in the newly independent States of the former Soviet Union. They initially focused on such issues as constitutional law, judicial restructuring, and criminal law, but quickly expanded to focus on a series of additional legal issues such as media, commercial, property and land use law. Unlike IRIS, which depends on government funding, CEELI draws for its funding on non-State sources. CEELI's work in the area of commercial law provided support and assistance to governments, judges, and lawyers in host countries by, for example, assessing draft laws, organising interactive workshops, and bringing long-term resident commercial law practitioners and legal specialists into the country. Much of CEELI's work focused on educating local legal professionals in the commercial concepts embodied in the new laws and economic systems being developed. On secured transactions CEELI drafted a comprehensive 'Concept Paper' providing a conceptually thorough analysis of the background to the drafting of a new statute, identifying the various public policy choices and priorities and highlighting the different options available to the policy makers.[48]

From Model to Assessment – the Continuing Role of EBRD

As well as producing the Model Law on Secured Transactions' EBRD has also produced an annual transition report that assesses the performance of its 'client' countries using a range of performance indicators.[49] The intention was to appraise the status of the transition from a centrally planned economy to a market economy though EBRD itself was conscious of the difficulty in making such an appraisal, stating that '[p]rogress is measured against the standards of advanced industrial economies, recognising that there is no perfectly functioning market economy and that the institutional diversity among market economies does not present a unique endpoint for the transition'.[50] The method of assessment initially adopted by EBRD suffered from certain flaws. On the methodological front, it was far from scientific, being made on the basis of a questionnaire survey distributed to selected large private law firms, academics and other experts familiar with commercial law in the countries of the region. EBRD has admitted that:

48 Available on-line at: www.abanet.org/ceeli/papers.

49 See generally 'Focus on Secured Transactions' *Law in Transition* (Autumn 2000); F Dahan and J Simpson 'Secured Transactions in Central and Eastern Europe: European Bank for Reconstruction and Development (EBRD) Assessment' (2004) 36 Uniform Commercial Code Law Journal 77.

50 *1997 Transition Report* (London, EBRD) at p 12.

> much of the material that forms the basis of the Table is not readily verifiable and reflects the subjective assessments of survey respondents. Similarly, the information and views provided by respondents were not always consistent, and the EBRD has been selective in using material provided by the survey. . . . [C]are must be taken in reading and interpreting the results.[51]

The marking scheme adopted also was not free from fundamental conceptual problems. Marks from 1 to 4+ were awarded to each country for the extensiveness and effectiveness of its secured transactions, corporate and bankruptcy laws, alongside an overall mark. In the secured transactions sphere, a mark of 1 was given when laws 'impose substantial constraints on the creation, registration and enforcement of security over movable assets, and may impose significant notarisation fees on pledges'.[52] This seems unproblematic but when it comes to the granting of a 4+ mark, the criteria became much more controversial. In the first place, a 4+ requires that the legal rules 'closely approach those of more developed countries in respect to pledge, bankruptcy and company law'. But the rules in the 'more developed countries' themselves show no sign of uniformity and it is not clear how this can be the case.[53] Legal sociologist Terence Halliday has not stinted with the criticism, stating that:[54]

> EBRD's legal transition survey, begun in the mid-1990s, was essentially a diagnostic instrument constructed by a very small group of mostly in-house experts. It relied almost entirely on persuasion of nation-states to take it seriously, something it did by ranking countries against each other and effectively shaming them into reforms. But it had several defects. Its legitimation warrants were limited – it relied almost entirely on a few technical experts and its . . . technology was primitive and not at all defensible by social science standards. Moreover its technology was not accompanied by an articulated normative standard.

Perhaps acknowledging the limitations in the assessment strategy and the Model Law, EBRD has articulated and refined a less prescriptive set of general principles designed to inform and guide law makers in framing

---

51 *Ibid* at p 17.

52 *Ibid* at p 19.

53 The point is made by F Dahan 'Secured Transactions Law in Western Advanced Economies: Exposing Myths' [2001] Butterworths Journal of International Banking and Financial Law 60.

54 See T Halliday 'Legitimacy, Technology and Leverage: The Building Blocks of Insolvency Architecture in the Decade Past and the Decade Ahead' (2007) 32 Brooklyn Journal of International Law 1081 at 1088. See also A Ramasastry 'What Local Lawyers Think: A Retrospective on the EBRD's Legal Indicator Surveys' in *Law in Transition: Ten Years of Legal Transition* (London, EBRD, Autumn 2002).

'modernised' laws on secured transactions.[55] It has also formulated 'Guiding Principles for the Development of a Charges Registry (2005) and 'Core Principles for a Mortgage Law' (2008) and adopted a more sophisticated list of questions for evaluating progress made in this area. It is still committed to the proposition that an appropriate legal environment can, at a minimum, facilitate the transition process to a more free market economy and, ideally, can promote the development of financially healthy and competitive enterprises. But while embodying a general philosophy of maximum flexibility and minimum restrictions, the later emanations from EBRD are fairly broad brush and acknowledge a plurality of possible approaches, recognising that not all 'recipes' work for all cases.[56] Moreover, EBRD is mindful of the fact that getting effective laws on the statute book is less than half the battle. The quest for effective enforcement is a perennial one. Effective implementation in practice is the standard by which the progress made by a particular legal system is ultimately to be assessed. It has been remarked elsewhere that a 'jurisdiction can have the most modern law possible dealing with creation, registration, and priorities, but unless it provides for an efficient and effective system for enforcement, the entire raison d'etre of secured financing is defeated and secured financing will not occur other than on a very limited scale'.[57]

---

55 See J-H Röver above, note 13 chapter 8. EBRD's Core Principles of a Modern Secured Transactions Law are available at www.ebrd.com, and are as follows:

1. Security should reduce the risk of giving credit leading to an increased availability of credit on improved terms.
2. The law should enable the quick, cheap and simple creation of a proprietary security right without depriving the person giving the security of the use of his assets.
3. If the secured debt is not paid the holder of security should be able to have the charged assets realised and to have the proceeds applied towards satisfaction of his claim prior to other creditors.
4. Enforcement procedures should enable prompt realisation at market value of the assets given as security.
5. The security right should continue to be effective and enforceable after the bankruptcy or insolvency of the person who has given it.
6. The costs of taking, maintaining and enforcing security should be low.
7. Security should be available (a) over all types of assets (b) to secure all types of debts and (c) between all types of person.
8. There should be an effective means of publicising the existence of security rights.
9. The law should establish rules governing competing rights of persons holding security and other persons claiming rights in the assets given as security.
10. As far as possible the parties should be able to adapt security to the needs of their particular transaction.

56 See J-H Röver above, note 13 at 318: 'reform of secured transactions law in central and eastern Europe cannot start from a simple, one-size-fits-all solution. Each country evidently needs a tailor-made solution which is suited in particular to its property law.'

57 See *Secured Transactions Systems and Collateral Registries* (International Finance Corporation, Washington, 2010) at 17.

OAS MODEL LAW

Background and General Philosophy

In 2001 the Organisation of American States (OAS) produced a Model Law on Secured Transactions.[58] Boris Kozolchyk, one of the progenitors of the Model Law, has said that its first objective

> is to create a non-possessory security interest that permits debtors to retain possession of the collateral while allowing secured creditors to enforce their security interest, extra-judicially whenever possible, in case of default. It also facilitates the creation of a regional credit market by laying the legal groundwork for a network of electronic registries. The model law would create a single registry database for each country.[59]

While almost a decade later than the EBRD Model Law, it is not very apparent from the text that the OAS Model Law was in any way derived from the former. The OAS Model is much closer, not just in tone and terminology, but also in substance to the American Article 9.[60] From the terminological perspective, there is a switch between the EBRD and OAS Model Laws from charge to security interest; chargor to secured debtor; chargee to secured creditor and charged property to movable property collateral. In all this, the influence of Article 9 is evident and so too in the non-recognition by the OAS Model of the concept of an unpaid vendor's charge found in the EBRD Model. The OAS Model, like Article 9 but unlike the EBRD Model, also has the concept of the purchase

---

[58] See generally B Kozolchyk and J Wilson 'The Organisation of American States: The New Model Inter-American Law on Secured Transactions' (2002) 7 Uniform Law Review 69; J Wilson 'Secured Financing in Latin America: Current Law and the Model Inter-American Law on Secured Transactions' (2000) 33 Uniform Commercial Code Law Journal 43, and for background references see A Garro 'Harmonization of Personal Property Security Law: National, Regional and Global Initiatives' (2003) 8 Uniform Law Review 357; 'Difficulties in Obtaining Secured Lending in Latin America: Why Law Reform Really Matters' in J Norton and M Andenas eds above, note 16 at 251. Valuable preliminary material can be found at (2001) 18 Arizona Journal of International and Comparative Law.

[59] See B Kozolchyk and D Furnish 'The OAS Model Law on Secured Transactions: A Comparative Analysis' available on the World Bank Global Insolvency Laws Database – www.worldbank.org text accompanying fn 69.

[60] B Kozolchyk in 'Secured Lending and Its Poverty Reduction Effect' (2007) 42 Texas International Law Journal 727 relates how he was asked by a Mexican NAFTA negotiator 'why it was that Mexico's law of secured transactions had to resemble that of the United States and Canada, my reply was that the proper question was not what law Mexico had to emulate but whether Mexico did in fact desire secured lending. If it did, its law had to be based on principles that reflected those practices tried and tested in active financial marketplaces and thus capable of universal usage.'

money security interest. Moreover, following the American, but not the European precedent, the OAS Model Law contains separate and distinct rules on the formalities required for the creation of a security interest and for its effectiveness against third parties (perfection).

In terms of the creation of a security interest, the OAS Model requires an agreement between security giver and security taker which in the case of a non-possessory security interest must be in writing and contain various details, including information as to the maximum amount secured.[61] Effectiveness against third parties requires that the security interest should be publicised by registration, or by delivery of possession or control to the creditor, or to a third person on its behalf.[62] A single filing may cover multiple security transactions between the same parties.[63] There are detailed rules on priorities and on enforcement, with the basic rule giving priority in accordance with the order in which publicity is effected.[64] There is also a special priority rule that favours a possessory security interest in a document of title or negotiable instrument.[65] The OAS Model permits the creation of security in all types of property including receivables and other intangibles. The architects of the Model Law have spoken of it as a 'bridge between the most effective institutions in the common and civil law systems', but it is more a bridge with one-way traffic permitting colonisation of traditional civil law domains by common law concepts.[66]

The imprint of Article 9 over the OAS Model is clear but the latter is a much simpler and more direct instrument. It lacks some of the sophisticated conceptual apparatus of the revised Article 9, such as the concept of perfection by control applicable in the case of certain types of financial collateral. It has been said:[67]

> Because of its clarity and logical organization, the model law is a didactic enactment that can be used as a primer of secured transactions law for the uninitiated. It addresses some of the thornier concepts and their application with spare, fluid language, trusting the legally trained reader to derive appropriate implications. In contrast,. . . Article 9 is for the adept practitioner, familiar with the various transactions, but wishing to search for answers to virtually every specific factual situation and contingency imaginable. . . . The OAS model law's statement of the basic priority rule takes less than one line. By contrast, Revised Article 9 buries its fundamental priority rule in a bramble patch of language.

61 Articles 5–7 of the Model Law.
62 Article 10.
63 Article 38.
64 Article 48.
65 Article 52.
66 B Kozolchyk and J Wilson above, note 58.
67 See B Kozolchyk and D Furnish above, note 59.

> One can emerge the wiser from it only after negotiating several disentanglements and carefully tracking down various references to other provisions.

In short, the OAS Model and the revised version of Article 9 have fundamentally different drafting styles. In this respect they have been likened to an odd couple no matter how harmonious their goals might be.[68] 'In its casuistry, Revised Article 9 continues to provide groundbreaking concepts and rules. The OAS model law, on the other hand, emerges as a concise, sharply-focused and even elegant statute, albeit rudimentary in scope and untested in operation.'

Moreover, the OAS Model embodies much the same facilitative and enabling philosophy that is contained in the EBRD Model. For this reason it has been argued that the principles and policies which the two Models have in common largely exceed these differences.[69]

General Features of the OAS Model – Scope of Application

The OAS Model is limited to consensual security interests.[70] A secured creditor who perfects its security interest by publicising it in the prescribed manner is given, in the language of the Model Law, a 'preferential right', which means that the secured creditor has the preferential right to payment from the collateral sale proceeds.[71] While legislating for a general security interest, the Model Law also recognises that special laws should govern security interests in certain types of property, and States are allowed to exclude certain types of collateral from the general scheme.[72] The preparatory materials suggest that investment property is envisaged as falling within that exception.

Article 7 contains the formalities for a non-possessory security interest. The relevant agreement must be in writing and, as a minimum, must contain information as to (1) date of execution; (2) the debtor and creditor including the debtor's signature which may be electronic; (3) the maximum amount secured by the security interest; (4) a description of the collateral though this may be generic; (5) a description of the secured obligations which may also be generic and (6) express intimation that the property described serves as collateral for the secured obligation.

---

68 *Ibid* at 37.

69 See A Garro 'Harmonization of Personal Property Security Law: National, Regional and Global Initiatives' (2003) 8 Uniform Law Review 357.

70 Article 5.

71 Article 2.

72 Article 1.

The security interest envisaged by the Model Law is extremely flexible in scope and it is capable of reaching 'movable property . . . susceptible to pecuniary valuation at the time of creation or thereafter'.[73] 'Movable property collateral' is defined in a very broad way to encompass any asset of economic value that is not real estate.[74] The security interest may extend to future or after-acquired property from the moment that the debtor acquires rights in such property. The security interest may also extend to proceeds or fruits of the collateral, though this extension has to be indicated in the summary registration form provided by the Model Law. 'Proceeds' are referred to as 'attributable movable property . . . that can be identified as derived from the originally encumbered property, such as fruits, or other property resulting from its sale, substitution, or transformation'.[75] The language of the Model Law is sufficiently broad to validate what Article 9 would identify as a floating lien on shifting collateral or English law would identify more prosaically as the floating charge. The security interest may cover one or more specific items of movable property, generic categories of movable property, or all of the debtor's movable property, whether present or future, corporeal or incorporeal. While the maximum amount secured must be stated in the security contract, the parties can pitch this at a high figure to cover all possible contingencies.

The Model Law recognises that given the civil law antecedents of many countries in the Americas, it would be a step too far to legislate for the abolition of traditional security and quasi-security devices such as pledges, chattel mortgages and title retention mechanisms such as conditional sales. Instead it opts for the alternative approach of providing for a uniform publicity and priority system. The Model Law is very strong on the publicity principle and this is illustrated by the fact that in the case of possessory security interests it requires that possession is actually transferred to the creditor.[76] 'This rule endeavors to eliminate the use of "constructive possession pledges" where the debtor retains possession and use of the collateral – a mechanism that goes against true pledge requirements of delivering the collateral to the secured creditor.'[77]

All security devices are subject to the same publicity principle and subject to the same principle of priority being linked to the date of publicity. Article 48 sets out the basic priority rule in simple terms stating that

73 Article 2.
74 Article 3.
75 Article 3 V1.
76 Article 10 para 2.
77 See B Kozolchyk and D Furnish above, note 59 at 26.

the priority of a secured interest is determined by the time of its publicity. Article 2 states that the Model Law applies irrespective of the form of the transaction and regardless of whether ownership of the property is held by the secured creditor or the debtor. But this provision contains the seeds of ambiguity. There is no definition of security and one might argue that Article 2 by itself is insufficiently strong to warrant recharacterisation of retention of title clauses and finance leases as security interests, strictly so-called. The American Uniform Commercial Code (UCC) contains a similar pronouncement, but follows this up by a specific itemisation of transactions that are to be regarded as constituting security interests. There is nothing equivalent in the OAS Model and, in this absence, a degree of ambiguity about the scope of the OAS Model remains. The only type of 'quasi-security' transaction that the OAS Model deals with is the factoring or assignment of receivables, which is treated in the same way as security interests for publicity purposes and though this is unclear, maybe also for priority purposes.[78] The justification for this is stated to be that since 'assignment or factoring of accounts usually involves the sale of accounts from the account creditor to the secured creditor, there is little practical difference between the sale of accounts and the taking of a security interest in accounts'.[79]

The OAS Model also strikes out in an Article 9 direction by recognising purchase money security interests though with a change in nomenclature referring to them as acquisition security rights.[80] The validation of general security interests opens up the possibility of a security monopoly over the assets of the debtor. The first creditor on the block may have staked out a strong priority position by taking security over practically all items of value in the debtor's business, both existing and future. Article 9 creates an exception to the first-to-file-has-priority principle for purchase money security interests and the OAS Model does likewise. The justification for this exception is to improve the debtor's prospects of accessing low-cost credit. If the first creditor with the security monopoly refuses to make further advances, then the debtor may be starved of credit. Because of the security monopoly other creditors may be reluctant to lend except on costly terms. It is also argued that in general, second lenders may be prepared to offer more advantageous credit terms since they are lending

---

[78] See Article 13: 'The provisions of this Law concerning security interests over receivables are applicable to every type of assignment of receivables. If the assignment is not for security it must comply only with the publicity provisions of this Law; if it fails to so comply, it will be subject to the priority rules of this Law.'

[79] See B Kozolchyk and D Furnish above, note 59 at 27.

[80] Articles 12, 40 and 51 of the Model Law.

against specific risk rather than general risk. Purchase money lending, it is argued, is also beneficial to existing lenders because it adds to the pool of the debtor's assets and increases the prospects of the debtor's business generating sufficient profits to be able to repay earlier loans. The EBRD Model Law refuses to pay heed to the rationale. Subordination agreements whereby existing lenders may concede a higher priority position to new lenders are however permitted.[81] Implicitly at least, the EBRD Model subscribes to the view that if new lending is in reality beneficial to existing lenders, the latter can and may agree to it.

Under Article 9 the conditions for acquiring super-priority status vary depending on whether the property in question can be categorised as inventory or capital equipment.[82] Super-priority status in inventory is more difficult to obtain with the new financier required to notify existing lenders with a potentially conflicting security interest in the collateral that they intend to get a purchase money security interest. The prior notification requirement does not exist in the case of inventory and is designed to protect existing financiers who make periodic advances to the debtor upon the debtor's receipt of inventory. The OAS Model Law simplifies the Article 9 framework somewhat, though it makes super-priority to some extent more difficult to obtain by imposing a universal prior notification requirement. Article 40 provides that to obtain an acquisition security interest, a secured creditor must, before the debtor takes possession of the relevant property, register 'in the registration form a notation that indicates the special character of the acquisition security interest; and. . . [n]otify the holders of previously perfected security interests over property of the same kind that the secured creditor has or expects to acquire an acquisition security interest in the collateral described in the notice'. The super-priority of the acquisition security interest extends to cash proceeds but no further.

Enforcement of Security under the OAS Model Law

The existence of efficient enforcement mechanisms is crucial to the value of security. Cumbersome court procedures can slow down or render impracticable the enforcement of security with the consequence that the secured creditor is unable to realise the value inherent in the secured assets. Article 9 allows out-of-court enforcement of security, though the effect of this is somewhat tempered by the fact that the debtor can get an

---

81 Article 17.8 of the EBRD Model Law.

82 See generally Article 9.324 of the American Uniform Commercial Code.

automatic stay on creditor enforcement actions by making certain filings with the court under Chapter 11 of the US Bankruptcy Code. The secured creditor has to go to court to get relief from the stay and such relief is only available if the creditor can show that its interests have not been adequately protected.[83]

In England the traditional way of enforcing security is through the out-of-court appointment of a receiver by a secured creditor and the function of the receiver is to sell or otherwise realise the secured assets for the benefit of the secured creditor. At common law, there is no requirement that the secured creditor should give the debtor prior notice of the intention to appoint a receiver.[84] All that is required is that the creditor should give the debtor the short time necessary to effect the mechanics of payment. Other jurisdictions have introduced a longer notice period that is designed to give the debtor some breathing space in locating alternative sources of funding. Canada, e.g., introduced a notice requirement in 1992 in s 244 of the Bankruptcy and Insolvency Act which requires that a secured creditor who intends to enforce a security over all or substantially the whole of the debtor's property should send a prescribed notice to the debtor.[85] The security interest cannot be enforced until ten days after service of the notice.

The EBRD Model Law allowed out-of-court enforcement of security but only after a 60-day notice period. The OAS enshrines the same principle but the notice period is much shorter – three days. Article 54 provides that a secured creditor who intends to commence enforcement, in case of default of the secured debtor, shall register an enforcement form in the Registry and deliver a copy to the secured debtor, to the person in possession of the collateral and to any person who has publicised a security interest in the same collateral. The enforcement form must contain (1) a brief description of the default by the secured debtor; (2) a description of the collateral; (3) a statement of the amount required to satisfy the secured obligation and to pay the secured creditor's enforcement expenses as reasonably estimated; and (4) a statement of the remedies that the secured

---

[83] Section 361 US Bankruptcy Code. Examples of 'adequate protection' are provided by s 361 although the concept itself is not defined. The examples given are cash payments, additional or replacement security interests on other property and something that will give the creditor the 'indubitable equivalent' of its security interest.

[84] See *Bank of Baroda v Panessar* [1987] Ch 335; *Bunbury Foods Pty Ltd v National Bank of Australasia Ltd* (1984) 51 ALR 509. In most instances however, the Enterprise Act 2002 in the UK now prohibits the appointment of a receiver over the whole or substantially the whole of a company's assets.

[85] This follows judicial developments in Canada – see *Lister Ltd v Dunlop Canada Ltd* (1982) 135 DLR (3d) 1.

creditor intends to exercise. The debtor then has a period of three days to object by producing evidence before a court that full payment has been made, and no other defence can be entertained.

In the case of a non-possessory security interest over corporeal property, once the notice period has expired, the secured creditor is entitled to insist on an immediate order of possession from the court. Article 57 states that such an order should be granted forthwith, without granting a hearing to the debtor. The provision goes on to state that any exception or defence that the debtor wishes to make against such order must be initiated through an independent judicial action, and this independent judicial action should not prevent the secured creditor from exercising its enforcement rights against the collateral. Where the collateral consists of intangible property such as receivables the secured creditor is entitled to enforce the security without getting a court order provided that the notice period has expired, by collecting or enforcing the receivables against the third party obligated on the receivables.

The object of the OAS is clearly to provide a speedy enforcement procedure but how the process might work in practice is open to question. It is intended, e.g., that the secured creditor's possession action should be insulated from any consideration of the validity or indeed the enforceability of the underlying loan agreement. One could draw an analogy with the letter of credit as a payment mechanism in international sale of goods contracts. The liability of an issuing or confirming bank to honour a letter of credit undertaking is separate and autonomous from the underlying sales contract. In other words, a dispute between seller and buyer about performance of the sales agreement does not affect the liability of an issuer or confirmer under a letter of credit undertaking.[86] Letters of credits, however, are a well-recognised and internationally established payment mechanism. The autonomy principle is long established. In the enforcement of security context, however, there is no such history of 'separateness' and it is difficult to imagine disputes about the validity and merits of the underlying loan agreement not creeping into the process, especially in jurisdictions where the non-judicial enforcement of security is a novelty.

---

[86] See UCP 600 (2007) the revised version of the Uniform Customs and Practices for Documentary Credits. These are the internationally recognised contractual rules for letters of credits. They were first promulgated by the International Chamber of Commerce in 1933 and have since gained almost universal acceptance by bankers worldwide. Judicial acknowledgement of the UCP is reflected in cases such as *Edward Owen v Barclays Bank* [1978] 1 QB 159 at 171.

CONCLUSION

One strategically placed member of the UNCITRAL Secretariat has spoken of the EBRD and OAS Models as precursors to the UNCITRAL Legislative Guide.[87] The same could also be said of sector-specific agreements. All these instruments share the same basic philosophy that long-standing legal traditions, concepts and techniques, such as requirements of specificity in collateral descriptions, must now be modified so as to be responsive to the needs of commerce and finance. Financial need is said to call for the minimum degree of formality and the maximum degree of flexibility, including the authorisation of global security. Although this feature is less pronounced, these instruments also share something of a common vocabulary and common concepts, such as validation of receivables financing without any need for notice to debtors as a constitutive element in the creation of the security interest. In addition, they share a publicity principle and a commitment to publicity as a primary reference point for determining priorities between competing security interests in the same collateral.

But there are differences in the Model Laws, some subtle and others more pronounced. The models differ on whether a functional approach to security should be adopted with broadly similar treatment of security interests narrowly so-called and transactions that in economic terms perform a roughly equivalent function, including sales under reservation and certain types of finance lease. Mechanisms for the enforcement of security also differ, and this divergence only partly obscures even larger differences on insolvency-related questions, including recognition of preferential claims and stays on the enforcement of security.

The Model Laws and Conventions, on the other hand, have almost uniformly been sold on the basis that they will increase the availability and reduce the cost of credit. Put in a crude way, it is an example of the developed world helping the developing world by making available the benefit of their accumulated knowledge and experience as well as their technical know-how and expertise. The less developed world can make use of 'shortcuts' in the transition process through availing of the wisdom being passed on. Less visible have been the interests of the developed world in all this. But it is a feature, though usually veiled beneath a mask of benevolence and bonhomie. It did however surface during US Congressional debates on the ratification of the Cape Town Convention on International

[87] S Bazinas 'Harmonisation of International and Regional Trade Law: The UNICTRAL Experience' (2003) 8 Uniform Law Review 53.

Interests in Mobile Equipment and the associated Aircraft Protocol. As a US public official testified,[88] the Convention would clearly benefit creditors who financed the purchase of aircraft in foreign countries with the Convention in force by giving them needed protection; this, in turn, would benefit the US sellers of aircraft by increasing their markets. For countries such as the US that manufacture aircraft, those reduced costs should encourage increased exports and export-related economic growth – not just by major manufacturers, but also by smaller companies that make the parts and provide related aviation services. In addition, the Convention and Aircraft Protocol will benefit them by significantly reducing the risk they now incur when financing aircraft in countries whose laws do not meaningfully protect creditors in the event of a default or insolvency.

Outright opposition to international harmonisation efforts is seldom expressed in terms of the notion that it is all about those in the developed world trying to help themselves. These sentiments, however, come to the fore occasionally. For instance, the relative lack of success of the OAS Model Law has been spoken of in the context of a 'fundamental and long-standing suspicion that transplanting "modern law", sold under the label of establishing an ideal environment for business and economic growth . . .will only benefit foreign multinationals'.[89] Fears about the role of the creditor are said to be difficult to dispel 'especially because they are often based on unfortunate experiences'.[90]

---

88 See A Boss 'The Future of the Uniform Commercial Code Process in an Increasingly International World' (2007) 68 Ohio State Law Journal 349 at fn 175.

89 See D Fernandez Arroyo and J Kleinheisterkamp 'Inter-American Model Law on Secured Transactions' (2002) 4 Yearbook of Private International Law 246 at 251–252.

90 *Ibid* at 252.

6. The UNCITRAL Secured Transactions Guide

The Secured Transactions Guide went through the UN General Assembly approval process in December 2008,[1] though the editorial revisions were only completed in 2009 and an intellectual property annex was 'pre-released' on 15 July 2010. In this chapter it is intended to provide a critical evaluation of the main provisions of the Guide, looking at the Guide in the context of other international and national secured transactions instruments including the EBRD Model Law and Article 9. The discussion is divided into six parts. The first part looks at the overall philosophy of the Guide and how this is exemplified in particular provisions, including the scope of assets that may be collateralised. It also notes, in this connection, important limitations on the scope of the Guide. The second part looks at all-assets security and possible carve-outs for unsecured creditors. The third part considers the creation and third party effectiveness of security rights. The fourth part addresses the treatment of quasi-securities. The fifth part considers the principles for working out priorities between competing securities, including the extent of the super-priority status afforded to quasi-securities. This is followed by a conclusion which attempts to summarise some of the central themes in the discussion.

THE SECURED TRANSACTIONS GUIDE – OVERALL PHILOSOPHY

The Secured Transactions Guide is a detailed document and the details were increased in 2010 with the addition of a separate annex that applies to security over intellectual property rights.[2] Subject to certain limitations, the Guide is designed to be comprehensive in its reach, both in terms of the range of persons to whom it may apply and also in terms of the assets that may serve as security. Essentially the Guide is an exhortation to States

1 UN General Assembly Resolution 63/121.

2 See on the UNCITRAL website – www.uncitral.org – 'Supplement on Security Rights in Intellectual Property' the Final Draft of which was pre-released on 15 July 2010.

to be as comprehensive as possible in the process of framing their secured credit law and not to leave inadvertent gaps in coverage.

The first recommendation in the Guide sets out this key objective stating that the law should be designed:

> (a) To promote low-cost credit by enhancing the availability of secured credit; (b) To allow debtors to use the full value inherent in their assets to support credit; (c) To enable parties to obtain security rights in a simple and efficient manner; (d) To provide for equal treatment of diverse sources of credit and of diverse forms of secured transactions; (e) To validate non-possessory security rights in all types of asset; (f) To enhance certainty and transparency by providing for registration of a notice of a security right in a general security rights registry; (g) To establish clear and predictable priority rules; (h) To facilitate efficient enforcement of a secured creditor's rights; (i) To allow parties maximum flexibility to negotiate the terms of their security agreement; (j) To balance the interests of all persons affected by a secured transaction; and (k) To harmonize secured transactions laws, including conflict-of-laws rules relating to secured transactions.

The Guide is broad and sweeping in its remit insofar as the kinds of assets that may be 'collateralised' (used as security) are concerned. All types of movable property, both property presently owned by the debtor and property that may be acquired by the debtor in the future, can be the subject of security.[3] Moreover, a security right in assets extends to the proceeds, unless otherwise agreed.[4] An important aspect of the Secured Transactions Guide is to facilitate receivables financing and security may be created over future, fluctuating and conditional obligations owed to the debtor.[5] In addition, security rights may be created in bank accounts despite any contrary agreement between the grantor of the security interest and the depositary bank but, by virtue of the security agreement, no duties are thereby imposed on the depositary bank.

The Guide applies essentially to contractually created property rights. Security rights that arise by operation of law rather than from the agreement of the parties are outside its sphere of operation.[6] There is also a

---

3 See Recommendation 2(a) stating that the law should apply to 'Security rights in all types of movable asset, tangible or intangible, present or future, including inventory, equipment and other tangible assets, contractual and non-contractual receivables, contractual non-monetary claims, negotiable instruments, negotiable documents, rights to payment of funds credited to a bank account, rights to receive the proceeds under an independent undertaking and intellectual property'.

4 Recommendation 19.

5 See Recommendation 2(c).

6 See Recommendation 2 stating that the law should apply to 'all rights in movable assets created by agreement that secure payment or other performance of an obligation, regardless

statement in the Guide to the effect that the law should apply equally to legal and natural persons, i.e. to both companies and individuals. The extension envisaged by the Guide to persons that do not necessarily transact business through the corporate form carries with it however the caveat that the scope of consumer protection legislation should not be affected.[7]

At first, the reason for recommending the application to non-business-oriented transactions seems obvious – it complicates the law if differing requirements apply to the creation and recognition of security interests depending on whether the security giver acts for business purposes, or as a consumer. The difficulty with the recommendation, however, is that a particular jurisdiction may not have a very developed consumer protection regime to offset against the risks in the grant of security. Consumers may grant security without a full appreciation of the consequences in terms of the control that the creditor may exercise over their assets. Depending also on the bankruptcy laws in the jurisdiction, debtors may find themselves losing assets that are essential to their livelihood or sense of personality, e.g. a family home. If there are no developed consumer protection principles in play, a more primitive form of protection is simply to deny the possibility of individuals creating security over certain types of property. A blanket ban of this nature is undoubtedly a blunt tool and may restrict the availability of credit. On the other hand, it provides consumers with a degree of respite from certain types of creditor enforcement action and in a world where 'consumer overindebtedness' is seen as a pressing social problem, limiting consumer credit availability may be no bad thing.

Limitations on Scope

The Guide does not apply to security rights in 'securities' (in other words, investment intangibles such as shares or bonds). This is a very significant omission and stems from a desire to avoid overlap with the work of other international organisations, in particular the Hague Conference on Private International Law.[8] The law relating to intermediated securities, including security rights in the same, was considered to fall within the domain of the Hague Conference and UNCITRAL did not wish to duplicate its efforts.

The Secured Transactions Guide also does not apply to immovable property with the exception of chattels that are attached to land and

---

of the form of the transaction, the type of the movable asset, the status of the grantor or secured creditor or the nature of the secured obligation'.

7 Recommendation 2(b).

8 On which see www.hcch.net.

become so-called 'fixtures'.[9] The reasons for this exclusion appear pragmatic. Real property is often considered to be an area where sovereignty issues are particularly important. National governments, or even provincial or regional governments, guard jealously their legislative competence in this field. Article 9 applies only to personal property and against this backdrop it appeared logical to have a similar limitation on the sphere of application of the Guide. On the other hand, if the overall philosophy of the Guide is to facilitate the taking of security with a view to promoting the availability of low-cost credit, should this same philosophy not permeate the law relating to security over real estate? Certainly, the European Bank for Reconstruction and Development (EBRD) seems to think so, for its Guide to Mortgage Law applicable to real estate is virtually identical in terms of substantive content to its Secured Transactions guidelines applicable to personal property.[10]

ALL-ASSETS SECURITY AND POSSIBLE 'CARVE-OUTS'

Under the Guide it is perfectly permissible to create 'all-assets security', i.e. the equivalent of a floating security or universal business security over the entirety of the business operations of an enterprise.[11] In many jurisdictions, it is perhaps only a slight exaggeration to speak about a wilderness of single instances when talking about the taking of security. For instance, in one comparative study it is suggested that[12]

> none of the jurisdictions of the EU Member States has developed a comprehensive, functional approach to security rights in movables. Instead, there exists in each jurisdiction a wide range of security devices, which differ from each other with respect to the character of the secured debt, the collateral that may be used, and the legal concept on which the security rights are based: title-based

[9] Recommendations 4 and 5. There are other exceptions in Recommendation 4.

[10] See *Mortgages in Transition Economies – the Legal Framework for Mortgages and Mortgage Securities* (2007) available at www.ebrd.com/pubs/legal/mit.htm and for discussion see J Simpson and F Dahan 'Mortgages in transition economies' in F Dahan and John Simpson eds *Secured Transactions Reform and Access to Credit* (Cheltenham, UK and Northampton, MA, USA, Edward Elgar Publishing, 2008) 172.

[11] Recommendation 17 providing that a security interest may encumber all assets of the debtor.

[12] See E-M Kieninger ed *Security Rights in Movable Property in European Private Law* (Cambridge, CUP, 2004) at 648. See also U Drobnig 'Present and Future of Real and Personal Security' [2003] European Review of Private Law 623; C Bourbon-Seclet 'Cross-border Security Interests in Moveable Property' [2005] JIBLR 419; MC di Luigi 'Divergences of Security and Property Law in the European Union: the Need for Action' [2008] JBL 526.

> security rights such as retention of title, security transfer of ownership or leasing exist side by side with the possessory pledge and various devices that are based on the idea of the pledge such as non-possessory registered charges in individualised property or entities of assets.

Often we have sector-specific legislation that permits security in certain situations. This legislation may have been passed at the prompting of important political constituencies or pressure groups and it may be difficult to explain on more principled grounds. Interest groups who find their needs satisfied have no particular need to urge the enactment of more universal security instruments.

There are at least two arguments against the recognition of universal security rights.[13] The first is the proposition that a debtor should have a cushion or margin of 'free' assets that are available to satisfy claims by unsecured creditors. The second is the proposition that certain assets can never serve as the subject of security. For instance, many non-lawyers may find baffling the concept that a debtor can create security over assets that it does not yet own. On the other hand, Article 9 freely permits the creation of such security and the English common law does likewise through the medium of the floating charge.[14]

The arguments against the recognition of universal security rights have also been made in the US. While Article 9 has no truck with the arguments, this outcome represents the result of a long process of historical development.[15] Pre-Article 9 US law did not have any place for a universal security right.[16] This conclusion comes through in a leading case – *Zartman v First National Bank of Waterloo*[17] where the security, in express terms, covered after-acquired property but the court, nevertheless, denied effectiveness to the provision. It was said that a borrower could not create

---

13 For other arguments see P Wood *Law and Practice of International Finance* (London, Sweet & Maxwell, 2008) at 259–260.

14 See generally on the floating charge R Nolan 'Property in a Fund of Assets' (2004) 120 LQR 108; E Ferran 'Floating Charges – the Nature of the Security' [1988] CLJ 213; S Worthington 'Floating Charges – an Alternative Theory' [1994] CLJ 81.

15 One of the architects of Article 9, Grant Gilmore, has said in 'Security Law, Formalism and Article 9' (1968) 47 Nebraska LR 659 at 672: 'Article 9 draftsmen argued from the premise that, under existing security law, a lender could take an enforceable interest in all of a debtor's present and future personal property to the conclusion that the new statute should provide for the accomplishment of this result in the simplest possible fashion.'

16 Grant Gilmore has argued that if floating charges had been accepted in the US, then some of the pressure for change which brought about Article 9 would have been absent – see G Gilmore *Security Interests in Personal Property* (2 vols, Boston, Little Brown, 1965) volume 1 at 359–361.

17 (1907) 189 NY 267.

security over property that it did not yet own and secondly, the borrower's freedom of disposition sanctioned by the security meant that the security was fraudulent as against other creditors.

This line of authority was confirmed at the highest judicial levels in the United States.[18] Over time however, a sophisticated avoidance industry developed which had the effect of permitting large-scale receivables and other financing.[19] This resulted in most types of personal property, including both tangible and intangible property, becoming available to serve as security. Like the current situation in Europe, this was often the result of legislative initiatives mounted by interest groups in the individual States.[20] Article 9 rationalised and systematised this state of affairs. The relevant terminology was simplified with the effective abolition of the multiplicity of separate security devices and their replacement by the concept of a single security interest that could exist in all a grantor's property. Article 9 implements the idea that there is no necessary incompatibility between the existence of a security interest in property and the debtor's freedom to dispose of the secured assets in the ordinary course of business. So, amongst other things, Article 9 brings together a multiplicity of separate security devices as well as permitting universal security. The Secured Transactions Guide does likewise but a number of jurisdictions, including France, continue with an incremental approach, adding to the number of security devices and leaving it to the market place to sort out those that will be made use of in practice.[21]

Carve-outs for Unsecured Creditors

The validation of 'all-assets security' is one of the most significant features of the Guide.[22] This reflects an Article 9 approach but one might also argue that it merely legislates for the equivalent of an English-style floating charge, which has functional analogues in other countries.[23] These other

---

18 *Benedict v Ratner* (1925) 268 US 353.

19 See generally Grant Gilmore above, note 16, volume 1, chapters 1–8.

20 Article 9 has been described as 'an anthological collection of the most celebrated security law controversies of the preceding forty years' in Grant Gilmore 'Security Law, Formalism and Article 9' above, note 15 at 671.

21 See Marie-Elodie Ancel 'Recent Reform in France: The Renaissance of a Civilian Collateral Regime?' in F Dahan and J Simpson eds *Secured Transactions Reform and Access to Credit* (Cheltenham, UK and Northampton, MA, USA, Edward Elgar, 2008) at 259.

22 See Recommendation 17 providing that a security right may encumber all assets of a grantor.

23 See P Wood above, note 13 at 264, with a list of statutory general business charges of varying scope.

countries however, including the UK, generally carve out a proportion of all-assets security for the benefit of unsecured creditors.[24]

Under English law, a certain percentage of floating charge realisations are set aside for the benefit of unsecured creditors. The percentage is calculated by secondary legislation on a sliding scale, but subject to a global ceiling of £600 000.[25] Moreover, the carve-out is inapplicable if the company's net property is less than a prescribed minimum and where the insolvency representative considers that the cost of making a distribution to unsecured creditors would be disproportionate to the benefits. Defenders of the English provision suggest[26] it constitutes a fair concession to unsecured creditors without destroying the notion of security in its entirety. It is admittedly a blunt instrument since it benefits all unsecured creditors and not merely non-adjusting creditors, i.e. those who are unable to adjust the explicit or implicit lending terms to take into account the fact that the borrower has granted security.[27] The fixed ceiling, however, allows attendant risks to be calculated.

The Guide does not however recommend this approach of setting aside a proportion of security, or all-assets security, for the benefit of unsecured creditors. This clearly indicates a preference for the US approach where the idea of 'carve-outs' for the benefit of unsecured creditors failed to gain acceptance in the Article 9 revision process. Carve-out advocates pointed out that while the US Bankruptcy Code recognised security rights to their fullest, nevertheless there were a number of rules, doctrines and practices that effectively operated to erode the priority of secured claims in bankruptcy.[28] For example, Chapter 11, which governs proceedings for the restructuring of ailing businesses, imposes restrictions on the

---

[24] See what is now s 176A Insolvency Act 1986 and the Insolvency Act 1986 (Prescribed Part) Order 2003 which fixes the proportion of collateral set aside. See generally G McCormack *Secured Credit under English and American Law* (Cambridge, CUP, 2004) at 46–48 and 108–112 and see also P Wood above, note 13 at 260: 'The monopolistic scope of the [universal] charge tends to attract legislative diminutions in order to protect unsecured creditors . . .'.

[25] See Insolvency Act 1986 (Prescribed Part) Order 2003.

[26] D Milman and D Mond *Security and Corporate Rescue* (Manchester, Hodgsons, 1999) at 52. The 1982 Department of Trade and Industry Committee on Insolvency Law and Practice (the 'Cork Committee') which recommended a carve-out for unsecured creditors specifically rejected the proposition that any such diminution of credit would occur (Cmnd 8558 at para 1535).

[27] See V Finch 'Security, Insolvency and Risk: Who Pays the Price?' (1999) 62 MLR 633 at 652.

[28] See L Bebchuk and J Fried 'The Uneasy Case for the Priority of Secured Claims in Bankruptcy' (1996) 105 Yale LJ 857; L Bebchuk and J Fried 'The Uneasy Case for the Priority of Secured Claims in Bankruptcy: Further Thoughts and a Reply to Critics' (1997) 82 Cornell L Rev 1279; E Warren 'Making Policy with Imperfect Information: The Article 9 Full Priority Debates' (1997) 82 Cornell L Rev 1373 at 1377.

enforcement of security interests and during this time the value of the collateral may fall.[29] State legislatures also had power to sanction the creation of statutory liens with priority over the claims of secured creditors and this power was increasingly exercised.[30] Advocates of a carve-out were sceptical at suggestions that their proposals would lead to a diminution in credit. They pointed out that a partial priority regime already obtained to a degree and that, in the final analysis, matters might turn on the extent of the carve-out.

Carve-out critics suggested, however, that it would be factored into the borrowing base and secured creditors would extend less credit as a result. This would have a particularly adverse impact on marginal businesses, resulting in further bankruptcies.[31] The lawyers responsible for the drafting of Article 9, Steven Harris and Charles Mooney,[32] took on board these concerns. In their view, even a partial subordination of secured credit would cause many potential lenders to refuse to advance loans. They urged caution since the social and economic benefits of priority rights were indirect.[33] In their assessment, the denial of full priority might detract from the capacity of entrepreneurs to attract investors, although it was impossible to identify those companies that never came into existence as the result of a particular change in priority rights. Unpaid workers were easier to spot than workers who were never able to find a job because a particular project had not received start-up financing.[34] It was suggested that while secured creditors might lose profits under a carve-out regime,

---

29 See D Baird and T Jackson 'Corporate Reorganizations and the Treatment of Diverse Ownership Interests: A Comment on Adequate Protection of Secured Creditors in Bankruptcy' (1984) 51 U Ch L Rev 97 at 112–114.

30 See K Klee 'Barbarians at the Trough: Riposte in Defense of the Warren Carve-Out Proposal' (1997) 82 Cornell L Rev 1466 at 1474–1475.

31 *Ibid* at 1472: 'For example, where the debtor is in a risky start-up venture or on the verge of insolvency, the risk to unsecured creditors might be so great that instead of seeking a high interest to compensate for increased risk, they simply will not extend new credit. The resulting liquidity crisis will force the debtor into bankruptcy, where unsecured creditors will recover less than if the debtor had not filed.'

32 See SL Harris and CW Mooney 'A Property-Based Theory of Security Interests: Taking Debtors' Choices Seriously' (1994) 80 Va L Rev 2021; 'Measuring the Social Costs and Benefits and Identifying the Victims of Subordinating Security Interests in Bankruptcy' (1997) 82 Cornell L Rev 1349.

33 For a strong riposte to this see E Warren (1997) 82 Cornell L Rev 1373 n 62: 'Harris and Mooney state: "For example, data may confirm that small businesses (and, accordingly, minority-owned businesses) would disproportionately comprise that group [that would face constriction of credit]" . . . their support? Anecdotal evidence. This argument can be rephrased to say that banks want full priority to help their minority friends. Some critics may demand more than anecdotes to support this proposition.'

34 See D Baird 'The Importance of Priority' (1997) 82 Cornell L Rev 1420 at 1421.

the biggest losers would be debtors, who would receive less funding, and potential contracting parties with such debtors.[35]

The US Attorney General's Office concurred with this general assessment, stating that the carve-out proposal[36] 'could have detrimental effects on many highly leveraged sectors of the economy, such as small businesses and agriculture'. Political realities meant that carve-out proposals fell by the wayside in the United States. But the political realities are different in the rest of the world, and what plays well in Peoria, Illinois may not necessarily play well in Beijing or St Petersburg or Poitiers.[37]

CREATION AND THIRD PARTY EFFECTIVENESS OF SECURITY RIGHTS

The Guide provides that a security right is created by an agreement concluded between the grantor and secured creditor. The relevant agreement may be oral if it is accompanied by dispossession of the grantor pursuant to the agreement.[38] Otherwise, however, it must be in writing or evidenced in writing. The Guide is nevertheless medium neutral and the writing requirement can be met by something that serves as its electronic equivalent.[39] The security agreement must identify the parties and also reasonably describe both the secured obligation and the assets to be encumbered by the security interest.[40] The Guide cautions however against overly exact description requirements and suggests that a generic description of the secured obligation and the encumbered assets is sufficient. A security agreement may relate to property that is not yet in existence, or not yet owned by the grantor.[41] In those circumstances, the security right is deemed to have been created when the grantor acquires rights in the asset, or the power to encumber the asset.[42] It is also the case that a security right

---

35 SL Harris and CW Mooney 'Measuring the Social Costs and Benefits and Identifying the Victims of Subordinating Security Interests in Bankruptcy' (1997) 82 Cornell L Rev 1349 at 1357.

36 *Ibid* at note 49.

37 Perhaps one can add that playing well in Peoria – the epitome of heartlands America – is often considered to be a barometer of acceptability and commercial success for the Hollywood movie industry.

38 Recommendation 15.

39 See Recommendation 11 stating that where the law requires that a communication or a contract should be in writing, or provides consequences for the absence of a writing, that requirement is met by an electronic communication if the information contained therein is accessible so as to be usable for subsequent reference.

40 Recommendation 14.

41 See Recommendation 17.

42 Recommendation 13.

may be effective as between the grantor and the secured creditor even if it is not effective against third parties.[43]

As far as receivables financing is concerned, the Guide tracks the provisions of the United Nations Convention on the Assignment of Receivables in International Trade.[44] Bulk assignments, for example, are permissible and so too is the assignment of future receivables and parts of, and undivided interests in, receivables.[45] An assignment is declared to be effective despite a non-assignment clause in the contract creating the receivable.[46] With respect to the secured party, the Guide tries to limit liability for breach of a non-assignment clause. A third party who took an assignment notwithstanding the non-assignment clause is not liable say for inducing a breach of contract on the 'sole ground that it had knowledge of the agreement'.[47] It should be noted also that knowledge, in the context of the Guide, means 'actual knowledge' and not 'constructive knowledge', i.e. the knowledge that one would have acquired had one deigned to make reasonable inquiries.[48]

Security Rights and Publicity

Under the Secured Transactions Guide, third party effectiveness of security rights generally requires registration of the security in a general security rights register.[49] Of itself, this notion is pretty controversial in that many jurisdictions, mostly notably Germany, are committed to the concept of registrationless regimes of personal property security. Even someone not ill-disposed towards the US Article 9 approach like

---

43 Recommendation 30.

44 See http://www.uncitral.org/uncitral/ed/uncitral_texts/payments/2001Convention_receivables.html.

45 Recommendation 23: 'The law should provide that: (a) An assignment of a contractual receivable that is not specifically identified, a future receivable or a part of or an undivided interest in a receivable is effective as between the assignor and the assignee and as against the debtor of the receivable as long as, at the time of the assignment or, in the case of a future receivable, at the time it arises, it can be identified to the assignment to which it relates; and (b) Unless otherwise agreed, an assignment of one or more future receivables is effective without a new act of transfer being required to assign each receivable.'

46 Recommendation 24. Certain common contracts where non-assignment clauses are often found are however excluded from the ban – see Recommendation 24(c).

47 Recommendation 24(b). Nothing in the recommendation affects any obligation or liability of the assignor for breach of the non-assignment agreement, but the other party to such agreement may not avoid the original contract or the assignment contract on the sole ground of that breach.

48 See Legislative Guide 'Terminology'.

49 See Recommendations 32–35.

Ulrich Drobnig has downplayed the importance in this connection of the publicity principle, asking

> is the complicated technical system really necessary if all the information it offers is a notice that there may exist a security interest, so that intending creditors are put on notice but have to turn to the debtor in order to verify the true state of affairs. Is not nearly the same effect achieved in countries without a registration system where the courts proceed from a general presumption that business people must know that any major piece of equipment is bought on credit?[50]

On the other hand, one might argue that a registrationless regime of personal property security only works well in a relatively closed credit market like Germany where there are a number of powerful players with a quasi-monopolistic control on credit.[51] In a closed credit market, leading banks have detailed information on the financial behaviour and credit needs of businesses. This is much less likely in a global credit market with financial institutions operating across national frontiers. Potential lenders simply do not have the business background and information on potential borrowers. If one does not have information that is publicly available through a filing system, then financial institutions who are trying to enter the credit market are also effectively excluded. They do not have the fund of built-up knowledge and experience and have to rely more on credit reference agencies who may operate less transparently than a public filing system. Advocates of the American approach argue that it is more facilitative of entrepreneurial endeavour than the German one, i.e. it opens the availability of credit to persons who were previously not on first-name terms with bankers.[52] On the other hand, this approach has been criticised for resting on an outdated philosophy that stresses the need for publicity in order to

---

50 See U Drobnig 'Present and Future of Real and Personal Security' [2003] European Review of Private Law 623 at 660.

51 For a somewhat sarcastic panegyric to the American system see J White 'Reforming Article 9 Priorities in Light of Old Ignorance and New Filing Rules' (1995) 79 Minnesota Law Review 529 at 530: 'The filing system is an integral part of the most sophisticated secured lending system known to mankind. Only by an effective filing system can a secured lender know of other lenders and only by it can later secured lenders and unsecured lenders be encouraged to lend. Without such a system, lenders would grow wary, commerce would be hobbled, and the manifold commercial ends that are met by commercial lenders would be stunted, rendered more costly, or stymied altogether. . . . I can see generations of law students writing this down and repeating this incantation in negotiations, in court, and elsewhere. This view even extends to Americans abroad who approach the English, Dutch and Germans with an air of superiority, asserting the superiority of our filing system and belittling the European efforts to put together a filing system worthy of the name.'

52 See A Dunham 'Inventory and Accounts Receivable Financing' (1949) 62 Harvard Law Review 588 at 611: 'One banker thought the questions [about sources of debtor infor-

thwart the appearance of false wealth: 'creditors and others dealing with the debtor . . . do not want to have to search registers and it would disturb the market dealings if they had to on each occasion.'[53]

Methods of Achieving Third Party Effectiveness

Article 9 uses the expression 'perfection' as a general synonym for third party effectiveness of security rights. Filing is the standard method of perfecting an Article 9 security interest though other methods of perfection are permissible in certain circumstances, including possession where physical possession of the property used as security is handed over to the security taker. Of course the transfer of physical possession is not practicable in most situations. The assets may be intangible, or the debtor may need them for the carrying on of its business. In deference to the needs and wants of the capital markets, the revised Article 9 makes use of a notion of perfection by control.[54] In the case of certain types of financial collateral, including dematerialised or immobilised shares, the security taker can perfect the security through taking control of it. An example of control is where a securities intermediary agrees to respond to instructions from the secured party rather than from the debtor.

In its approach to the third party effectiveness of security rights, the Guide follows the basic tenor of Article 9. Filing or registration is given pride of place notwithstanding the general lack of appeal of this construct to civil law jurisdictions. The Guide also contains asset-specific recommendations along the lines of Article 9 that validate alternative methods of achieving third party effectiveness of security rights in relation to particular types of collateral.[55]

In the Guide moreover, it is the US concept of notice filing that finds favour, rather than the concept of transaction filing found in English law, and also more familiar to other jurisdictions.[56] Under the notice filing

---

mation] "silly" because his bank did not make a loan unless the borrower "was properly introduced" and therefore a fraudulent borrower was an impossibility.'

[53] See P Wood above, note 13 at 278 and also 314, arguing that the international trend is away from the 'obsolete concept of false wealth'.

[54] For the definition of control see Article 9-106. 'Control' is recognised as a superior method of perfection over financial collateral than filing. Article 9-328 lays down that a secured party who is perfected by control will have priority over an earlier secured party who has perfected its security interest by filing.

[55] Recommendations 48–53.

[56] See Recommendations 54 and 57 of the Legislative Guide. For a succinct explanation of the distinction between notice filing and transaction filing see the Scottish Law Commission discussion paper *Registration of Rights in Security by Companies* (Edinburgh, TSO, October 2002) at p 8.

regime, it is not the security agreement itself that is filed but a so-called 'financing statement' providing limited information.[57] The filed notice merely indicates that a person may have a security interest in the collateral concerned, and further inquiry by a searcher from the potential creditor and/or debtor will be necessary to ascertain the true state of affairs. Notice filing is party-specific rather than transaction-specific. The information filed is an invitation to further inquiry rather than being a synopsis of the transaction. The notice may be filed either before, or after, a particular transaction and a single filing is effective to cover multiple transactions.[58]

Advance registration allows a secured party to mark out its intentions in advance of the conclusion of the agreement and while negotiations between the parties are continuing. It is claimed that this is more convenient and flexible than 'after the event' transaction filing.[59] The parties are given more time to attend to registration rather than having to do it post-transaction when there may be a lot of other formalities to deal with. Moreover, the facility whereby a single filing covers multiple transactions renders more concrete the possibility of extending registration requirements to trade credit transactions where there may be a number of separate transactions between the same buyer and seller. If each one required individual registration, then cost and inconvenience would militate against registration being achieved in practice.

Many observers, and indeed legislatures, however, remain to be convinced about the merits of notice filing. Registration in advance of a transaction seems relatively small beer and, in any event, its benefits can largely be secured through a modification of a transaction-based filing system that allows registration in advance but under which the registration lapses if a confirmatory filing is not made within a particular period of time. Divorcing registration from particular individual transactions opens up the possibility that the register may become less reliable as a source of information. A searcher cannot be sure whether a particular

---

57 According to the Scottish Law Commission, the only civil law jurisdictions to have introduced notice filing are Quebec and Louisiana; see the discussion paper *Registration of Rights in Security by Companies* above, note 56 at para 1.28, and see further T Harrell 'A Guide to the Provisions of Article 9 of Louisiana's Commercial Code' (1990) Loyola Law Review 711; M Bridge, R Macdonald, R Simmonds and C Walsh 'Formalism, Functionalism and Understanding the Law of Secured Transactions' (1999) 44 McGill LJ 567.

58 Recommendations 67 and 68.

59 The EBRD has been sceptical about the merits of allowing advance registration or pre-registration stating that 'the advantages of allowing a potential creditor to take priority during the negotiations are debatable' – see *Publicity of Security Rights: EBRD Guiding Principles for the Development of a Charges Registry* (December 2004) at p 14, available on the EBRD website www.ebrd.com/st.

entry on the register relates to an actual transaction between the parties or whether it relates to a transaction that was contemplated but never in fact materialised. The information that is publicly available is less than under a transaction filing system and, in the modern information age, this state of affairs hardly seems justifiable. The internet and modern methods of data capture should also allow easy registration of security instruments, and any loss of financial privacy associated with such a procedure could be alleviated by the hiving off of commercially sensitive information to a separate document.

THE TREATMENT OF QUASI-SECURITIES

In nailing its colours to the mast of notice filing, the Guide demonstrates the US influence in its drafting. This influence is also evident in the Guide's treatment of quasi-securities. Quasi-securities are legal devices or arrangements that strictly speaking, in terms of the law, do not constitute securities but serve many of the same economic functions in terms of releasing funds to an entity in need of finance.

Article 9 and legal regimes modelled upon it, such as those in New Zealand and in the common law provinces of Canada, adopt a 'recharacterisation' approach towards quasi-security. Attention is paid to what is perceived to be the economic substance of a transaction rather than to its legal form.[60] Article 9 is also specifically stated to apply to certain transactions like factoring of debts and retention-of-title clauses that, in traditional legal terms, do not involve the creation of security but nevertheless, in economic terms, serve the same financing purpose. In its deeming provision, Article 9 seems to be consciously extending the concept of security. Certain transactions are redesignated as security rights and the security rights regime is then applied to them subject to certain modifications.[61]

The Guide takes the same functional track. It provides that the law should treat all devices that perform security functions as secured transactions, including the transfer of title to tangibles or the outright assignment

---

[60] Article 9-109 states the scope of application of Article 9 and Article 1-201(37) defining 'security interest' as meaning an interest in personal property or fixtures that secures either payment or else the performance of an obligation.

[61] See J Ziegel 'The Travails of English Chattel Security Law Reform – a Transatlantic View' [2006] LMCLQ 110 at 116: 'a conditional sale agreement is only a short form of chattel mortgage and that in each case the seller or mortgagee merely retains or obtains title as security for performance of the buyer's obligation.'

of receivables for security purposes.[62] This comprehensive approach would cover more or less all title transfer 'security' devices, i.e. rights of a proprietary kind that secure payment or the performance of obligations. There is a general principle enshrined in the Guide that public notice of quasi-security interests must be given by means of filing in a register that is open to public inspection.[63]

The European approach is very different.[64] The dividing line between security strictly so-called and 'quasi-securities' may be a thin one in particular cases, but it is a line that is generally respected. In the main, quasi-securities do not have to be publicised through registration as a condition of third party effectiveness. By and large, European jurisdictions, both civil and common law, do not apply registration requirements to quasi-securities.

The Guide has the general rule of registration for quasi-securities. Moreover, while certain exceptions are allowed, these are much more in keeping with American Article 9 sentiments than with European legal traditions. Under Article 9 there is a certain grace period for registration of a quasi-security – 20 days from the date of creation – and this provision finds its way into the Guide.[65] One might ask rhetorically why does the Guide mirror Article 9 in this respect? There are other international parallels close at hand, such as the EBRD Model Law on Secured Transactions under which a simple retention-of-title clause is categorised as an unpaid vendor's charge and is valid for six months without registration.[66]

More fundamentally, one might criticise the Article 9 approach for ignoring and overriding the parties' intentions.[67] The parties never intended to create a security interest but are deemed by legislation to have done what they never intended to do. Critics say that this approach does not so much involve looking to the substance of the transaction. The intention of the parties, as manifested in the form that they have drawn up, represents the substance of the transaction and what Article 9 does is to

---

[62] Recommendation 2(d) which states that the law should apply to 'all property rights created contractually to secure the payment or other performance of an obligation, including transfers of title to tangible assets for security purposes or assignments of receivables for security purposes, the various forms of retention-of-title agreements and financial leases'.

[63] See Part IX of the Legislative Guide 'Acquisition Financing' with Option A Unitary Approach and Option B Non Unitary Approach.

[64] See generally E-M Kieninger ed above, note 12.

[65] See Recommendations 180(a)(ii) and 192(a)(ii).

[66] See Article 9 of the EBRD Model Law, which can be consulted on the 'secured transactions' section of the EBRD website: www.ebrd.com.

[67] See P Wood above, note 13 at 298–299 on recharacterisation, arguing that the issue is 'whether there should be freedom or restriction, whether the bird should fly free from the cage or be slapped back in and the key thrown away'.

disregard that substance.[68] Even some supporters of Article 9-type regimes have acknowledged this argument:[69]

> There are two features of the UCC, Article 9 approach that appear to be troublesome even to those who are attracted to it. The first is the total reconceptualisation that it requires in the context of types of transactions that traditionally are not viewed as secured financing devices. . . . The second feature . . . is the extent to which it requires a bifurcated approach to the characterisation of certain types of transactions. Since a title-retention sales contract or a lease falls within a secured financing regime because it functions as a security device, it follows that the seller or lessor is not the owner of the goods sold or leased. . . . What is troublesome is that outside this regime, the recharacterisation might not be acceptable with the result that the same transaction is viewed differently depending on the legal issues being addressed.

In the same vein Roderick MacDonald has argued that the 'boosterism of Article 9 norm entrepreneurs needs to be tempered by a realistic assessment of what can actually be accomplished in transnational commercial law reform'. He also suggests that the 'claim to universalism in accounts of modernization must be given up in favour of more differentiated analyses and prescriptions for particular times and for particular places'.[70]

Perhaps recognising these realities, there is a twist to the tale in that the Guide admits the possibility of a 'non-unitary approach'. Under this approach, the substantive treatment of functionally similar transactions would be the same as for security rights strictly so-called but the legal characterization would remain different.[71] In deference to primarily civilian sensibilities, and with a view to gaining greater international acceptance, the UNCITRAL Guide is more subtle in its approach than is the blunt tool of Article 9. Two options are available, with one option (the unitary approach) being an Article 9-style regime with all its trappings. Another possibility, however, is the non-unitary approach. The latter approach would entail States still applying a different formal characterisation to

---

[68] See the comment by I Davies 'The Reform of English Personal Property Security Law' [2004] LS 295 at 321: 'The difficulty with the functionalism as applied in Article 9-type regimes is that it can be both over-inclusive and also under-inclusive at the same time. A more appropriate approach in any reform of English personal property security law is to operate within the existing legal landscape rather than to seek to transform it.'

[69] R Cuming 'The Internationalisation of Secured Financing Law' in R Cranston ed *Making Commercial Law: Essays in Honour of Roy Goode* (Oxford, OUP, 1997) at 522–523.

[70] See R MacDonald 'Article 9 Norm Entrepreneurship' (2006) 43 Canadian Business Law Journal 240 at 291 who also states that 'we need to locate our evaluations of commercial law reform within a better understanding of how local entrepreneurial networks and credit institutions function on the ground'.

[71] See generally recommendation 192 of the Legislative Guide.

quasi-security devices. States nevertheless would effectively be obliged to apply the same legal rules to both security and quasi-security. Both types of transaction would be subject to filing or registration obligations for third party effectiveness.[72]

One might argue that the non-unitary approach flows from the methodology adopted in the OAS Model Law, though it is less clearly articulated in the earlier instrument. The OAS Model imposes uniform publicity requirements for all types of security interest although it preserves the different methods of creating security and the application of the OAS Model to quasi-security is not expressly stated.

PRIORITY RULES

One of the perceived advantages of Article 9 is the presence of clear and rationally determined priority rules. There is the general principle that the first security interest to be filed has priority over competing security interests in the same property, subject to an exception for purchase money security interests.[73] The latter outrank general security interests that extend to the same property. The purchase money security interest is basically the provision of funds to enable a debtor to acquire particular property, with the debtor obtaining a security interest in the property. Under Article 9, there is a distinction drawn between general security interests and purchase money security interests, with the latter enjoying a form of super-priority that has traditionally been enjoyed by those relying on quasi-securities such as title-retention devices. Other financiers extending credit to facilitate the acquisition of property can now enjoy this super-priority status in certain circumstances. If, e.g., a debtor has created security over all its assets, including future property, then despite the general first-to-file priority principle, a financier whose credits facilitated the acquisition of 'new property' by the debtor will take priority over the earlier creditor in respect of the new property.[74]

---

[72] Recommendation 192 of the Guide. Both would also constitute an exception to the general first-to-file-has-priority principle underlying the Guide.

[73] Article 9-324 deals with the priority of purchase money security interests and see generally on this area P Shupack 'Defining Purchase Money Collateral' (1992) 29 Idaho Law Review 767; K Meyer 'A Primer on Purchase Money Security Interests under Revised Article 9' (2001) 50 Kan LR 143. For an argument against the PMSI super-priority rules see A Schwartz 'A Theory of Loan Priorities' (1989) 18 J Legal Stud 209 at 250–254.

[74] Under Article 9-324(g) the holder of a purchase money security interest that secures the unpaid purchase price of collateral will prevail over the holder of a conflicting purchase money security interest that enables the collateral to be acquired. This means that a reten-

In its provisions in this area, the Guide once again sticks to the contours of Article 9.[75] There is a first-to-file priority principle but subject to a special priority treatment of purchase money security interests. In the associated commentary, purchase money lending, or acquisition financing as it is referred to, is spoken of as potentially a more competitive source of financing than all-assets financing. The provisions on acquisition financing are said to embody the general policy objective of providing a source of affordable credit particularly for small/medium-sized enterprises, ensuring the equal treatment of all acquisition financiers and creating transparency.[76] There is a broad definition of 'acquisition security rights' to encompass all security rights in an asset that secure the obligation to pay any unpaid portion of the purchase price or other obligation incurred to enable the grantor of the security right to acquire the asset. The definition includes retention-of-title rights, financial lease rights and 'hire-purchase' agreements (lease agreements with the option to purchase the goods).[77]

Pursuant to the 'equivalence of treatment' principle, the same general rules on the creation of general security rights apply to the creation of acquisition security rights.[78] But the idea of requiring registration for third party effectiveness of finance lease and title-retention mechanisms is likely to be controversial for many jurisdictions.

The economic justification for investing acquisition security rights with super-priority status focuses on the fact that the debtor's total pool of assets has been increased. Existing debt is not simply being refinanced. With the infusion of funds the debtor is acquiring new assets, and if existing security interest holders were allowed to claim priority in these new assets then, it is argued, they would receive a windfall benefit as they had done nothing to fund the acquisition.[79] Moreover, if an all-assets financier is allowed to obtain priority with respect to the debtor's after-acquired assets, then that financer may have an effective credit monopoly. If the financier is unwilling to advance any further funds, then it may be very difficult for the debtor to procure financing from other creditors who may be loath to accept lower-ranking security or to lend on an unsecured basis. Moreover, financiers who are lending against specific assets may be in a position to offer more competitive interest rates than general

tion-of-title seller has priority over a lender that makes an enabling loan. For a similar rule under the Secured Transactions Guide see Recommendation 182.

75 Recommendations 180 and 192.

76 See the statement of purposes in Part IX of the Guide.

77 See the 'Terminology' section of the Guide.

78 Recommendations 178 and 187 of the Guide.

79 For a law and economics perspective on this view see H Kanda and S Levmore 'Explaining Creditor Priorities' (1994) 80 Virginia LR 2103 at 2138–2141.

all-assets financiers. The financiers who are lending against specific assets are lending against specific risk rather than general risk. They may be able more easily to establish the risk associated with specific assets including risk of default etc.[80]

There are counter-arguments. For instance, it might be argued that lenders against discrete assets are more likely to be smaller, secondary lenders and less likely to provide competitive interest rates than general lenders. Moreover, attributing a privileged status to acquisition loans seems premised on the assumption that the advance of funds which is specifically tied to the purchase of 'new' assets is somehow more valuable for the debtor's business than the advance of funds for non-acquisition reasons, such as to pay the wages of employees.[81] One might question whether this is necessarily the case and whether paying the wages of employees should not be regarded at least as equally socially valuable.

Acquisition security rights exist in embryonic form in many jurisdictions through the recognition of quasi-securities. In the main, these quasi-securities have priority over security interests, strictly so-called, over the same property.[82] The move to an Article 9 regime, however, would greatly expand the boundaries of purchase money super-priority. This would have implications for other creditors, both secured and unsecured, that are not always fully appreciated. Moreover, purchase money super-priority is not an ever-present feature of international model laws on secured transactions. The mechanism is not contained, e.g., in the EBRD Model Law on Secured Transactions. Under this Model Law however, like many national laws, creditors are free to vary the order of priorities amongst themselves, though without prejudicing the position of third parties. One might argue that if purchase money super-priority is really beneficial to existing lenders then existing lenders should be perfectly prepared, on a voluntary basis, to consent to a new lender having super-priority.

---

80 See A Schwartz 'The Continuing Puzzle of Secured Debt' (1984) 37 Vand LR 1051.

81 See the comments in WJ Gough *Company Charges* (London, Butterworths, 2nd edn 1996) at 436.

82 See also R MacDonald above note 70 at 283: 'Collapsing the distinction between owing and owning, between true security and title deployed to secure the performance of an obligation, does not relieve a legislature of the need to determine whether, in a competition between secured creditors, a distinction should be drawn between a creditor who was once an owner (a vendor) and a creditor who is merely a financier (a lender). Indeed, the priority afforded to the vendor's hypothec (or a "purchase money security interest") merely replicates the logic of an instalment sale or a sale under a resolutory condition in regimes that continue to distinguish between security and title devices.'

The Extent of Super-priority and Enforcement

Under the Guide, like in Article 9, there is a special rule to deal with purchase money security interests in consumer goods. Such a security right – an acquisition security right in the language of the Guide – becomes automatically effective against third parties upon creation and has super-priority over any claims by third parties even though the latter may have secured their claim by a prior filing. This result, although express in complex conceptual language, seems eminently sensible. If, say, an individual buys a computer from a retailer for personal use and the retailer retains ownership of the computer until it is paid for, then the retailer under the Guide is deemed to have an acquisition security right. Ordinarily such a right should be registered in a public register against the name of the purchaser to be effective against third parties such as a prior creditor with a claim against the consumer's after-acquired property. This result, however, would seem to run counter to the expectations of the parties and to make credit sales fraught with hazards for the retailer. The Guide avoids this inconvenient conclusion by deeming the retailer to have an acquisition security right which has automatic third party effectiveness and is given super-priority status.

Leaving aside consumer goods, in Article 9 and PPSA regimes there are difficult questions more generally about the conditions that must be satisfied before super-priority status can be obtained and whether a distinction should be drawn, as in some schemes, between inventory and capital equipment. It is also debatable how far the super-priority of the acquisition financier should extend into proceeds of the original goods supplied. The Secured Transactions Guide, while specifying the required outcomes in considerable detail, allows for alternative approaches on both these issues. Basically the possibility of alternative approaches is carried through into both the unitary and non-unitary treatment of acquisition security rights.

One alternative laid out in Recommendations 180 and 192 is to make super-priority in inventory more difficult to establish. In the case of inventory, before delivery of goods to grantor/buyer etc., the holder of potentially competing and already registered security rights should be notified of the acquisition financier's intentions. On the other hand, to acquire super-priority in 'non-inventory', registration of the acquisition rights within a 20 to 30-day grace period after delivery of the goods to the grantor/buyer is all that is required. The justification for the difference in the legal treatment of inventory and 'non-inventory' can be accounted for by differences in the risk equation insofar as new financing is concerned. As Hideki Kanda and Saul Levmore have remarked in respect of similar rules in Article 9: 'The rules intimate that the acquisition of new inventory and its associated debt is more threatening to earlier creditors than the debt-financing of new equipment but that debt tied to new inventory is still less threatening than new money unlinked to particular assets.'[83] The Official Comment to Article 9-324 of the Uniform Commercial Code explains that the purpose of a notification requirement is to protect a non-purchase money inventory secured party which, under an arrangement with the debtor, is typically required to make periodic advances against incoming inventory, or periodic releases of old inventory as new inventory is received. If the inventory-secured party receives notice it may not make an advance. The notification requirement is not the same as giving the existing secured party a veto on the new financier having super-priority, but it may function in roughly the same way through the existing secured party exerting pressure on the debtor.

One might object to a notification requirement, however, on the basis that it complicates the law unnecessarily, and that the distinction between inventory and non-inventory is somewhat arbitrary. Recognising these realities, UNCITRAL admits the possibility of an alternative approach which does not discriminate between inventory and other types of collateral. Under this alternative approach, there would be no prior notification requirement for inventory. A supplier etc. could acquire super-priority simply by filing a general notice in the security rights register without having to contact existing financiers on the register individually.[84]

The Secured Transactions Guide is also pluralistic when it comes to the extension of super-priority of the acquisition financier into proceeds. The alternative approaches are set out in Recommendation 185 dealing with unitary treatment of acquisition and non-acquisition security and Recommendation 199 (non-unitary). The second, and simpler, alternative is to deny the possibility of super-priority in proceeds, thus limiting it to the original assets financed. The first alternative is more complex. Basically it again makes the distinction between inventory and non-inventory, with super-priority in proceeds of the latter easier to establish. There is also a distinction in part between different kinds of proceeds. For non-inventory, the principle is that super-priority should extend into proceeds. For inventory, the same principle obtains except where the proceeds consist of receivables etc. In the latter scenario, super-priority is conditional on the

---

83 See H Kanda and S Levmore above note 79 at 2139 and see generally M Bridge, R MacDonald, R Simmonds and C Walsh 'Formalism, Functionalism and Understanding the Law of Secured Transactions' (1999) 44 McGill LJ at fnn 99–108.

84 See Recommendations 180 and 192 'Alternative B'.

acquisition financier notifying secured creditors that have already filed notice of a security interest that would cover the receivables.

The justification for not extending the super-priority of the inventory financier into proceeds consisting of receivables is to encourage a receivables financier to provide credit against the receivables. The proceeds of this credit would then be used to pay the inventory financier. In many jurisdictions, including England where retention-of-title clauses are recognised, the supplier's super-priority is limited in practice to the physical goods supplied and does not extend to receivables arising from the resale of those goods.[85]

The unitary/non-unitary divide also comes into play when it comes to the enforcement of acquisition security rights. Under the unitary approach, the Secured Transactions Guide takes the line that enforcement of acquisition security rights should conform to the law that applies to the enforcement of security rights generally.[86] Moreover, in the case of insolvency proceedings with respect to the debtor, the provisions that apply to security rights should apply also to acquisition security rights.[87] The non-unitary approach is less prescriptive however. In the insolvency context, it allows for the possibility that the law governing retention-of-title rights or financial lease rights could be made compatible with the regime applicable to the enforcement of ownership rights of third parties rather than with the security rights regime.[88] The same recognition of alternative possibilities carries through to the principles governing post-default enforcement of acquisition security rights under the non-unitary approach.[89] It stipulates however that the law should specify whether a retention-of-title seller or financial lessor has any right to retain surplus value if goods subject to retention of title or financial lease were repossessed by the seller or lessor and resold for more than the outstanding debt plus expenses. But there is also a statement that the regime applicable to the post-default enforcement of security rights applies to the post-default enforcement of retention-of-title or financial lease rights,

---

[85] See *Pfeiffer GmbH & Co v Arbuthnot Factors Ltd* [1988] 1 WLR 150; *Compaq Computer Ltd v Abercorn Group Ltd* [1991] BCC 484. See more generally G Monti, G Nejman and W Reuter 'The Future of Reservation of Title Clauses in the European Community' (1997) 47 ICLQ 866; J-H Dalhuisen 'The Conditional Sale Is Alive and Well' in J Norton and M Andenas eds *Emerging Financial Markets and Secured Transactions* (London, Kluwer, 1998); and also E Kieninger 'Securities in Movable Property within the Common Market' (1996) 4 European Review of Private Law 41.

[86] Recommendation 178.

[87] Recommendation 186.

[88] Recommendation 202.

[89] See Recommendation 200.

except to the extent necessary to preserve the coherence of the overall sale and lease regime.[90]

CONCLUSION

The UNCITRAL Secured Transactions Guide adds to the toolbox for States wishing to reform their law on secured transactions. In broad terms, the Guide follows an Article 9 functional approach towards security with the treatment of title-retention devices assimilated to that of traditional security rights. Registration is required for third party effectiveness of the rights in question. There is a subtle twist however in the recognition and development by the Guide of a 'non-unitary' approach to so-called acquisition security rights such as title-retention devices. Under the 'non-unitary' approach, in the strict sense, title-retention mechanisms may still be labelled somewhat differently by the law of a particular jurisdiction than security rights would be, but the same outcomes would result irrespective of the classification exercise. This 'non-unitary' approach is designed to make the contents of the Secured Transactions Guide more acceptable to Civil Law Jurisdictions.[91] It remains to be seen, however, whether the apparent sleight of hand in the Guide will prove convincing in practice.

Just as the Guide builds on the earlier receivables Convention, UNCITRAL is in the process of parlaying the guide into further 'modernisation' work in the secured transactions sphere. In this work it decided to give priority to the preparation of a 'text' on registration of security rights in movable assets on the basis that secured transactions law reform cannot be achieved in practice without an efficient, publicly accessible security rights registry.[92] The Guide was not considered to be sufficiently detailed on the various legal, administrative, infrastructural and operational questions that needed resolving before a registry could be implemented successfully.[93]

Generally however, the Secured Transactions Guide is a much more detailed instrument than, say, the EBRD Model Law on Secured Transactions or EBRD's Core Principles on Secured Transactions

90 See Recommendation 200(b).

91 See R MacDonald above, note 70 at 291.

92 See UN Doc A/CN 9/702 (April 2010) and A/CN 9/WG VI/WP 44 – 'Registration of Security Rights in Movable Assets' (August 2010).

93 See UN General Assembly Official Records Sixty-fifth session, Supplement No 17 (A/65/17) at para 265.

Laws.[94] The Core Principles cover the same ground as the UNCITRAL Guide, and embody many of the same points, but they are on the whole much less prescriptive. The Core Principles do not track the content of Article 9 to the same degree. There is much greater flexibility and tolerance of divergence in the Core Principles than in the Guide. For example, while the Core Principles talk about having an effective means of publicising the existence of security rights, unlike the UNCITRAL Guide they do not come down in favour of notice filing as distinct from transaction filing. Article 9 enthusiasts extol the virtue of notice filing to the nth degree but this book suggests that the arguments are not all one way. The same considerations apply in relation to priority rules. Article 9 has a specific set of priority rules that may facilitate the extension of credit in an American context, but these rules are not exactly replicated in Europe. The UNCITRAL Guide, in the main, however, follows the straight-down-the-line prescriptions of Article 9.

94 See generally F Dahan and J Simpson 'The European Bank for Reconstruction and Development's Secured Transactions Project: A Model Law and Ten Core Principles for a Modern Secured Transactions Law in Countries of Central and Eastern Europe (and Elsewhere!)' in E-M Kieninger ed above note 12 at 98.

7. The Insolvency Legislative Guide

This chapter compares the UNCITRAL Secured Transactions Guide with its Guide on Insolvency. The main part of the chapter is taken up with examining the main features of the Insolvency Guide and analogies between it and the key features of the American Bankruptcy Code. A central message is that the Insolvency Guide is not as closely aligned with US law as the Secured Transactions Guide. The Insolvency Guide is not beyond reproach – arguably it imposes too heavy a legalistic framework on corporate restructurings and fails to pay sufficient heed to context. Nevertheless, there appears to be greater recognition of diversity and greater accommodation of different approaches than in the Secured Transactions Guide. The last part of the chapter tries to explore the reasons why this may be the case.

THE INSOLVENCY GUIDE – ITS CENTRAL PHILOSOPHY AND KEY COMPARISONS

The Insolvency Guide contains a central underlying philosophy of promoting business rescue as well as providing the appropriate balance between reorganisation and legislation.[1] These are stated to be key objectives of the Guide. The Guide also lists other objectives: certainty in the market to promote economic stability and growth; maximising asset values; ensuring equitable treatment of similarly situated creditors; timely, efficient and impartial resolution of insolvency; preservation of the insolvency estate to allow equitable distribution of assets and equitable treatment of creditors; ensuring a transparent and predictable insolvency law with incentives for gathering and dispensing information; establishing clear rules for the ranking of priority claims and a framework for cross-border insolvency.[2] These are high-order principles and address potentially ever-present

[1] The Insolvency Legislative Guide can be found on the UNCITRAL website, www.uncitral.org.

[2] Recommendation 1. Recommendation 6 provides that the recommendations in the Legislative Guide have been designed to address each of the key objectives and achieve an appropriate balance between them.

problems in the functioning of national insolvency regimes. They seek to reduce fears that the Guide is solely concerned with protection of creditor rights, or alternatively debtor interests, and they also seek to balance liquidation with reorganisation. Such statements can easily be dismissed as 'motherhood and apple pie' rhetoric but the notion of balance is important to the Guide. The Guide is explicitly committed at the outset to some balance between the divide in global insolvency systems and also some balancing of the interests of different economic actors within the insolvency process.[3]

The Insolvency Guide appears to have drawn much of its inspiration from the US Bankruptcy Code and in particular Chapter 11 on the restructuring of ailing businesses. As one US court put it, 'the purpose of [Chapter 11] is to provide a debtor with the legal protection necessary to give it the opportunity to reorganize, and thereby to provide creditors with going-concern value rather than the possibility of a more meagre satisfaction of outstanding debts through liquidation'.[4] The Guide contains a central concept that favours corporate reorganisation but the principle is not prioritised above all others.

It is common to divide up legal systems of the world into pro-debtor and pro-creditor regimes, with the US being assigned to the pro-debtor camp and the UK to the pro-creditor camp, though there is much to be said for the view that these labels are nothing more than a potentially misleading over-simplification.[5] The pro-debtor label is used in connection with the US Bankruptcy Code, and especially Chapter 11, for a number of reasons. These include the fact that the Chapter 11 process is normally begun by the company itself seeking protection from its creditors; the existing management are not displaced in favour of some court-appointed outsider; the management itself can prepare a reorganisation plan and put it to creditors and shareholders; there is a specific mechanism for the financing of the company during the Chapter 11 period which may include the 'priming' or 'trumping' of existing security interests; and finally, in certain circumstances, secured creditors can be crammed down, i.e. forced

---

[3] See generally S Block-Lieb and T Halliday 'Harmonization and Modernization in UNCITRAL's Legislative Guide on Insolvency Law' (2007) 42 Texas International Law Journal 481 at 506 and see also S Block-Lieb and T Halliday 'Legitimation and Global Lawmaking' (2006) Fordham Law Legal Studies Research Paper No 952492 and also T Halliday 'Legitimacy, Technology, and Leverage: The Building Blocks of Insolvency Architecture in the Decade Past and the Decade Ahead' (2006) 32 Brooklyn Journal of International Law 1081.

[4] *Canadian Pacific Forest Products Ltd v JD Irving Ltd* (1995) 66 F 3d 1436 at 1442.

[5] See generally G McCormack *Corporate Rescue Law: An Anglo-American Perspective* (Cheltenham, UK and Northampton, MA, USA, Edward Elgar, 2008).

to accept a reorganisation plan against their wishes.[6] The Insolvency Guide incorporates some of these features but not others. For instance, there is no presumption in favour of debtor-in-possession reorganisation procedures.[7] The Insolvency Guide permits, but does not require, debtor-in-possession. It is not a slave to US fashion in this respect.

Neither is the Guide a slave to US terminology. Indeed it makes use of terminology in a way that is not peculiar to any legal system. For example, it talks about an 'insolvency representative' as the person administering the debtor's estate, whether in a reorganisation or liquidation context. The US talks about a 'bankruptcy trustee' whereas the general UK approach is to refer to the relevant person as a 'liquidator' in the terminal liquidation context and as an 'administrator' in the reorganisation setting. It is suggested that the Insolvency Guide terminology is more appropriate and useful. It also seems more 'fit for purpose' than the language employed in the EC Regulation on Insolvency Proceedings,[8] which refers to the expression 'liquidator' indiscriminately in a sense that does not accord with its meaning under UK law. The Insolvency Guide consciously avoids use of language that is overly associated with one particular legal system. For example, it does not use the US language of 'automatic stay' to refer to the prohibition on creditor enforcement actions during insolvency proceedings. Sometimes the modifications are subtle. US bankruptcy law refers to 'adequate protection' of proprietary interests during the course, say, of restructuring proceedings,[9] while the Insolvency Guide embraces the same concept but couches it in terms of 'protection of value'.

---

[6] See generally R La Porta, F Lopez-De-Silanes, A Shleifer and R Vishny 'Law and Finance' (1998) 106 Journal of Political Economy 1113. It should also be noted that under s 365 of the US Bankruptcy Code so-called 'ipso facto' clauses, e.g. a clause in a contract stating that a supplier's contractual commitments to a company will come to an end once the company enters bankruptcy proceedings is generally of no effect, unlike the position in the UK. Section 541(c) also strikes at ipso facto clauses. It invalidates contractual provisions or provisions of non-bankruptcy law 'conditioned on the insolvency or financial condition of the debtor' that restrict or condition the transfer of property to the bankruptcy estate.

[7] See Recommendation 7(c).

[8] Council Regulation (EC) 1346/2000, OJ 2000 L 160/1. See generally on the Regulation G Moss, I Fletcher and S Isaacs, *The EC Regulation on Insolvency Proceedings* (Oxford, OUP, 2nd edn 2009); M Balz (1996) 70 American Bankruptcy Law Journal 485; I Fletcher (1997) 23 Brooklyn Journal of International Law 25; I Fletcher (1998) 33 Texas International Law Journal 119; H Rajak [2000] Company Financial and Insolvency Law Review 180.

[9] Section 361 of the US Bankruptcy Code, which provides three examples of ways in which adequate protection may be given: (1) periodic cash payments; (2) additional or replacement liens; and (3) other relief amounting to the 'indubitable equivalent' of the person's interest in the property.

Structure and Shape of the Insolvency Guide

The Insolvency Guide consists of almost 200 recommendations divided into 20 topics and a detailed commentary, and there is occasionally a commentary but no recommendations as with the insolvency of corporate groups. The commentary serves various purposes. It may stress the importance of a particular issue or principle and then justify a series of recommendations that give effect to that principle. It may contain something of a comparative analysis in situations where there is considerable cross-country variation on a particular topic, presenting and discussing alternative approaches and endeavouring to evaluate them in a comparative light. Where there is no preferred approach, the commentary may explain how the different approaches operate in practice and the relationship between these approaches. The commentary engages in what has been described as the 'rhetoric of self-validation'.[10] General claims are made about the merits of the guide in promoting investment and economic development as well as integration of a country into the global economy, and more specific claims are made about the advantages of adopting particular recommendations. Some recommendations are said to reflect universal or near-universal consensus. For other provisions, the Guide invokes a quantitative criterion referring to the fact that many laws follow a particular course or that such a standard is used extensively. In a minority of cases the Guide refers to a trend in support of particular recommendations, emphasising the fact that such a trend is increasingly recognised. The commentary also serves an important validation function by registering the fact that the views advanced by particular delegates have been listened to, even if they were not ultimately adopted, and also by setting out the reasons that favour particular approaches.

The Insolvency Guide has been praised for employing a sophisticated repertoire of rules. These are organised in a hierarchy of specificity that depends on the type of consensus that could be reached on a particular issue. It is suggested that this array of rule-types contains ample flexibility to deal with cross-national variability on issues. For instance, where consensus could not be reached on the content of a rule, it was possible to reach agreement that there should be a rule on a particular topic (architectural recommendations) plus a commitment that the rule

---

[10] See generally S Block-Lieb and T Halliday 'Harmonization and Modernization in UNCITRAL's Legislative Guide on Insolvency Law' above, note 3 at 501.

should be set out with clarity and purpose in the insolvency law (norms of disclosure).[11]

Block-Lieb and Halliday suggest that the recommendations in the Insolvency Guide can be grouped along a 'spectrum of specificity that ranges from broad statements of commercial norms to explicitly detailed language ready for enactment'.[12] At the most prescriptive end of the spectrum are imperative recommendations suggesting national legislation with a detailed content that is expressly set out in each recommendation. But imperative recommendations do not all conform to the same pattern. They may be substantive, procedural or indeed conditional in nature. Conditional recommendations are predicated upon a particular procedure being enacted and specify that if one has this provision then it should have this content. For instance, according to Recommendation 151, where the insolvency law does not require a plan to be approved by all classes, it should address the treatment of those classes not voting to approve a plan that has otherwise been approved by the requisite classes. Conditional recommendations are said to give UNCITRAL 'the capacity to acknowledge local contingencies and variations in an orderly way'.[13]

Constraining recommendations are inclined to point in a particular direction but then leave choices up to local legislation. They can set out a base standard stipulating that there should be a rule on a topic, and then set out certain elements that should be included. Permissive recommendations are in the form that a country may adopt a rule that contains certain things. Imperative plus permissive elements are sometimes combined in the same substantive rule. The Guide also contains norms of minimalism specifying that if there is to be a rule on a particular topic, or an exception to a rule, it should be kept to a minimum. For example, Recommendation 188 on secured claims provides:

> The insolvency law should specify that a secured claim should be satisfied from the encumbered asset in liquidation or pursuant to a reorganization plan, subject to claims that are superior in priority to the secured claim, if any. Claims superior in priority to secured claims should be minimized and clearly set forth in the insolvency law.

Weaker still are focusing recommendations that seek merely to sharpen the focus of insolvency law. These may take the form of architectural

---

11 See generally *ibid* at 509: 'the range of available rule-types permitted the Working Group to avoid issues on which consensus was unlikely and which were likely to stall or impede production of the Legislative Guide'.

12 *Ibid* at 502.

13 *Ibid* at 503.

recommendations suggesting the existence of a rule on some specific topic of insolvency law without specifying the content of the rule. Recommendation 185 can be pointed to in this connection. It refers to the need to specify classes of creditors and to make clear what priority they should be accorded, but it does not set out how this should be done. Norms of disclosure are another example of focusing recommendations. These call for transparency and greater specificity in particular provisions of insolvency law.

Flexibility and Form in the Insolvency Guide

The Insolvency Guide carefully navigates its way around potential political hot potatoes. It treads carefully using norms of minimalism and disclosure rather than imperative recommendations.[14] For example, Recommendation 7 provides that an effective and efficient insolvency law should identify the debtors that may be subject to insolvency proceedings, including those debtors that may require a special insolvency regime. In many jurisdictions, banks and other financial institutions may be subject to a special insolvency regime. In other jurisdictions, state-owned enterprises may be exempt, wholly or in part, from the operation of normal insolvency processes, whether as a matter of law or practice. In certain countries, particular types of entity, such as joint venture companies, may be excluded from the law. These exclusions may be the product of history or path-dependent legal development but may also respond to deep-seated national sensitivities. The Legislative Guide respects these differences. It calls for clarity in the scope of application of the relevant law but adds that exclusions should be 'limited'.[15] In general the Guide speaks softly where issues of significant social, political or cultural import overlap with insolvency law, such as over the priority of employee claims.[16]

Detailed Content of the Legislative Guide – Commencement and Nature of Insolvency Proceedings

The Legislative Guide contemplates the commencement of insolvency proceedings on application either by the debtor or by creditors.[17] Creditor

---

[14] See generally *ibid* at 509: 'We find that the Working Group used softer, less constraining rule-types to minimize the likelihood that dissenting nations might abandon the central tendency of the Guide, particularly where cultural and social issues were at stake.'

[15] See generally the discussion at pp 38–41 of the commentary attached to the Legislative Guide, which is available on the UNCITRAL website: www.uncitral.org.

[16] See generally *ibid* at pp 272–273.

[17] See Recommendations 8–13.

initiation of proceedings is predicated upon the insolvency of the debtor being established either by the debtor being generally unable to pay its debts as they mature, or the debtor's liabilities exceeding the value of its assets. Provision is made for interim relief of a provisional nature to protect and preserve the value of the assets of the debtor or the interests of creditors, between an application being made to commence insolvency proceedings and the commencement of such proceedings. But, during this period, the debtor is entitled to continue in business and to use and dispose of assets in the ordinary course of business, except to the extent restricted by the court. Upon the commencement of insolvency proceedings, a stay or moratorium comes into force.[18] The commencement or continuation of individual actions concerning the assets of the debtor is stayed and the right to transfer, encumber or otherwise dispose of any assets of the estate is suspended. In general, the stay continues for the duration of the insolvency proceedings, though for secured creditors in liquidation proceedings it is contemplated that the stay should be for a shorter fixed period.

A secured creditor is entitled to relief from the stay if the encumbered asset is not necessary to a prospective reorganisation or sale of the debtor's business. Moreover, while the stay lasts, a secured creditor is entitled to protection of the value of the asset in which it has a security interest.[19] Appropriate measures of protection include cash payments by the debtor's estate, provision of additional security interests, or such other means as the court determines. All this is pretty similar to Chapter 11 of the US Bankruptcy Code, though the latter uses the language of 'adequate protection' rather than protection of value. In both instruments there are no definitions of what constitutes 'protection' but examples are given. In the US, there are many legislative and judicial statements to the effect that secured creditors should not be deprived of their bargain.[20] It may be necessary for the company to make use of the secured property in the reorganisation process but secured creditors and other property rights holders should be protected – in particular against the risk that the property may depreciate in value. There is no adequate protection if the security is depreciating during the period of the stay. In *Re Bermec*[21] the court suggested that the object of the adequate protection requirement is to leave a secured creditor with the equivalent in value of what was bargained for.[22] The

[18] See Recommendations 39–51.

[19] Recommendation 50.

[20] See HR Rep No 595, 95th Congress, 1st Session 339 (1977).

[21] (1971) 445 F2d 367.

[22] But see *Re Alyucan* (1981) 12 BR 803 where the court rejected the view that the preservation of a certain collateral-to-debt ratio was part of the creditor's property interest that warranted protection. See also *United Savings Association of Texas v Timbers of Inwood*

US Congress, it seems, left the concept deliberately vague so as to facilitate 'case-by-case interpretation and development. It is expected that the courts will apply the concept in light of [the] facts of each case and general equitable principles.'[23]

In the UK, by contrast, there is no unambiguous statutory statement that secured creditors are entitled to receive 'adequate protection' or 'protection in value' of their proprietary rights. The leading case of *Atlantic Computers*[24] calls for a balancing exercise between proprietary rights and the socially desirable goals of administration. It was suggested however, that strong weight should normally be accorded to proprietary rights and only where disproportionate loss would be caused to unsecured creditors by the exercise of proprietary rights should the exercise of such rights be stayed. There was nothing specific about compensating secured creditors for a decline in the value of the secured property during the administration period though, no doubt, this would be factored into the equation in an appropriate case.

The Legislative Guide reflects the view that to allow recovery procedures by creditors to operate without restraint could frustrate the overall socially desirable goal of rescue. Since going-concern value may be a lot more than breakup value, reorganisation proceedings are designed to keep a business alive so that this additional value can be captured. This goal will be compromised, however, if creditors are able to seize assets that are essential to the carrying on of the company's business. Consequently, we have a stay or moratorium on actions by creditors to collect debts or repossess property in the ailing company's possession. The rescue strategy seems to be founded upon the utilitarian pillar that the interests of a few may need to suffer in service of the needs of the many, with this pillar being transformed into a legal mechanism through the moratorium.[25] Property rights are simultaneously sacrificed but also protected to a degree. Moreover, relief from the stay is available where the property is not needed for a successful reorganisation. The language of the Insolvency Guide is close to Chapter 11 but the underlying premise is one that finds a mirror in many jurisdictions including the UK.

Forest Associates Ltd (1988) 484 US 365 where the Supreme Court held that the adequate protection provision did not entitle an undersecured creditor to compensation for the delay caused by the stay in enforcing the security. There is an argument that Recommendation 50 is worded more broadly thereby allowing US commercial interests to achieve what they have been denied by judicial interpretations of the 'adequate protection' provision.

[23] See HR Rep No 595, 95th Congress, 1st Session 339 (1977).

[24] [1992] Ch 505.

[25] See generally D Milman 'Moratoria on Enforcement Rights: Revisiting Corporate Rescue' [2004] Conv 89.

Post-Commencement Finance

The Insolvency Guide makes provision for financing companies after the commencement of insolvency proceedings; in certain circumstances, this would involve super-priority new financing. Super-priority new financing is often seen as necessary to resolve 'debt overhang', i.e. existing assets being fully secured, and to cure 'underinvestment' problems, i.e. lack of incentives to finance value-generating projects.[26] The provisions in the Guide closely mirror those in the US. The UK in fact lacks a dedicated statutory regime for the financing of ailing companies.[27] One must rely on inferences from general legislative provisions, though Canadian courts have spelled out a vibrant new financing regime on the basis of statutory materials that are more slender than those found in the UK.[28]

In the US, new financing is dealt with in s 364 of the Bankruptcy Code, which lays down that credit extended during the reorganisation process has priority over pre-petition unsecured claims. If the extension of credit is in the ordinary course of business, then priority is automatic, whereas if the extension of credit is outside the ordinary course, then the priority must be authorised by the court prior to the granting of credit. If the lender does not agree to the contrary, a company can get a reorganisation plan confirmed only by ensuring that the new lender is paid in full at the confirmation stage and even if the plan fails, 'new' debts have priority over unsecured pre-filing debts in the ensuing liquidation. There may be a lot of cases where a company's assets are secured to such an extent that mere priority over pre-filing unsecured creditors offers new lenders little chance of recovery in any subsequent liquidation. In these circumstances, meaningful priority means priority over pre-filing secured creditors and s 364(d) provides that the court may authorise this in narrowly defined circumstances. The pre-filing secured creditor is safeguarded by the fact that the

---

[26] See generally GG Triantis 'A Theory of the Regulation of Debtor-in-Possession Financing' (1993) 46 Vanderbilt Law Review 901 and see the paper prepared by George Triantis for the Corporate Law Policy Directorate of Industry Canada 'Law and Economics of Debtor-in-Possession Financing' – available on the Industry Canada website www.strategis.gc.ca. See also on the benefits of DIP financing S Dahiya, K John, M Puri and G Ramirez 'Debtor-in-Possession Financing and Bankruptcy Resolution: Empirical Evidence' (2003) 69 Journal of Financial Economics 259.

[27] The concept of an administrator's liability on contracts may be broad enough to catch repayment obligations under financing agreements entered into on behalf of the company – see para 99 Schedule B1 Insolvency Act 1986.

[28] For the Canadian experience see J Sarra 'Debtor in Possession (DIP) Financing: The Jurisdiction of Courts to Grant Super-Priority Financing' (2003) 21 Dalhousie Law Journal 337; M Rotsztain 'Debtor-in-Possession Financing: Current Law and a Preferred Approach' (2000) 33 Can Bus LJ 283.

company must prove that it cannot obtain the loan without granting such a security interest and that the secured creditor is adequately protected against loss. The case law suggests that the statutory requirements are strictly applied and that the 'priming' of prior secured lending is permitted only in infrequent and exceptional instances.[29]

The provisions in the UNCITRAL Guide are said to have a threefold purpose.[30] The first is to facilitate the flow of finance for the continued operation or survival of the debtor's business or the preservation or enhancement of the value of the assets of the estate. The second is to ensure appropriate protection for the providers of post-commencement finance, and the third is to ensure appropriate protection for those parties whose rights may be affected by the provision of such finance. Post-commencement finance should rank ahead of existing unsecured creditors or it can be secured on unencumbered assets or the subject of lower-ranking or equal-ranking security on already encumbered assets. In a regime that closely mirrors the US position, it is also provides that post-commencement finance may trump existing security interests if certain conditions are met including (a) existing security interest holders were given the opportunity of being heard; (b) debtor can show that it cannot obtain the finance in any other way and (c) the interests of existing secured creditors will be protected.

The US model is not the only one that could have been drawn upon in the Insolvency Guide. UNCITRAL appears consciously to have opted for the US approach in preference to the Canadian one. Canadian courts have used a 'balance of prejudices' test to authorise super-priority new financing and this test has now been put on a statutory footing.[31] This test appears wider, less tightly controlled and less respectful of existing securities than that in the US under s 364 of the Bankruptcy Code. The US regime in effect requires that existing creditors should not lose under new lending arrangements whereas the Canadian approach authorises DIP financing even where existing creditors might lose, provided that others stand to gain even more. The courts can evaluate the benefit and

---

[29] See generally G Kuney 'Hijacking Chapter 11' (2004) 21 Bankruptcy Developments Journal 19 at 48–49.

[30] See p 111 of the commentary attached to the Legislative Guide, which is available on the UNCITRAL website: www.uncitral.org.

[31] See the *Sky Dome* case (1998) 16 CBR (4th) 118 at 123 where the court said: 'This is not a situation where someone is being compelled to advance further credit. What is happening is that the creditor's security is being weakened to the extent of its reduction in value. It is not the first time in restructuring proceedings where secured creditors – in the exercise of balancing the prejudices between parties which is inherent in these situations – have been asked to make such a sacrifice.' Other leading cases include *Re Dylex Ltd* (1995) 31 CBR (3d) 106 and *Re United Used Auto & Truck Parts Ltd* [2000] 5 WWR 178.

risks of new financing and, based upon that evaluation, determine whether the financing is appropriate, without having to ensure any protection for existing creditors.[32]

Executory Contracts

The Insolvency Guide also shows some similarities to the US position in its treatment of so-called 'executory' contracts or contracts that are not yet fully performed by the insolvent party.[33] US law contains provisions allowing a company in the bankruptcy process to assume or reject executory contracts, and under s 365 of the US Bankruptcy Code so-called 'ipso facto' clauses, for example a clause in a contract stating that a supplier's contractual commitments to a company will come to an end once the company enters bankruptcy proceedings, are generally of no effect. This is unlike the position in the UK. Section 541(c) of the US Bankruptcy Code also strikes at ipso facto clauses. It invalidates contractual provisions or provisions of non-bankruptcy law 'conditioned on the insolvency or financial condition of the debtor' that restrict or condition the transfer of property to the bankruptcy estate.

The Insolvency Guide embodies the same underlying philosophy in these respects as the US Bankruptcy Code, although Recommendation 69 is merely in general terms and provides that insolvency law should specify the treatment of contracts under which the debtor and its counterparty have not yet fully performed their respective obligations. But there is a further set of more prescriptive recommendations. Recommendation 70 deals with automatic termination and acceleration clauses in contracts and stipulates that any contractual clause providing for the automatic termination or acceleration of a contract upon the occurrence of an

---

[32] For criticism see D Light 'Involuntary Subordination of Security Interests to Charges for DIP Financing under the Companies' Creditors Arrangement Act' (2002) 30 CBR (4th) 245. See also K Yamauchi 'The Courts' Inherent Jurisdiction and the CCAA: A Beneficient or Bad Doctrine?' (2004) 40 Canadian Business Law Journal 250.

[33] The standard definition of 'executory contract' is that offered by Vern Countryman, who calls it a contract under which the obligations of the debtor and the other party are so far unperformed that the failure of either to perform would constitute a material breach excusing the performance of the other – see 'Executory Contracts in Bankruptcy Part 1' (1973) 57 Minn L Rev 439. More recently a functional test suggested by Jay L Westbrook has found favour. This test looks at what performance remains for the debtor and decides whether it makes economic sense for the debtor-in-possession to assume or reject or, in other words, to perform or not to perform. The focus is on whether it benefits the bankruptcy estate to perform whatever remains for the debtor to do under the contract. 'The trustee may, indeed must, assume or reject every pre-bankruptcy contract of the debtor that is not completely performed or satisfied on the date of bankruptcy' – see JL Westbrook 'A Functional Analysis of Executory Contracts' (1989) 74 Minn L Rev 227 at 235.

insolvency event is unenforceable against the insolvency representative and the debtor. Recommendation 71, though, allows exceptions to this general rule such as in the case of financial contracts or labour contracts. Recommendation 72 specifies that an insolvency representative may decide to continue the performance of a contract where continuance would be beneficial to the insolvency estate, though a counterparty is entitled to insist upon a swift decision on continuance or rejection of the contract. Likewise Recommendation 84 provides that the insolvency representative can decide to assign a contract, notwithstanding restrictions in the contract, provided that the assignment would be beneficial to the estate.

Avoidance Provisions

The provisions on transactional avoidance in the Insolvency Guide are much less constrained by US norms.[34] Recommendation 87 states that the insolvency law should contain provisions that apply retroactively and are designed to overturn transactions, involving the debtor or assets of the estate, and that have the effect of either reducing the value of the estate or upsetting the principle of equitable treatment of creditors. This provision gets at three kinds of transactions. The first is transactions intended to defeat, delay or hinder the ability of creditors to collect claims where the effect is to put assets beyond the reach of creditors, or potential creditors, or otherwise prejudice the interests of creditors. The second are transactions at an undervalue where an insolvent debtor received inadequate value in exchange for the transfer of property or the performance of an obligation etc. The final type is preferential transactions where a creditor received more than its pro rata share of assets from an insolvent debtor.[35] Transactions with related persons may be subject to a longer avoidance period than transactions with unrelated persons, but there is no requirement that this be the case. The Insolvency Guide is permissive in this respect as it is in relation to other aspects of avoidance proceedings, though it does stipulate that the costs of avoidance proceedings should be paid as administrative expenses. Insolvency law is allowed, however,

---

[34] For a UK/US comparison in this area see G McCormack 'Swelling Corporate Assets: Changing What Is on the Menu' (2006) JCLS 39.

[35] Vern Countryman put the point well when he said in 'The Concept of a Voidable Preference in Bankruptcy' (1985) 38 Vanderbilt Law Review 713 at 748: 'Statements in the legislative history also mention preserving the bankruptcy policy of "equality" of distribution. But, with creditors classified for distribution purposes on the basis of liens and priorities, no bankruptcy policy of "equality" exists. A policy of preserving classes and of preserving equality within classes does exist, however, and the preference concept is designed to preserve this policy.'

to provide alternative approaches that address the pursuit and funding of avoidance proceedings.[36]

The Guide is flexible on time limits for the commencement of avoidance proceedings as it is on the elements that need to be proven to avoid a particular transaction and on defences. It is stated, however, that legitimate defences may include the fact that the transaction was entered into in the ordinary course of business prior to commencement of insolvency proceedings. It is permissible also for the law to establish presumptions and permit shifts in the burden of proof to facilitate the conduct of avoidance proceedings.

US law under s 547 of the US Bankruptcy Code adopts an 'effects'-based test for invalidating allegedly preferential transactions.[37] The test asks whether the effect of the transaction was to give the creditor more than it would have received in a liquidation case. There are then various defences to an avoidance action such as the 'ordinary course of business' defence. Other jurisdictions may focus on the motives or intentions of either the debtor or the creditor. Did, for example, the debtor intend to give a preference or did the creditor know that it was receiving a preference? Under English law encapsulated in s 239 of the Insolvency Act 1986 a transaction can only be set aside if the debtor was influenced by a desire to prefer, and in the leading case of *Re Mc Bacon*[38] a distinction was drawn between desire and intention. According to the court, desire was subjective while intention was objective. A transaction could only be set aside if the debtor consciously wished to improve the creditor's position in the debtor's insolvency. Criticisms may be levelled at this test. It is not easy to decipher a person's mind, making the transactional avoidance process fraught with difficulty. Very few preferences are properly challengeable under the test. The test does little to promote a level playing field among creditors.

---

[36] See generally on this S Wheeler 'Swelling the Assets for Distribution in Corporate Insolvency' [1993] JBL 256.

[37] See generally on the US position V Countryman above note 35; R Weisberg 'Commercial Morality, the Merchant Character, and the History of the Voidable Preference' (1986) 39(3) Stanford Law Review 11–16; M Shanker 'The American Bankruptcy Preference Law: Perceptions of the Past, the Transition to the Present, and Ideas for the Future' in J Ziegel ed *Current Developments in International and Comparative Corporate Insolvency Law* (Oxford, Clarendon Press, 2004) 313.

[38] [1990] BCC 78. For a rare case where a preference challenge was successful see *Re Agriplant Services Ltd.* [1997] BCC 842, on which see D Milman and R Parry 'Challenging Transactional Integrity on Insolvency: An Evaluation of the New Law' (1997) 48 NILQ 24; R Parry *Transaction Avoidance in Insolvencies* (Oxford, OUP, 2001); A Keay *Avoidance Provisions in Insolvency Law* (Sydney, LBC Information Services, 1997); A Walters 'Preferences' in J Armour and H Bennett eds *Vulnerable Transactions in Corporate Insolvency* (Oxford, Hart Publishing, 2003) 123.

On the other hand, the US 'effects' test subject to an 'ordinary course of business' defence has not escaped criticism. Certainly, any such defence needs to be framed with circumspection and caution. It has been said that any[39] 'semi competent creditor's lawyer should be able to present at least a colorable ordinary course defense. The prospect of daunting litigation costs in having to counter an ordinary course argument undoubtedly deters trustees from bringing many potentially meritorious preference actions and influences them to settle many more.' The Insolvency Guide in this area does come down explicitly in favour of the US approach or any other with a number of different approaches permitted.

Set-off and Netting

Can mutual debts and obligations between counterparties be set off against one another so as to reduce the net amount payable from one party to another? Can set-off operate where one of the parties is insolvent or is it confined to situations outside the insolvency context? Globally there are a number of different approaches among jurisdictions on set-off rights and netting of obligations.[40] There seems to be a growing trend, however, as evidenced by the EC Financial Collateral Directive,[41] of allowing set-off and netting in an insolvency and isolating financial market participants from some of the general effects of insolvency law.

The Insolvency Guide is imperative when it comes to set-off and netting rights, stating that insolvency law should protect a pre-existing general right of set-off operative prior to the commencement of insolvency proceedings.[42] Moreover, the law should permit the netting of outstanding obligations under financial contracts.[43] Once the financial contracts of the debtor have been terminated by a counterparty, the counterparty is free to net or set off obligations under those terminated financial contracts to establish a net exposure position relative to the debtor. The counterparty in the case of financial contracts is also allowed to terminate contracts or enforce automatic termination clauses notwithstanding any provisions of the general insolvency law prohibiting this course of action. The purpose

---

39 See C Tabb 'Rethinking Preferences' (1992) 43 South Carolina Law Review 981 at 1032.

40 See P Wood *English and International Set-Off* (London, Sweet & Maxwell, 1990) and also P Wood *Law and Practice of International Finance* (London, Sweet & Maxwell, 2008) chapter 14.

41 Directive 2002/47/EC of the European Parliament and of the Council of 6 June 2002 on financial collateral arrangements.

42 See Recommendation 100.

43 See Recommendations 101–107.

of this provision is stated to be to allow market participants to extend credit based on 'net' positions, making it impossible for the debtor to 'cherry-pick' contracts by performing some and breaching others. This is considered to be especially important in the context of financial markets because of systemic risk.[44]

Debtor-in-Possession versus Management Displacement

The Insolvency Guide is at its most flexible when it comes to debtor-in-possession versus management displacement in the context of reorganisation proceedings. It is specifically stated that different approaches may be taken on this issue including[45]

(a) retention of full control by the debtor, i.e. debtor-in-possession with appropriate safeguards including varying levels of control of the debtor and debtor displacement in certain circumstances;
(b) limited displacement where the debtor operates the business subject to the supervision of an insolvency representative with an appropriate division of responsibilities between the two;
(c) total displacement of the debtor in favour of an insolvency representative.

The UNCITRAL Guide does not in any way mandate the US Chapter 11 debtor-in-possession approach to corporate restructuring.[46] Under Chapter 11 an outside trustee can only be appointed to take over management of a company for cause, and their appointment in Chapter 11 is exceptional.[47] In *Re Marvel* Entertainment Group[48] it was stressed that the appointment of an outside trustee should be the exception rather than

[44] See generally the discussion at pp 157–158 of the commentary attached to the Legislative Guide, which is available on the UNCITRAL website: www.uncitral.org.
[45] See Recommendation 112.
[46] See the statement at p 162 of the commentary attached to the Legislative Guide above, note 44 'In reorganization proceedings, there is no agreed approach on the extent to which displacement of the debtor is the most appropriate course of action and, where some level of displacement does occur, on the ongoing role that the debtor may perform and the manner in which that role is balanced with the roles of other participants.'
[47] The legislative statements in s 1104 that a trustee can be appointed only for cause such as fraud, dishonesty or gross mismanagement and that sheer size or large numbers of bondholders or shareholders are not enough have successfully warned the courts away from appointing trustees. It has been held that simple mismanagement is not a sufficient reason for an appointment – *Re Anchorage Boat Sales* (1980) 4 Bankr 635.
[48] (1998) 140 F 3d 463 at 471.

the rule. The court also enunciated the policy reasons behind the debtor-in-possession principle stating that

> current management is generally best suited to orchestrate the process of rehabilitation for the benefit of creditors and other interests of the estate. . . . The debtor-in-possession is a fiduciary of the creditors and, as a result, has an obligation to refrain from acting in a manner which could damage the estate, or hinder a successful reorganization. The strong presumption also finds its basis in the debtor-in-possession's usual familiarity with the business it had already been managing at the time of the bankruptcy filing, often making it the best party to conduct operations during the reorganization.

In UK administration, by contrast, the board of directors is automatically displaced from its management powers and functions in favour of an outside administrator. Many reasons have been offered to explain the difference. These reasons relate to different attitudes towards entrepreneurship and risk-taking in the UK and US; a different jurisdictional mix of carrots and sticks in encouraging early invocation of corporate rescue procedures; different conceptions of the nature of the two processes as well as their aims and objectives; path-dependency and the continued gravitational pull of historical circumstances and finally, differences in the nature of the lending markets, and in particular the bond markets in the two countries.

As the Insolvency Guide itself recognises, the choice between debtor-in-possession and management displacement is not necessarily an 'all-or-nothing' one. Some jurisdictions have formal legislative procedures that are in some sense halfway between debtor-in-possession and manager-displacing corporate restructuring. The 'examinership' procedure in Ireland is an example.[49] Under this procedure, an examiner may be appointed by the court to an ailing company to investigate and report and to prepare a restructuring plan, but there is a presumption that the existing management should continue to direct the affairs of the company during the period of examinership.[50] The examiner does not have functions

---

[49] The relevant law is contained in the Companies (Amendment) Act 1990 as amended principally by the Companies (Amendment) (No 2) Act 1999. There was significant American influence on the legislation – on this see 'Foreword' to Weil, Gotshal & Manges LLP *Reorganizing Failing Businesses* (American Bar Association, 1999): 'Weil, Gotshal & Manges LLP was privileged to help the country of Ireland draft its Companies Act of 1990 to help attract investment by assuring investors a reorganization statute that would help businesses, notwithstanding defaults, if a healthy core business could emerge.' See generally on the legislation TB Courtney *The Law of Private Companies* (Dublin, Butterworths, 2nd edn 2002) chapter 23.

[50] See the comments of Costello J in *Re Clare Textiles Ltd* [1993] 2 IR 213. Under s 24 of the Act the court has no power to confirm proposals which do not provide for the survival of the company and at least part of its undertaking as a going concern.

equivalent to those of a liquidator or administrator, nor does s/he have any executive functions.

It should be noted however that there are risks associated with co-determination models like the Irish one. It may be the case that the division of authority caused by the dual decision-making structure could create an arena for clashes of opposing egos and interests:

> First, one of the fallibilities of shared authority and collective decision-making is human miscommunication. The flow of information between the various decision-makers is susceptible to errors, miscommunication and hence distortion. Secondly, between management and the trustee, the former enjoys superior access to information concerning the debtor. Because the two decision-makers represent different interest groups, management has an incentive to withhold information from the other representative (the trustee), undermine the latter's effective decision-making and thus tip the scale of power and risk taking in favor of its own constituency, the equityholders.[51]

Representation of Creditors

The Insolvency Guide seeks the active involvement of creditors in the insolvency proceedings but does not mandate the form of involvement.[52] It mentions various possibilities such as a creditors' committee, a special representative or other representation mechanism. There are even alternatives set out for the appointment of a creditors' committee such as directly by creditors, or by the court or an administrative body. The Guide gives illustrative examples of the kinds of functions a creditors' committee may perform including:[53]

(a) providing advice and assistance to the insolvency representative or debtor-in-possession;
(b) participating in the development of a reorganisation plan;
(c) being consulted on asset sales outside the ordinary course of business.

Subject to approval by the court, the creditors' committee is allowed to select, employ and remunerate professionals that assist in enabling it to perform its functions. There is no prescription, however, on how the costs and remuneration of these professionals should be met.

---

[51] D Hahn 'Concentrated Ownership and Control of Corporate Reorganizations' (2004) 4 Journal of Corporate Law Studies 117 at 52.

[52] Recommendations 126–136.

[53] Recommendation 133.

In both the US and UK there are mechanisms for creditor participation in insolvency decision making. While the mechanisms differ in the two countries, in both countries the rhetoric does not always match the reality.[54] In the US, in theory, at the start of every Chapter 11 case, a committee of unsecured creditors is appointed. According to s 1102, ordinarily this shall consist of the seven largest creditors who are willing to serve, though the US trustee often goes to great pains to ensure a representative committee.[55] Service on a creditors' committee may provide some informational benefits but in smaller cases it may not be worth the effort for creditors since they are not compensated for the time spent on committee work. A creditors' committee, however, may engage lawyers, accountants and other professionals whose fees and expenses are entitled to administrative expense status under s 507. These professionals, for example, may be tasked by the committee with evaluating the merits and feasibility of a proposed reorganisation plan. Creditors' committees are intended to be primary negotiating bodies for the formulation of reorganisation plans and their powers in this regard are spelled out by s 1103.[56] They can act as sounding boards for a debtor-in-possession who wants to see whether a particular plan will fly.

Under the administration procedure in the UK, the assumption is that an administrator should put his proposals before the creditors for approval. But it has been held that while creditors should normally be consulted, the administrator is free to take major decisions such as disposing of the bulk of a company's assets in advance of a creditors' meeting. In the relevant parliamentary debates in the UK, the government resisted a proposal that would make a creditors' meeting mandatory in all instances.[57] A government spokesperson suggested that the proposal would 'add unnecessarily to costs, burden the courts and reduce the returns for those creditors who did have a financial interest. . . . [T]he virtues of creditors' meetings are grossly exaggerated. It costs a lost of money for the boss of a small company to attend a creditors' meeting, possibly more than he

---

[54] See generally S Wheeler 'Empty Rhetoric and Empty Promises: The Creditors' Meeting' (1994) 21 Journal of Law and Society 350.

[55] On the role of the US Trustee in bankruptcy cases see generally the US Department of Justice website www.usdoj.gov/ust.

[56] See also HR Rep No 595, 95th Cong 1st Session 401–402 and see generally D Bussel 'Coalition-Building Through Bankruptcy Creditors' Committees' (1996) 43 UCLA L Rev 1547.

[57] HL Debates 29 July 2002 at col 783. It was said 'Creditors must be given a chance to voice their concern and they should not be denied that right, particularly where the administrator thinks the company has insufficient property to enable a distribution to be made to unsecured creditors. These creditors will recover nothing and they . . . must be satisfied that nothing can be done for them and to be able to test that at the meeting.'

is owed.' There is subsequent empirical evidence in the UK to the effect that unsecured creditors have little desire to play a central role in insolvency decision making. One study conducted on behalf of the Insolvency Service said:[58] 'Interviewees unanimously reported that creditor meetings are always very poorly attended, and that they strongly suspected that when reports, proposals and progress reports were sent out these were dispatched without ceremony to a cylindrical filing cabinet under the desk which is emptied daily.'

Reorganisation Plans

The Insolvency Guide goes into detail as to the kinds of provisions that may and should be included in a reorganisation plan. In the main these provisions track those of US Chapter 11 but are by no means an exact copy.[59] The rationale of the regime is said to facilitate rescue of businesses thereby preserving employment and protecting investment, identifying those businesses that are capable of reorganisation and maximising the value of the estate.[60] In certain cases, however, there may be a conflict between these stated objectives. For example, the value of the debtor's estate may be maximised through a going-concern sale of the assets rather than attempting a potentially complex restructuring. The goal of Chapter 11 has been articulated as the confirmation of a reorganisation plan,[61] and while Chapter 11 has often proved a convenient vehicle for achieving an efficacious going-concern sale, this objective has been neglected in the official history.[62] The mantra of reorganisation assumes pride of place, and this is the same with the Legislative Guide.

---

58 'Report on Insolvency Outcomes' at p 54 – a paper presented to the Insolvency Service by Dr Sandra Frisby – see www.insolvency.gov.uk and for a synopsis 'Not Quite Warp Factor 2 Yet? The Enterprise Act and Corporate Insolvency' (2007) 22 Butterworths Journal of International Banking and Financial Law 327.

59 See s 1129 of the US Bankruptcy Code for the provisions on confirmation of a reorganisation plan.

60 Recommendations 139–159.

61 See Stevens J in *Bank of America v 203 North LaSalle Street Partnership* (1999) 526 US 434 at fn 4 of his judgment.

62 But see the National Bankruptcy Review Commission Report, *Bankruptcy: The Next Twenty Years* (E Warren, Reporter, 1997) at pp 609–660. The report is available at http://govinfo.library.unt.edu/nbrc. It acknowledges that reasonable people differ about how to define 'success' in Chapter 11 cases (see p 611): 'Some argue that a Chapter 11 case in which no plan is confirmed should be considered successful where the case produces an orderly sale of assets or a negotiated solution without a formal plan. Creditors may define success in terms of distribution amounts or in terms of preserving future dealings with the debtor. The debtor, on the other hand, may define success in terms of job preservation, enhancement of going-concern value, or future returns to equity. The public may define success in terms of overall fairness.'

But the Chapter 11 model is not followed in other respects. For instance, the debtor is given an exclusive right to propose a Chapter 11 reorganisation plan for a certain period, normally 120 days, after the commencement of the case.[63] The Insolvency Guide has no such period of debtor exclusivity. The recommendations are silent on who may propose the plan. The proposal, like in Chapter 11, is however required to be accompanied by a disclosure statement that enables those who are entitled to vote on the plan to make an informed judgement on the issue. The Guide does not go into great detail on the content of the plan, though it does require identification of each creditor class and the treatment provided for the class by the plan, such as how much they will receive and the timing of payment.[64]

For voting on the plan, the Legislative Guide is fairly prescriptive. For instance, a creditor or shareholder whose rights are modified or affected by the plan is not bound by the plan unless given the opportunity of voting on its terms. In the corollary case, where creditor or shareholder rights are not adversely affected by the plan, they should not have the opportunity of voting. The Guide appears to require the division of creditors into classes with separate classification of creditors according to their respective rights as well as voting in classes. The Guide permits, but does not require, 'cramdown' – a mechanism whereby the dissent of a class of creditors may be overcome if at least one class whose rights are adversely affected by the plan signifies approval.

In the US the cramdown rules set the ultimate parameters for all Chapter 11 plan negotiations. The availability of cramdown limits the ability of a creditor to hold out for better treatment and also permits viable businesses to reorganise even if a few creditors object strenuously. The cramdown rules can work to hold the interests of a small group of powerful creditors in check.[65] Chapter 11 requires court approval for cramdown and the Guide appears to follow this approach. It also embodies two fundamental Chapter 11 principles, namely the 'liquidation' or

---

63 Section 1121 of the US Bankruptcy Code. This period may be extended for cause. In *Re Public Service Company of New Hampshire* (1988) 88 BR 521 the US Bankruptcy Court concluded that 'size and complexity must be accompanied by other factors pertinent to the particular debtor and its reorganization to justify extension of plan exclusivity, except perhaps in the very early, initial stages of the chapter 11 proceedings. Such factors include . . . the likelihood of an imminent consensual plan if the debtor retains control, no alternate substantial plan being held off by debtor exclusivity, and the general balancing analysis to avoid allowing the debtor to hold the creditors and other parties in interest "hostage" so that the debtor can force its view of an appropriate plan upon the other parties.'

64 Recommendations 148–152.

65 National Bankruptcy Review Commission Report *Bankruptcy: The Next Twenty Years* (1997) at pp 546–547.

'best interests' test and secondly, the absolute priority rule. The 'best interests' test requires that a creditor should receive at least as much under the plan as it would in liquidation. The 'absolute priority' rule requires that insolvency priorities should be respected; in other words, that creditors should be paid in the same order as they would in liquidation with creditors paid out before shareholders and senior creditors before junior creditors etc.

The Guide, however, also permits as an alternative the UK company voluntary arrangement (CVA) approach whereby restructuring plans do not have to go to court for approval but a dissenter is allowed to challenge the plan on procedural grounds or on grounds of substantial unfairness by making a court application within a prescribed time limit.[66] In the CVA context there are no separate classes. Approval of a CVA requires a majority in excess of 75 per cent in value of creditors present at the creditors' meeting, but a resolution is invalid if those voting against it include more than half in value of independent creditors. A CVA, however, may not affect the rights of secured creditors without their consent, nor the rights of preferential creditors to be paid ahead of unsecured creditors. There is no procedure whereby the objections of secured creditors can be overcome unlike Chapter 11 cramdown. There are a number of other significant differences between reorganisations under Chapter 11 and by means of a CVA. For example, the percentages required for obtaining creditor approval at the relevant meetings are different under the two procedures. Chapter 11 requires a majority in number of creditors representing two-thirds of value whereas CVAs need 75 per cent in value. Moreover, in Chapter 11 the court has to make a determination on whether a reorganisation plan is 'feasible',[67] but no such judicial determinations are required for CVAs where it is up to the creditors and shareholders of the relevant company to decide on the economic merits of a proposed restructuring.[68]

---

66 Recommendations 153, 154. Under s 6(7) UK Insolvency Act a procedural irregularity does not invalidate the approval given at a meeting unless it is the subject of a successful statutory challenge.

67 For a critical perspective on the merits of a feasibility requirement see L LoPucki *Courting Failure: How Competition for Big Cases Is Corrupting the Bankruptcy Courts* (Ann Arbor, University of Michigan Press, 2005) at p 105, who quotes a bankruptcy judge: 'You must have seen some of these plans. Some of them are as big as the New York telephone book. How is a judge who is foreclosed from participating in the reorganization ever going to read that plan and find anything wrong with it?... I don't care how smart you are, you wind up talking to yourself, challenging your own assumptions and driving yourself crazy. The judge isn't going to be allowed to call in and examine a bunch of expert witnesses. That's not a typical judge's role. It may be the judges' responsibility, but as a practical matter they can't do it.'

68 See generally G McCormack *Corporate Rescue Law* above, note 5 chapter 8.

Expedited Reorganisation Proceedings

So-called prepacks are a conspicuous feature of the corporate landscape in both the US and UK, though there substantial differences in what is meant by 'prepacks' in the two countries. Prepacks, whatever the precise form they may take, build on the insight that there is likely to be a substantial saving of cost and convenience if the company minimises the time that it spends in formal insolvency procedures. The longer and more drawn out the procedure, the greater the costs and expenses that are likely to be incurred.[69] Moreover, a company may suffer a loss of goodwill and a defection of valuable customers upon the commencement of formal insolvency procedures. It can be difficult to achieve a voluntary out-of-court restructuring, however, because of holdout problems. Voluntary processes have no means of binding dissentients. If the dissenters are small in number or significance, they can be paid off in full or left out of the restructuring equation but this ceases to be a viable option the greater their size and significance.[70]

In a prepackaged Chapter 11, substantial negotiations are held with creditors prior to the commencement of the formal process. In some cases the creditors actually vote on the proposed restructuring beforehand, whereas in other cases the contours of the plan are merely worked out. But in both scenarios the formal Chapter 11 process is activated as means of binding dissentient individuals or groups to the plan. While some of the standard procedural safeguards do not operate, a Chapter 11 prepack will still come before the court for approval. Prepackaged administrations in the UK, on the other hand, are usually a means of accomplishing the sale of a substantial part of the company's undertaking to a buyer that has been identified in advance, rather than carrying out a restructuring in the strict sense. Prepacks in administration need not come before the court

---

69 See generally the Chrysler and General Motors restructurings in the US and the US Congressional Oversight Panel report on the same (September 2009) 'The Use of TARP Funds in the Support and Reorganization of the Domestic Automotive Industry' available at http://cop.senate.gov/documents/cop-090909-report.pdf.

70 See generally SC Gilson 'Managing Default: Some Evidence on How Firms Choose between Workouts and Chapter 11' in JS Bhandari and LA Weiss eds *Corporate Bankruptcy: Economic and Legal Perspectives* (Cambridge, CUP, 1996) 308 and also J McConnell and H Servaes 'The Economics of Pre-packaged Bankruptcy' in the same collection. Prepackaged bankruptcies are also more likely to have financing arrangements in place. On this see generally S Dahiya, K John, M Puri and G Ramirez 'Debtor-in-Possession Financing and Bankruptcy Resolution: Empirical Evidence' (2003) 69 Journal of Financial Economics 259 at 269–270 and see also S Chatterjee, S Dhillon and G Ramirez 'Debtor-in-Possession Financing' (2004) 28 Journal of Business and Finance 3097.

and additionally, the sale may be held in advance of a creditors' meeting and without getting approval from creditors.

Despite their perceived advantages there have been substantial criticisms of 'prepacks' on both sides of the Atlantic. For example, it has been suggested in some empirical studies that companies with prepackaged Chapter 11s[71] are more likely to go forum-shopping, i.e. to file for bankruptcy in what is perceived to be the most advantageous jurisdiction rather than the centre of the company's operations, and that such companies have a greater propensity to refile for Chapter 11 protection at some later stage.[72] In the UK there have also been criticisms. In a prepack the corporate assets are normally sold off to an existing management team. The secured creditors are paid out of the sale proceeds but agree to maintain lending facilities in place with the new corporate entity that has taken over the company assets. To many observers, the old company is trading on, albeit under a slightly different guise, but having shed its unsecured debt.[73] Prepacks, therefore, may function as a means 'by which powerful players can bypass carefully constructed statutory protections'.[74] It is argued that in a prepack the market may not have been properly explored and consequently, the business may be sold at an undervalue.[75] In certain circumstances it may be commercially justifiable to sell the business back to management or some other connected party, but the suspicion is that corporate insiders are benefiting at the expense of outside unsecured creditors. In other words, that prepacks generally enhance the interests

---

71 See T Eisenberg and LM LoPucki 'Shopping for Judges: An Empirical Analysis of Venue Choice in Large Chapter 11 Reorganizations' (1999) 84 Cornell L Rev 967 at 976–977.

72 *Ibid* and see also L LoPucki and S Kalin 'The Failure of Public Company Bankruptcies in Delaware and New York: Empirical Evidence of a "Race to the Bottom"' (2001) 54 Vanderbilt Law Review 231. But for different perspectives see R Rasmussen and R Thomas 'Timing Matters: Promoting Forum-shopping by Insolvent Corporations' (2000) 94 Northwestern University Law Review 135, arguing that the US Bankruptcy Code would be more efficient if the law facilitated more forum shopping for bankruptcy venues; D Skeel 'What's So Bad about Delaware?' (2001) 54 Vanderbilt Law Review 309; H Miller 'Chapter 11 Reorganization Cases and the Delaware Myth' (2002) 55 Vanderbilt Law Review 1987; T Zywicki 'Is Forum-Shopping Corrupting America's Bankruptcy Courts? (2006) 94 Georgetown Law Journal 1141.

73 P Walton 'Pre-packaged Administrations: Trick or Treat?' (2006) 19 Insolvency Intelligence 113 at 116.

74 See V Finch 'Pre-Packaged Administrations: Bargains in the Shadow of Insolvency or Shadowy Bargains' [2006] JBL 568.

75 *Ibid* at 570 and Stephen Davies QC 'Pre-pack – He Who Pays the Piper Calls the Tune' Recovery (Summer 2006) at p 16. See now Statement of Insolvency Practice (SIP) 16 prescribing procedures for IPs to follow in relation to prepacks, particularly in sales to connected parties. The Joint Insolvency Committee consultation on SIP 16 (2000) (available on the Insolvency Service website, www.insolvency.gov.uk) canvasses various possibilities for reform of SIP 16.

of insiders, professional advisers and secured creditors at the expense of smaller unsecured creditors and outside shareholders.[76]

The Legislative Guide, however, waxes lyrical on the merits of 'pre-packs', acclaiming the general advantages of expedited reorganisation procedures, and uses this specific language rather than the language of prepacks. It refers to preserving the benefits of voluntary restructuring negotiations where a majority of each affected class of creditors agree to a plan; binding minority members; minimising time delays and expense and ensuring that the plan negotiated and agreed in voluntary restructuring negotiations is not lost.[77] The Guide in this area tends to track the heavy-duty machinery of Chapter 11. For instance, the court in the expedited process is required to confirm the plan if (a) it satisfies the substantive requirements for confirmation of a plan in full reorganisation proceedings and (b) the information given to affected parties during the voluntary restructuring negotiations was sufficient to enable them to make an informed decision about the plan and pre-commencement solicitation of acceptances to the plan complied with applicable law.[78] One wonders however why there should be a need for the complicated paraphernalia of court confirmation. If the law in a particular jurisdiction requires that standard plans should come before the court for approval, then it makes sense that expedited plans should be subject to a modified version of this court-backed procedure. But if the standard procedure does not require court involvement, then it is hard to see why this should automatically be required in the case of the expedited procedure.

One might also criticise the Guide on the basis that it is unduly concerned with expedited restructuring procedures and not enough with expedited procedures that may lead to a going-concern sale of all, or part, of an ailing company's assets. The Guide may lack a certain nimbleness of foot, which leaves it liable to be outflanked by market developments of the kind seen in the Chrysler and General Motors (GM) restructurings in the US.[79]

---

[76] See S Frisby 'Interim Report to the Insolvency Service on Returns to Creditors from Pre- and Post-Enterprise Act Insolvency Procedures' – see www.insolvency.gov.uk at pp 39–40: 'One very tentative contention is that whilst pre-packs save more jobs they probably realise less, purely because they save more jobs. The purchaser of a business who accepts its actual and contingent employee-related liabilities will be inclined to apply an appropriate discount on what he would have been prepared to offer for the business without its employees. This, therefore, results in less funds being available to the company's creditors, with its unsecured creditors inevitably bearing the brunt of the discount.'

[77] Recommendations 160–168.

[78] Recommendation 166.

[79] On the Chrysler and General Motors restructurings see the US Congressional Oversight Panel report on the same (September 2009) 'The Use of TARP Funds in the Support and Reorganization of the Domestic Automotive Industry' available at http://cop.

The rationale behind reorganisation procedures is that the going-concern value of company assets may be greater than the liquidation value. In the UK the emphasis has normally been on business rescue and maintaining value through going-concern sales of the company's business, whereas in the US the traditional way of capturing the going-concern surplus has been through corporate rescue via restructurings. In the Chrysler and GM cases, however, huge auto manufacturers and distributors were effectively reorganised through a sale of potentially the profitable part of the company's businesses to newly created shell companies. The shell companies paid a certain amount for the assets of the 'old' car companies and also agreed to assume certain workforce-related liabilities. The detailed structure and funding arrangement in respect of the shell companies had been hammered out in advance of the bankruptcy filings, and essentially the US government provided most of the funding.[80] It was argued by certain creditors that the purported 'business sales' amounted to de facto reorganisation plans and also upset the normal scheme of bankruptcy priorities. But the Bankruptcy Court would have none of this, stating that s 363 of the US Bankruptcy Code permitted sales of corporate assets outside the normal course of business if there was a business justification for the sale.[81] A speedy sale was justified because business and customers would melt away if there were continued uncertainty about the fate of the car companies.[82]

The Legislative Guide acknowledges the possibility of going-concern sales of all or part of corporate assets but does not do much to regulate the practice and seems to contemplate reorganisations as the main vehicle for preserving value.[83]

Priorities and Distribution of Proceeds

Different jurisdictions have different approaches to the distribution of corporate assets in insolvency. In the US according to s 507 of the Bankruptcy Code, the order of distribution of assets in an insolvency is broadly as

senate.gov/documents/cop-090909-report.pdf. This report contains a perceptive analysis of US bankruptcy law and attached papers that are both supportive and critical of the Chrysler/GM de facto rescues.

[80] It appears that this was done for political reasons as the US government otherwise feared the collapse of the domestic auto industry with unpredictable economic and social consequences.

[81] On the 'business justification' test for s 363 sales see *In re Lionel Corp* (1983) 722 F2d 1063.

[82] See *In re Chrysler LLC* (2009) 405 BR 84.

[83] Recommendations 52 and 55–57.

follows: (1) secured claims (2) preferred claims and (3) unsecured claims, whereas in the UK it is broadly (1) secured claims other than those secured by a floating charge (2) preferential creditors (3) claims secured by a floating charge with a capped amount of these claims set aside for the benefit of unsecured creditors and (4) unsecured creditors. What counts as a preferred claim also differs between the US and UK. In general terms, in the US both tax and employee claims fall under this head subject to certain restrictions, whereas in the UK the preferential status of tax claims was abolished by the Enterprise Act 2002 and now basically only employee claims are entitled to preferential status in certain circumstances. Other jurisdictions may have much more expansive notions of preferred claims and, more importantly, such claims may have a much more elevated priority position, ranking ahead of all secured claims. There is a diversity of approaches across the world and the Guide endorses this pluralistic position though subject to certain caveats. It makes the point that increases in the categories of priority creditors will enlarge the scope for other groups to claim that they also deserve priority treatment.[84] The overall amount available for distribution to creditors is limited. One is talking about a 'zero sum' game and the greater the number of creditors that receive priority treatment, the less beneficial such treatment will become.

It acknowledges that distribution policies very often reflect choices in favour of important public interests such as the protection of employment, but it counsels that where these broader public interests compete with private interests, they may lead to a distortion of normal commercial incentives.[85] The Guide calls for transparency and predictability and suggests that where public interests are given priority, the policy reasons for establishing that priority should be clearly stated in the insolvency law. The Guide also refers to the practice in some States of establishing a wage guarantee fund, or insurance scheme, that provides a separate source of funds to ensure the settlement of employee claims.

Moreover, the Guide also notes the approach in some laws of capping the amount that can be recovered in priority by secured creditors. The UK is not specifically referred to in this connection but it is commented that in some laws a distinction is drawn between security interests over essentially all the assets of a business (an enterprise or floating charge) and other types of security interest, with the carve-out in favour of unsecured creditors being confined to the universal security. In the UK under the Enterprise Act, a proportion of recoveries under the floating charge

---

[84] See p 271 of the commentary attached to the Legislative Guide, which is available on the UNCITRAL website: www.uncitral.org.

[85] *Ibid* at p 267.

is reserved for the benefit of unsecured creditors.[86] The proportion is calculated on a sliding-scale basis and consists of 50 per cent of the first £20 000 of net recoveries, then 20 per cent of the remainder but subject to an overall ceiling of £600 000. The Guide suggests that the 'adoption of these types of exception to the rule of first priority of secured creditors has the potential to create uncertainty with respect to the recovery of secured credit, thus discouraging the provision of secured credit and raising the associated costs'.[87] Therefore, it is argued that the use of such exceptions in insolvency should be limited. Presumably, the provisions of the UK Enterprise Act come within the UNCITRAL strictures since the carved-out amount is subject both to percentage limits and to restrictions in terms of absolute monetary amount.

COMPARISONS BETWEEN THE INSOLVENCY GUIDE AND THE SECURED TRANSACTIONS GUIDE

The merits of the Insolvency Guide have been extolled as an exercise in smart law making.[88] UNCITRAL effectively narrowed the grounds of debate and took particularly contentious or potentially intractable issues off the table for decision. In a classic case of agenda setting, the odds of achieving consensus were increased by a focus on tackling only those issues that the agenda setters considered to be feasible. An example of this is the treatment, or non-treatment, of a matter that has proved contentious in the context of the Secured Transactions Guide, namely characterisation of retention of title provisions in insolvency proceedings and whether such provisions should be regarded as creating a security interest. The Insolvency Guide avoids controversy by deferring to the non-insolvency law of the enacting State rather than setting out a solution to the issue in the context of insolvency law. Issues of directorial liability for the company trading while insolvent are central to some insolvency systems, but the Insolvency Guide ducked out of firm pronouncements on this topic by discussing the matter in the commentary but not reaching any recommendations.[89] The same approach was adopted with respect

---

[86] Section 252 of the Enterprise Act which introduces a new s 176A into the Insolvency Act.

[87] See pp 269–270 of the commentary attached to the Legislative Guide above, note 84.

[88] See generally S Block-Lieb and T Halliday above, note 3 at 509.

[89] See however A/CN.9/WG.V/WP.96 – Directors' responsibilities and liabilities in insolvency and pre-insolvency cases (August 2010) on possible future work by UNCITRAL in the area of insolvency law.

to the proper treatment of corporate groups in insolvency proceedings.[90] In general, UNCITRAL declined to tread on sensitive national toes by skipping over imperative recommendations on matters likely to lead to stalemate or polarisation such as creditor priorities and the treatment of preferential claims.[91]

In certain respects it is undoubtedly the case that the provisions in the Insolvency Guide mirror those in the US Bankruptcy Code. The provisions on the treatment of executory contracts, i.e. contracts not yet performed by the debtor and financing the debtor during the restructuring period – post-commencement finance – are examples in point. Moreover, the provisions on the mechanisms for getting approval of a restructuring plan including cramdown have American likenesses though these provisions are not cast in imperative form. But the appearance of the Guide is not all American or even mainly American. A central feature that distinguishes the US from probably most other corporate restructuring regimes worldwide is the debtor-in-possession norm. The Legislative Guide does not express a preference for such a norm and concedes the possibility of a number of different approaches. This can be contrasted with the Secured Transactions Guide where the central features of the US Article 9 are all present – no carve-outs for unsecured creditors, recharacterisation of quasi-security, notice filing and the first-to-file priority principles with an exception for purchase money security interests.

---

90 UNCITRAL more recently however revisited this issue and on 21 July 2010 'pre-released' certain recommendations on the treatment of enterprise groups in insolvency – see www.uncitral.org. See generally I Mevorach *Insolvency within Multinational Corporate Groups* (Oxford, OUP, 2009).

91 See I Fletcher (2007) 'Maintaining the Momentum: The Continuing Quest for Global Standards and Principles to Govern Cross-Border Insolvency' 32 Brooklyn Journal of International Law 767 at 775, stating that 'it is probable that the UNCITRAL Legislative Guide on Insolvency Law will receive the closest consideration by policymakers and legislators, both on account of its institutional pedigree and also for the very reason that it appears to adopt a non-prescriptive approach that is free from any overt attempt to impose a legislative matrix upon states as a condition for economic acceptance or access to material benefits for the future.'

8. Conclusion

The UNCITRAL Legislative Guide contains a fairly detailed set of rules governing the creation and enforcement of security interests over personal property. Alternative possibilities are allowed in certain situations, but the document is more than a guide, it is a series of prescriptions. While the UNCITRAL instrument does not reproduce American terminology, the instrument does mirror the norms reflected in Article 9 of the US Uniform Commercial Code. The previous chapters have explained that this alignment with American law is much closer in the case of the UNCITRAL Secured Transactions Guide than the UNCITRAL Insolvency Guide. This concluding chapter tries to explain why this is the case. It also seeks to examine the possibility of the Secured Transactions Guide gaining widespread international acceptance.

THE INSOLVENCY AND AMERICAN PARALLELS

This book has made the point on a number of occasions that there are greater similarities between Article 9 of the US Uniform Commercial Code and the UNCITRAL Secured Transactions Guide than between the US Bankruptcy Code and the UNCITRAL Insolvency Guide. Why should this have happened? One possibility is that there was greater American influence on the drafting of the Secured Transactions Guide mediated through organisations such as the Commercial Finance Association (CFA); that this came through in the final product in the absence of any countervailing groups; and that American-centred organisations such as the CFA did not play an equivalently influential role in the formulation of the Insolvency Guide. It is difficult, however, to provide concrete proof in support of this proposition. American-based groups like the American Bar Association and the American Bar Foundation played a role in the process leading up to the promulgation of the Insolvency Guide. It may be the case that their influence was not as great as that of the CFA in the Secured Transactions Guide enactment process and it was at least partly offset by the London-based International Association of Insolvency Practitioners, INSOL, but this is largely a matter of speculation.[1]

Perhaps a more plausible explanation is that US bankruptcy law is much more of an outlier than US secured transactions law when viewed from a creditors' rights perspective. Those who address bankruptcy and secured transactions law at the UNCITRAL level, particularly private sector groups, are more likely to address it from a creditor perspective and therefore are likely to favour the enactment of provisions that advance creditor interests. US bankruptcy law, as distinct from secured transactions law, does not provide a suitable model in this respect, for the US Bankruptcy Code has traditionally been seen as very 'pro-debtor' compared, for example, with UK law which is seen as 'pro-creditor'. In the US, corporate reorganisation proceedings are governed by Chapter 11 of the Bankruptcy Code[2] and are almost always begun by a voluntary petition filed by the corporate debtor. The filing brings about a moratorium on enforcement proceedings against the debtor or its property, and the incumbent management normally remains in place during the early stages at least of the reorganisation proceedings. United States law is classed as pro-debtor rather than pro-creditor for it allows an automatic stay on assets; allows unimpeded petitions for reorganisation and allows the company's board of directors to remain in control during the reorganisation process.[3] One distinguished American commentator has observed:[4] 'if an American banker is very, very good, when he dies he will go to the United Kingdom. British banks have far more control than an American secured lender could ever hope to have.'

The importance of creditor rights particularly in bankruptcy proceedings

---

1 The annual reports of the UNCITRAL Working Groups set out the list of organisations that take part in its activities – see www.uncitral.org and internal links.

2 See generally on Chapter 11 G McCormack *Corporate Rescue Law: An Anglo-American Perspective* (Cheltenham, UK and Northampton, MA, USA, Edward Elgar, 2008). The economic efficiency etc. of Chapter 11 is discussed in M Bradley and M Rosenzweig 'The Untenable Case for Chapter 11' (1992) 101 Yale LJ 1043; E Warren 'The Untenable Case for Repeal of Chapter 11' (1992) 102 Yale LJ 437; T Eisenberg 'Baseline Problems in Assessing Chapter 11' (1993) 43 University of Toronto Law Journal 633; K Kordana and E Posner 'A Positive Theory of Chapter 11' (1999) 74 New York University Law Review 161.

3 *A Review of Company Rescue and Business Reconstruction Mechanisms* (London, DTI/HM Treasury 2000) at pp 38–41. At p 33 the review group however observes that 'it would be wholly inappropriate to attempt to replicate Chapter 11 in the UK, where the business culture and economic environment are quite different. . .'.

4 See J Westbrook ' A Comparison of Bankruptcy Reorganisation in the US with the Administration Procedure in the UK' (1990) 6 Insolvency Law and Practice 86 at 87 and see also J Franks and W Torous 'Lessons from a Comparison of US and UK Insolvency Codes' (1993) 8 Oxford Review of Economic Policy 70.

was stressed in the 'legal origins' or 'law matters' thesis developed by La Porta, Lopez de Silanes, Shleifer and Vishny.[5] The original creditor rights index constructed by La Porta et al. measured four powers of secured lenders in bankruptcy: whether there are restrictions, such as creditor consent, when a debtor files for reorganisation; whether secured creditors are able to seize collateral after the petition for reorganisation is approved, i.e. there is no 'automatic stay' or 'asset freeze' imposed by the court; secured creditors are paid first out of liquidation proceeds; and finally, whether an administrator, and not management, is responsible for running the business during the reorganisation period. Where a country's laws and regulations entrust each of these powers to secured creditors, a value of one is added to the creditor rights index. These scores are then aggregated and vary between 0 (poor creditor rights) and 4 (strong creditor rights). Nine countries, including the UK, have a 'perfect' score whereas the US only has a score of 1. Whereas in the US secured creditors are paid first out of bankruptcy proceeds, there are no restrictions on entering reorganisation and the debtor benefits from an automatic stay on assets while management runs the company during reorganisation.

The *Doing Business* reports issued annually since 2004 through the World Bank Group[6] build on the legal origins literature and employ a more sophisticated version of the same methodology employed by La Porta et al. In the 2010 *Doing Business* report the 'getting credit' indicator includes a 'legal rights' index that purports to measure eight features of collateral law and two aspects of bankruptcy law. The index assigns a score of 1 for each of the following aspects of the law in a particular jurisdiction:

- Any business may use movable assets as collateral while keeping possession of the assets, and any financial institution may accept such assets as collateral.
- The law allows a business to grant a non-possessory security right in a single category of revolving movable assets (such as accounts receivable or inventory), without requiring a specific description of the secured assets.
- The law allows a business to grant a non-possessory security right in substantially all of its assets, without requiring a specific description of the secured assets.

---

[5] See R La Porta, F Lopez de Silanes, A Shleifer and R Vishny 'Legal Determinants of External Finance' (1997) 52 Journal of Finance 1131 and by the same authors 'Law and Finance' (1998) 106 Journal of Political Economy 113. The first three named authors refine the 'legal origins' thesis and defend it against criticisms in 'The Economic Consequences of Legal Origins' (2008) 46 Journal of Economic Literature 285.

[6] See www.doingbusiness.org.

- A security right may extend to future or after-acquired assets and may extend automatically to the products, proceeds or replacements of the original assets.
- General description of debts and obligations is permitted in collateral agreements and in registration documents, so that all types of obligations and debts can be secured by stating a maximum rather than a specific amount between the parties.
- A collateral registry is in operation that is unified geographically and by asset type and that is indexed by the name of the grantor of a security right.
- Secured creditors are paid first (for example, before general tax claims and employee claims) when a debtor defaults outside an insolvency procedure.
- Secured creditors are paid first (for example, before general tax claims and employee claims) when a business is liquidated.
- Secured creditors are not subject to an automatic stay or moratorium on enforcement procedures when a debtor enters a court supervised reorganization procedure.
- The law allows parties to agree in a collateral agreement that the lender may enforce its security right out of court.

Scores are then aggregated with the higher scores signifying that the collateral and bankruptcy laws in a particular jurisdiction 'are better designed to expand access to credit'. In the 'legal rights' part of the 'getting credit' section in the 2010 *Doing Business* report, the US is given a score of 8 while the UK is given 9. This suggests that the gap between the two countries has narrowed because the index includes matters pertaining to collateral law. UK law however still comes out ahead because of the differences in respect of creditor rights on bankruptcy. Both the US and UK are in the creditor rights' mainstream when it comes to collateral law, but the US is an outlier in terms of creditor rights on bankruptcy, at least in countries with a common law legal origin.

There is further evidence for this proposition if one looks beyond the legal origins theory and the *Doing Business* reports to organisations such as the European Bank for Reconstruction and Development (EBRD). According to EBRD a modern law of secured transactions should be founded on five key elements:[7] a security right must confer property rights; the law should enable security to be taken in the widest possible

[7] See the 'secured transactions' section of the website of the EBRD website – www.ebrd.com and see generally J-H Röver *Secured Lending in Eastern Europe: Comparative Law of Secured Transactions and the EBRD Model Law* (Oxford, OUP, 2007); D Fairgrieve

range of circumstances; there should be effective publicity for security rights; there should be rapid, cost-effective means of recovering the debt from the secured asset; and it should be relatively inexpensive to create, maintain and exercise security rights.[8] US law (and English law too) scores well when judged against these benchmarks. The main pluses are the freedom to create security interests in almost all classes of assets and the general absence of procedural barriers in respect of the creation of security interests. On the other hand however, EBRD has also formulated Core Principles for an Insolvency Law Regime[9] which, in contrast with Chapter 11 of the US Bankruptcy Code, certainly leans in favour of a management displacement norm. Core Principle 9 states that the Insolvency Administrator should be an impartial third party and not a servant to the debtor or to any single or multiple creditors. The principle goes on to say that the

> liquidation or restructuring of an insolvent corporation impacts the debtor, the creditors, the employees, the state and the community. While these parties are accorded different levels of priority and importance in the insolvency process, the Insolvency Administrator must be seen as able to balance these competing interests so that the process itself is seen to be fair.

INFLUENCE OF THE SECURED TRANSACTIONS GUIDE

The Secured Transactions Guide is a detailed instrument and the product of detailed reflection over many years by highly informed and interested parties. It reflects modern financing techniques and incorporates the accumulated wisdom and practice as well as insights from highly developed and sophisticated economies at the cutting edge of global finance. It is a 'fuller', more contemporary and up-to-date product than either the EBRD or the Inter-American Model Law on Secured Transactions as well as being more widely consulted and reflected upon. For these reasons it is bound to be referred to as a source of inspiration and guidance by States when seeking to update their law on secured transactions. UNCITRAL is undoubtedly correct when it states that 'the Guide is a valuable resource tool because it discusses all issues to be addressed in a

---

'Reforming Secured Transactions Laws in Central and Eastern Europe' [1998] European Business LR 254.

[8] See also the Preface to the Model Law on Secured Transactions (1994) published by the European Bank for Reconstruction and Development (EBRD).

[9] http://www.ebrd.com/pages/sector/legal/insolvency/core_principles.html.

secured transactions law, explains all the workable approaches presenting their advantages and disadvantages and makes recommendations to the legislator'.[10] UNCITRAL has also claimed that the Guide has already influenced recent secured transactions law reform in Australia and South Korea, as well as the rules on proprietary security in movable assets in the Draft European Common Frame of Reference (DCFR) in respect of European Private Law.

The perceived influence on the DCFR is particularly interesting given the civil law antecedents of most European countries and the argument, often strongly voiced, that a Common Law Frame of Reference would involve marginalising the common law canon of experience in favour of the civil law. This proposition has been advanced forcefully by Pierre Legrand, who speaks of 'political correctness a l'européene' or the desire to eliminate difference across laws or to pretend that it is not there.[11] Legrand suggests the very existence of a European Civil Code means bowing to the civil law in preference to the common law. We have seen that the UNCITRAL guide is close to US Article 9. Its closeness also to the rules on proprietary security in the DCFR would seem not only to contradict Legrand's argument but more importantly to augur well for the transferability of the UNCITRAL Guide across frontiers and legal families.

At the institutional level the genesis of the proposal for a Common Frame of Reference (CFR) comes from the 2001 European Commission Communication on Contract Law[12] and a 2003 Action Plan that suggested

---

[10] See UN document A/CN.9/702/Add.1 – 'Possible future work on security interests' (2010) at para 51.

[11] See P Legrand 'On the Unbearable Localness of the Law: Academic Fallacies and Unseasonable Observations' [2002] European Review of Private Law 61 at 66 and see also P Legrand 'European Legal Systems Are Not Converging' (1997) 45 ICLQ 52; 'Against a European Civil Code' (1997) 60 MLR 44; 'The Impossibility of Legal Transplants' (2003) 4 Maastricht Journal 111; 'Antivonbar' (2006) 1 JCL 1.

[12] For background see the three primary European Commission documents: 'Communication from the Commission to the Council and the European Parliament on European Contract Law COM (2001) 398; 'A More Coherent European Contract Law, An Action Plan' COM (2003) 68; 'European Contract Law and the Revision of the Acquis: The Way Forward' COM (2004) 651. See now *Green Paper from the Commission on policy options for progress towards a European Contract Law for consumers and businesses* (Brussels, European Commission, July 2010). See also the von Bar Study Group on the European Civil Code: www.sgecc.net and the Acquis Group on European Private Law: www.acquis-group.org, and see also the Joint Network on European Private Law: www.copecl.org There is a vast academic literature, and for a taster see M Van Hoecke and F Ost eds *The Harmonisation of European Private Law* (Oxford, Hart Publishing, 2000); A Hartkamp et al. eds *Towards a European Civil Code* (Nijmegen, Kluwer Law International, 3rd edn 2004); H Collins *The European Civil Code* (Cambridge, CUP, 2008). See also M Kenny 'Constructing a European Civil Code: Quis Custodiet Ipsos Custodes?' (2006) 12 Columbia Journal of European Law 775.

possible avenues of development including a CFR. The CFR was envisaged as having various functions. One would be to provide a set of model terms for contracting parties. Another would be to serve as a toolbox or source of inspiration for European institutions (or even national legislatures) contemplating further legislative initiatives. Another possibility saw the CFR standing as an optional instrument applying to cross-border contractual relationships and expressly or impliedly selected by the parties, whether on an 'opt-in' or 'opt-out' basis. It should be noted that in the whole process the European Commission took great care to avoid use of the 'Code' word, but the task of producing the first draft of the CFR was given to an Academic Network led by a group called the Study Group on a European Civil Code.

The Study Group has now produced a comprehensive draft CFR covering broad areas of private law including secured transactions or 'proprietary security', as it is called in the language of the CFR.[13] The standard reason given for the inclusion of proprietary securities in the CFR seems to be that they are part of private law, being generally the product of contract, and have often been included in national Civil Codes though usually not in an exhaustive way.[14] In addition, it might be easier to find agreement on the content of such provisions than on, say, provisions of family law where moral and ideological differences run deeper. There have been objections to the CFR proposal on constitutional, economic and cultural grounds and it may be that the case for a CFR is ultimately a political case, based on advancing the goal of European legal integration. For instance, in the section on proprietary securities, the CFR proposal makes provision for a Europe-wide register of security interests. In a Europe of nation States the idea of replacing separate national registers with a single, unified European register seems unrealistic, especially given the fact that in the US, despite political unity, there is not a uniform national register. Registration in the US remains State-based. It is for the European political institutions to refine and develop the 'academic' CFR or DCFR into a political CFR. In this process some of the wider contractual and extra-contractual material such as proprietary securities could be excised from any product that eventually emerges. Moreover, while the chances of the CFR gaining acceptance as a binding instrument are likely to be stilled by

---

[13] A team headed by Professor Ulrich Drobnig (Hamburg) has produced the part of the Academic Common Frame of Reference dealing with credit securities: see www.sgecc.net.

[14] See generally J Basedow 'The Case for a European Contract Act' [2001] JBL 569. See also U Drobnig 'A Subsidiary Plea: A European Contract Law for Intra-European Border-Crossing Contracts' in S Grundmann and J Stuyck eds *An Academic Green Paper on European Contract Law* (The Hague, Kluwer, 2002) 343.

opposition on academic, political and popular levels, the CFR may live on in the sense of a toolbox, or source of ideas, for European and national legislators.[15]

The proposals on proprietary securities in the DCFR undoubtedly have some similarities with the UNCITRAL guide. They take a flexible approach towards creation and permissible limits of security, appearing to permit the creation of security over all sorts of property for all types of credit provider, though this goal is less clearly articulated in the DCFR. However, this is more a matter of inference in the DCFR than anything else. There is nothing equivalent to Recommendation 17 of the UNCITRAL Guide providing that a security right may encumber any type of asset, including parts of assets and undivided rights in assets. The DCFR, in line with the Guide, distinguishes between the creation and third party effectiveness of security rights. It also provides for different methods of perfection depending on the nature of the secured property, though registration is available as a matter of securing third party effectiveness in all instances. Registration is clearly envisaged as the standard method of achieving third party effectiveness. Other methods, however, may be more effective in certain circumstances in the sense that a secured party who has registered its security rights may potentially lose out in a priority battle to another secured party who has gained third party effectiveness in a different way. Again like the Guide, the DCFR adopts a recharacterisation approach, in essence treating retention of ownership devices as security interests by applying registration requirements to the same.[16] Retention-of-ownership devices include reservation-of-title clauses in sale-of-goods contracts, hire purchase contracts, consignment contracts and finance leases. The distinction between security rights strictly so-called and retention-of-ownership rights, however, is preserved in respect of default. On the realisation of the collateral, the holder of a security interest is not entitled to any 'surplus' over and above sums owing from the borrower. A 'retention-of-ownership' seller or lessee, on the other hand, is entitled to

---

[15] On 1 July 2010, the European Commission published a Green Paper that outlined seven different options for a European Contract law and invited views. These options range from a non-binding instrument for improving the consistency of EU legislation to a European civil code going beyond contract law that supersedes national law previously covering the field. In the Green Paper some of the advantages and disadvantages of each option are considered – see *Green Paper from the Commission on policy options for progress towards a European Contract Law for consumers and businesses* (Brussels, European Commission, July 2010) COM(2010) 348 final.

[16] See Rules 1.10 and 3.301 and also 3:303(1) 'For the purposes of the European register of proprietary security no distinction is made between retention of ownership devices and security.'

the surplus when the goods are repossessed and resold for more than the original purchase price.

The general line taken by the DCFR in respect of retention-of-ownership devices is the same as that in the Guide though some of the details are different. The Guide makes express provision for a greater range of cases and also entertains the possibility of alternative provision in certain instances. The same is true with the treatment of acquisition-financing devices. The latter are basically retention-of-ownership devices, and also security rights in property whose acquisition was facilitated by a loan made specifically for that purpose. Acquisition financing devices enjoy a privileged priority position under the DCFR, as they do under the Guide, but there are particular rules that must be complied with before this super-priority can be attained. The acquisition finance device is required to be registered within 35 days after delivery of the supplied asset, in which case super-priority is effective from the date of creation.[17] If registration takes place later than the 35 days, then the acquisition finance device becomes effective only at the time of registration and does not enjoy super-priority. Irrespective of the date of registration, super-priority does not extend to the fruits and proceeds of assets that are subject to an acquisition finance device.[18]

Both the DCFR and the Guide make provision for the general third party effectiveness of security rights through registration. The resemblances between the DCFR and the Guide are obvious in this respect but so too are the divergences. The DCFR is not as rigorously committed to the notion of notice filing and also disallows secured parties from relying on the benefits of the security in certain situations by making use of a concept akin to estoppel. Book IX – 3:305 of the DCFR echoes Recommendation 67 of the Guide, allowing entries to be made in the security rights register either before or after the contract for proprietary security has been concluded, but there is no provision that mirrors Recommendation 68 in stating that one notice is sufficient for multiple security rights arising from multiple agreements between the same parties.

The DCFR strikes out in a different direction from the Guide by imposing a duty on a registered security creditor to respond to requests by inquirers for information that concerns any security right covered by the entry so long as these requests are made with the security provider's approval.[19] This duty is owed both to the inquirer and to the security provider, and the secured creditor is liable in damages to both parties for any

17 Rule 3.107.
18 Rule 4.105.
19 Rule 3.319.

loss caused by breach of the duty.[20] But more significant than the liability in damages are the implications in terms of loss of priority if a secured party fails to handle information requests in the correct way. If the secured creditor incorrectly informs the inquirer that the assets concerned are not encumbered, the inquirer can within three months acquire a proprietary right in these assets in priority to the secured creditor despite the fact that there is an entry in the register covering the secured creditor's rights.[21] The inquirer also has a similar grace period of three months to acquire a superior-ranking security right if the secured creditor correctly informs the inquirer that the assets concerned are not encumbered.[22] A secured party on the register cannot avoid the loss of priority consequences attendant on failure to deal accurately with information requests simply by failing to respond, or delaying a response.[23] A failure to respond is treated as if the secured creditor had given the information that the assets concerned are not encumbered. Therefore the inquirer is free to take the benefit of a proprietary security that will have priority over an existing security right on the register. The inquirer is also entitled to take the benefit of a higher-ranking security during any period of delay when the secured party on the register has not yet dealt with an information request.[24] Therefore, it is incumbent upon a secured party to respond promptly and accurately to information requests.

Despite these differences it is probably fair to say that the similarities between the Guide and the DCFR outweigh the dissimilarities. The overall approach of the two instruments in significant respects is similar, although the general philosophy of the DCFR is not set out with the same clarity as the statement of key objectives in Recommendation 1 of the Guide. The DCFR, like the Guide, takes a facilitating and enabling approach towards the creation of security rights. Certain retention of ownership devices is deemed to create security rights. There is a general requirement of registration for third party effectiveness of security rights and also rules turning principally on the time of registration to determine priority between more than one security interest in the same collateral.

The UNCITRAL Secretariat is certainly correct to say that there are echoes of the Secured Transactions Guide in Book 9 of the Draft European Common Frame of Reference and in the Australian personal property security legislation, but there are two points in response. Firstly,

---

20 Rule 3.319(4).
21 Rule 3.322.
22 Rule 3.321.
23 Rule 3.323.
24 Rule 3.323(2).

the fate of the Common Frame of Reference as a binding instrument is very uncertain and most likely is destined to remain a political pipedream for the foreseeable future. Secondly, while the Australian legislation has been influenced by the Guide, to the extent that the Guide represents a distillation of principles that comes from the American Article 9, this influence is consistent with, and reinforces, the thesis advanced in Chapters 2 and 3 of this book of 'path-dependent' legal development and the notion that migration of legal concepts is most likely to occur within legal families.

The experience to date suggests that the Guide is not likely to succeed in the sense of producing formal or functional convergence between different jurisdictions in respect of secured transactions law. For instance, an influential sample by researchers linked to the World Bank of credit institutions in 129 countries over 25 years found no evidence that creditor rights were converging in respect of countries with different legal origins, or between rich and poor countries.[25] The evidence disclosed in this study (the 'Djankov study') was at variance with the hypothesis that institutions converged toward the more successful ones over time or that institutions in different countries, while distinct on the surface, functionally converged to accomplish the same goals. Convergence theorists may be able to dismiss the Djankov study on the basis that it measures mainly creditor rights in respect of insolvency law rather than creditor rights insofar as they are manifested in secured transactions law.[26] But this explanation does not really hold good in respect of a detailed study emanating from the Centre for Business Research at the University of Cambridge.[27]

This more recent and more rigorous but denser study by Armour et al. has come up with broadly similar conclusions to the Djankov study. The Armour study purports to measure shifts in shareholder, creditor, and worker protection in the UK, US, Germany, France, and India over

---

[25] See S Djankov, C McLiesh and A Shleifer 'Private Credit in 129 Countries' (2007) 84 Journal of Finance 299.

[26] For a somewhat different perspective see R Haselmann and K Pistor 'How Law Affects Lending' (2009) 23 Review of Financial Studies 549, whose paper investigates the effect of legal change on the lending behaviour of banks in twelve transition economies. The paper finds that banks increase the supply of credit subsequent to legal change but that changes to collateral law matter more for increases in bank lending than do changes in bankruptcy law.

[27] J Armour, S Deakin, P Lele and M Siems 'How Do Legal Rules Evolve? Evidence from a Cross-Country Comparison of Shareholder, Creditor and Worker Protection' (2009) 57 AJCL 579, and see also M Siems 'Numerical Comparative Law – Do We Need Statistical Evidence in Order to Reduce Complexity?' (2005) 13 Cardozo Journal of International & Comparative Law 521; P Lele and M Siems 'Shareholder Protection: A Leximetric Approach' (2007) 7 Journal of Corporate Law Studies 17.

the 1970–2005 period. The range of countries covered is obviously much narrower than in the Djankov study, and in the 'legal origins' study by La Porta et al., but the five countries include the parent systems for the legal origins theory (UK, France and Germany); the world's largest economy (US) and the world's largest democracy (India). The Armour study attempted a deeper analysis, with a wide range of regulatory materials being considered, including case law, functional equivalents to legislation and the role of default rules in addition to mandatory norms. It also attempted to provide a fuller picture of the dynamics of legal change in the five countries. Moreover, it disaggregated creditors' rights into three constituent measures representing respectively: (i) rules which limit the freedom of debtor firms to engage in activities that are potentially harmful to creditors; (ii) rules which facilitate creditors in contracting for greater protection; and (iii) rules which facilitate creditor power in bankruptcy proceedings.[28] The study suggested that variation in some aspects of creditor protection during the time period corresponded very weakly, if at all, to the civil/common law distinction. There was some support for the view that creditor contract rights were inclined to be stronger in common law than in civilian jurisdictions but another, more plausible, interpretation was that France was simply an outlier here in terms of 'weak' creditor protection. The strongest creditor protection came in the UK and Germany and the weakest in France and India. In terms of direction of change, the pattern was one of uneven development in all countries and there was little evidence of either functional or formal convergence.[29]

SUMMING UP

As pointed out in previous chapters, the UNCITRAL Secured Transactions Guide adds to the toolbox for States wishing to reform their law on secured transactions. The Guide also mirrors the content of Article 9 of the American Uniform Commercial Code fairly closely, though there are some variations that are intended to make the Guide more palatable to civil law jurisdictions in particular. The Guide is a detailed instrument and outstrips previous international efforts such as the EBRD Model Law on Secured Transactions in the breadth and comprehensiveness of its provisions.

---

28 J Armour et al. *ibid* at 604–606 and 612–615. The full index and dataset can be viewed online: http://www.cbr.cam.ac.uk/research/programme2/project2-20output.htm (project datasets).

29 J Armour et al. above, note 27 at 623–625.

One of the themes of this book is that the closeness in approach to Article 9 is likely to militate against the prospects of the Guide gaining widespread international acceptance. This is so for three interlocking reasons. The first is that the Guide may be technically deficient in certain respects or at least there are alternative models that offer equally, if not more plausible solutions. The second reason is the American imprint itself on the Guide, however subtle and disguised this may be in certain respects.[30] Frederick Schauer, for instance, comments that 'factors other than the receiving nation's own evaluation of the worth of legal ideas, and other than an objective assessment of the worth of legal ideas, are significant determinants of the patterns of legal transplantation and legal globalization'.[31] He also makes the point that 'copying' US law has a bad smell in numerous parts of the world, or in some political quarters at least, and therefore avoiding American influence, just because it is American, often appears to be a driving force. The third reason is the battering that American legal and financial norms have taken with the Crash of 2008. It is almost as if the Guide harks back to an 'age of innocence' before the Crash when belief in the self-correcting mechanisms of markets reigned supreme and American global financial hegemony went largely unchallenged.

[30] See J deLisle 'Lex Americana? United States Legal Assistance, American Legal Models and Legal Change in the Post-Communist World and Beyond' (1999) 20 University of Pennsylvania Journal of International Economic Law 179 at 269: 'efforts to export U.S. legal models are more likely to succeed if they eschew detailed, distinctively U.S.-derived prescriptions in favour of presenting advise or exemplars in terms of more "general" standards, "international" norms, "universal" principles. . .'.

[31] See F Schauer 'The Politics and Incentives of Legal Transplantation' (2000) Centre for International Development at Harvard Working Paper No 44 at p 24 – www.cid.harvard.edu/cidwp/044.htm.

Index